741.5   C832
Cou   c.2   WITHDRAWN

Onondaga County Public Library
Syracuse, New York

ART & MUSIC DEPARTMENT
Syracuse Public Library

a history of the comic strip

by PIERRE COUPERIE
MAURICE C. HORN
PROTO DESTEFANIS
EDOUARD FRANÇOIS
CLAUDE MOLITERNI
GÉRALD GASSIOT-TALABOT

translated from the French by EILEEN B. HENNESSY

created in conjunction with the exhibition of comic-strip art at
MUSÉE DES ARTS DÉCORATIFS / PALAIS DU LOUVRE

CROWN PUBLISHERS, INC., NEW YORK

TRANSLATION © 1968, BY CROWN PUBLISHERS, INC.
FIRST PUBLISHED IN FRANCE UNDER THE TITLE *Bande Dessinée et Figuration Narrative*
© 1967 BY SOCIETE CIVILE D'ETUDES ET DE RECHERCHES DES LITTÉRATURES DESSINÉES
LIBRARY OF CONGRESS CATALOG CARD NUMBER: 68-20471
PRINTED IN THE UNITED STATES OF AMERICA

Design by Sally Stein

acknowledgments

We should like to thank Paul Winkler and Gerald Gauthier of the Agence Opera Mundi, Paris; Sylvan Byck and John Brogan, Jr., of King Features Syndicate, Inc., New York; Robert Ahier of United Press International, Paris, and Albert Moody of United Features Syndicate, New York; Richard Clarke and Miss Slott of the Chicago Tribune–New York News Syndicate, Inc.; Cino del Ducca and Marcel Gros of Editions Mondiales, Hergé and Editions Casterman for the exhibition poster and reproduction of their documents; Bell Syndicate, Editor Press, Ledger Syndicate, McCay and Richardson Features, McClure Syndicate, McNaught Syndicate, Newspaper Enterprise Association Syndicate, Post Hall Syndicate, Publishers Newspaper Syndicate, The Rajah Press, and Walt Disney Productions for reproduction of their works; and Les Editions Armand Colin, Dargaud, Dupuis, Du Lombard, Gauthier-Languereau, Mondiales, S.P.E., and Stock, and the newspapers and newspaper organizations *Coq Hardi, Corriere dei Piccoli, Daily Mirror, Daily Mail, Evening Standard, Linus, London Express* Features, *Pierrot,* and *Vaillant*.

We especially wish to thank Alain Saint-Ogan, Crockett Johnson, G. H. Gallet, Crepax, Hulbert Burroughs, J. P. Gourmelen, Edouard Dejay, Arturo del Castillo, Robert Gigi, Louise Isel, Jules Feiffer, Woody Gelman, Milton Caniff, Burne Hogarth, Jacovitti, Rube Goldberg, Pellos, Sergio Tofano, J. F. Thevenon, Serge Voisembert, and Wallace Wood.

Our thanks also go to Arturo Ramos of Valence, France, and Pierre Horn of New York. And in particular we should like to thank David Pascal, representing the National Cartoonist Society for Europe, and George Fronval for help in the preparation of this work; the Galerie Ileana Sonnabend, Paris; the Leo Castelli Gallery, New York; the Moderna Museet, Stockholm; Studio Marconi, Milan; and the Comité Union Centrale des Arts Décoratifs. We make grateful acknowledgment to Mrs. Avonne Keller of the Newspaper Comics Council, Jerry Robinson, President of National Cartoonists Society, and Philip Seuling.

Full credit to the owners of copyright accompanies each illustration. With some of the older drawings, copyright confusion still exists, and a few individuals and organizations seem to have dropped out of sight altogether. If in our credits we have fallen short of legal perfection, we extend apologies. Our efforts to trace copyright owners were strenuous, and if errors or omissions exist we shall be happy to correct them in later editions.

preface

When the dedicated people in SOCERLID announced the coming show of comic strips at the Musée des Arts Décoratifs in Paris, it was an Everest moment for those of us who ply the inky trade. How did *we* ever make it to the Louvre?

Your instant replay whips recollection into action . . .

You're sitting in the spare room in the house on Walnut Street in Hillsboro, Ohio (or Illinois or Nebraska), with your mother's breadboard leaned against the sewing machine.

You have that first lesson from the Landon School spread out—and you're ready!

"Ambition of a thousand Caesars . . ."

A hundred years later you're sitting in an expensive Manhattan studio with a board leaning against a table; next week's continuity is spread out in front of you, and the fundamentals have changed very little.

Essentially your audience is the same—you!

Any success in the pariah world of the cartoon is an extension of those lonely attic hours. If you drew something that really pleased you, and you could eventually translate your virtuoso performance into the general acceptance beyond doting kin, you cracked a hymen of propagation.

Most of us remain loners, regardless of acquired skills and tricks of drawing in public. Reading the names of Americans recorded in this volume (and I assume the same is true with cartoonists around the world), I am impressed with the front runners who have never stopped auditioning. No matter how many assistants are employed in the production of a long-successful feature, the root quality is maintained by the head man keeping his hand on the throttle.

At some point, the individual who has the most to lose is, figuratively, back in that spare room on Walnut Street. The paper is just as white even when the syndicate list totals hundreds of newspapers; the stake is the same—a career apart from the lifetime of dull labor that will be the fate of most of his contemporaries at Webster School (or Ruskin or Washington).

The rewards are great, but without the burden of conscience resulting from having done someone in. If you win, it is because you have parlayed the hours spent in the attic by finding a world full of prototypes of yourself who keep you in the gilded slavery of feeding their habit.

MILTON CANIFF

New York
February, 1968

foreword

The comic strip, and particularly the American comic strip, which has produced from eight to twelve million pictures since its birth, has created the largest and most abundant iconographical field in history. Far from being simple, its content is the product of an incredible network of influences and traditions, both conscious and unconscious, all of which belong to the ensemble of a civilization and its past. Its immense distribution is unequaled by that of any other form of expression, artistic or literary; not even the film can boast, as can the comic strip, of reaching a third of humanity. Chic Young, the author of "Blondie," has more than 70 billion readers annually! In the course of his long career, George McManus drew nearly 80,000 pictures. . . .

And yet, in the eyes of some people, such a phenomenon does not exist, and cannot lay claim to a higher level of existence than the private work of some author whom no one reads! With the recent changes in thinking, some now admit its existence, but deny that it is of any interest. Their latest, and most unwittingly subtle, position is that the comic strip is not yet of any interest, but will be in the (undoubtedly distant) future; for the moment it has not progressed beyond the age of Georges Méliès. (Yet the comic strip has been in existence for seventy years!) Other, sometimes well-meaning, writers analyze its content on the basis of the most dubious examples, and its esthetics on the basis of the crudest pictures. Would literature pass this type of test if its historians haphazardly examined the whole of its production instead of concentrating their investigations solely on its masterpieces? We would discover that 75 percent of all literary production consists of the lowest type of penny dreadfuls, and 20 percent of mediocre works; possibly we would not even discover the 5 percent that consists of works of value. In the same way, if we lumped together all the buildings constructed in any given period, architecture would pass for a major art only with the greatest difficulty! But this is precisely what has been done with the comic strip. It would be only fair to equalize the criteria, and also to require that many of those who have been writing about the comic strip for some time should have some knowledge of the subject.

The conception of this book is an answer to these perplexities and deficiencies. Faithful to its desire to provide objective information, SOCERLID—the Société d'Etudes et de Recherches des Littératures Dessinées (Organization for the Study and Research of Pictorial Literatures)—has preferred to adhere closely to facts and figures, and to avoid abusive generalizations presented as facts to a public that is not capable of making a judgment. We have attempted to place the comic strip in its widest context, but only as a set of working hypotheses; we have avoided fashionable eccentricities and journalistic "psychoanalyses" and "psychopathologies." If the book goes far beyond the subject of the exhibition that it is intended to accompany and that is devoted to one aspect of the question (that of narrative technique), it is because the comic strip is an ensemble, and that ensemble is unknown to the public—its history as well as its practical, commercial, sociological, and esthetic aspects. We wished to reveal the innumerable aspects of an immense subject, some of which have never been discussed, some of which have been treated separately from various viewpoints. Although the historical chapters have been enlarged to the maximum, we have made a selection, and in this selection we have concentrated interest on the principal creative talents. We did not confine ourselves to the American comic strip, but we have accorded it the preeminent position that it has always occupied. The reader will be surprised by the illustrations; this was our intention. Even in the United States the public looks at the comic strip without seeing it. We have broken it up, analyzed it, and reconstituted it in accordance with the viewpoints taken by the various chapters, so that the public, torn away from its usual habits, may finally open its eyes.

If SOCERLID has been able to introduce the comic strip into the Musée des Arts Décoratifs, it owes its success to the liberal views of the museum's director, M. François Mathey. It is also indebted to those who were the first to understand its mission and to house its early exhibitions: the Société Française de Photographie, in the person of its president M. Robert Auvillain, and Mme. Christiane Roger.

introduction

Perhaps at no time in any historical period has so much scholarly commentary been written about the visual forms of mankind than in our own century. And of these, no art of any era, from any class or category, can surpass in output that of the modern cartoon—the comic panel and the comic strip.

If we were to assess these two large-scale art phenomena, we should expect some direct correlation between the enormous volume of critical literature and the impressive production of the art of the comic strip. One should anticipate at least a sizable reflection of opinion to mark the massive existence of this art.

But against this natural expectation, the record shows exactly the opposite.

What is the reason for this lack of inquiry, this dearth of comment? For some reason, among certain inner circles of the informed, especially among those who set the judgments of older approved and newer acceptable art, there has been an indifference to the comic strip, if not an assiduous avoidance of its presence. To some of the learned, where probative discussions of taste in art are entertained, to say even the words "cartoon" or "comic strip" is to incur a reaction of disdain, if not scorn; for the very name seems baneful, and projects a pejorative value of a debased art.

In another quarter, among the adherents of the recent Pop Art efflorescence, that segment which uses the cartoon as an archetypal form of mass culture in the mass media tends to disavow any serious connection with this form in its original state; that is to say, they do not create "cartoons" but "art."

What is this art that seems to be so offensive?

Perhaps the art we are talking about is not art at all, because even among its staunchest protagonists and practitioners there has developed no satisfactory definition that would place the cartoon and the comic strip in a relevant context with traditional art as art. Some will argue this form is not truly art because it depends in part upon its verbal content, that it may be a form of literature. But is it clearly literature if it often chooses to retreat entirely from verbal expression in its use of pantomime and mimicry, and therefore does not inhabit an authentic domain of literary territory. Is it drama, then? If so, to what place shall we assign its formal codes of form and structure, depiction and abstraction, its artistic and esthetic expression— its imagery, calligraphy and iconography? Certainly these are not the histrionic reflex of theatrical temperament. Yet surely in all this can we not find something of the comic and the tragic, the adventurous and the romantic, the prosaic and the poetic? True; but however it may be construed, in no categorical or classic sense can it be advanced that the comic strip offers valid comedy or tragedy, adventure or romance, prose or poetry. It does not assert the cosmic stress of the sublime or terrible, nor does it extol the universal, the heroic, the ideal; on a lesser human scale, it does not evoke the deeper throbbing rhythms of passion, toil, and suffering, or invite the felicitous sentiments of charm and kitsch. In its exercise of danger it is too reckless of reason, too void of feeling to be profound; and in its pursuit of the genial and the jocular it is possessed of a frenzy that is too bitter a remedy for the relief of pain. In short, it neither elicits the heights of the human dream nor probes the depths of the human soul nor promotes the catharsis of lighthearted laughter.

It is all these, yet none. It is everywhere contradiction and paradox; its underlying principle is uncertainty, the negation of coherent order. It is the model of the open-ended, the uncommitted, the undefined. Here we shall find the undisciplined and the unlearned taking potshots at authorities with merciless unconcern, seeking to unseat the jurisdiction of the elite.

Now perhaps we know why the scrupulous and the prudent cannot tolerate this thing called the cartoon; why it is hard for them to write it down as acceptable art. In a time of the ascendance of automation, of cybernetics and the multiplication of the anonymous, with the emergence of the dualisms of antimatter and antilogic, it is fitting there should also emerge a preoccupation with antiart and its many parallels, Neo-Dada, Pop, Op, Ob, and so on, and the comic strip. Against all the obscure extremes of Neo-Dada and the enigmatic fulminations of the avant-garde, these esthetic strategies are still the offshoots of respectability. For what we're dealing with in the comic strip is truth, in the guise of the village idiot, the boor and knave, the other, ugly side of ourselves.

Look hard, the next time you get the chance, into that art. You might find in it fuel for the kindling of fires, truth pursued by the gleam of conscience. Look, and you may find somewhere in the dross of the cartoon, something demonic, something malign but not fraudulent, on the dark side of the moon.

BURNE HOGARTH

New York, 1967

contents

    Preface by Milton Caniff   3
    Foreword   4
    Introduction by Burne Hogarth   5
 1. Background   7
 2. The Origins of the Comic Strip   11
 3. Period of Adjustment: 1910–1928   35
 4. The Upheaval of the Thirties   57
 5. The Crisis of the Forties: 1940–1948   83
 6. The Regeneration of the Comic Strip   103
 7. Production and Distribution   129
 8. The Comic-Strip Audience   147
 9. The World of the Comic Strip   155
10. Narrative Technique   179
11. Esthetics and Signification   205
12. Narrative Figuration   229
    Index   253

NOTE

The conception of this book, as well as chapters 1, 7, 8, 9, 11, and the notes for all the chapters (except chapters 10 and 12) were done by Pierre Couperie of the Ecole Pratique des Hautes Etudes Historiques.

Proto Destefanis and Edouard François have treated the Italian and the French-language comic strips, respectively, in chapters 2, 3, 4, 5, and 6.

The history of the American comic strip (in chapters 2, 3, 4, 5, and 6) was written by Maurice C. Horn, who also assisted in the final editing of the present book.

Claude Moliterni is the author of Chapter 10, devoted to narrative technique.

Gérald Gassiot-Talabot prepared Chapter 12, devoted to narrative figuration.

One of the first appearances of the balloon: the scroll. The Protat woodcut, 1370.

1

background

The advent of the comic strip marked the culmination of a long evolutionary process, the scope of which far surpassed the range of its early prototypes in the pictorial art. What is called (sometimes with undue exaggeration) "the civilization of the picture" is a nineteenth-century phenomenon that manifested itself in numerous forms. More generally, the progress of the picture paralleled that of the printed text, but technical problems retarded its development for two centuries, resulting in the divorce of the picture from the text.

Beginning in the last quarter of the fifteenth century, the woodcut was used in the illustration of books, and this technique underwent a remarkable development in the sixteenth century. Newssheets as well as books were decorated with engravings, which were very seldom genuine illustrations of the text in the newssheet. At best, stereotype pictures were used to represent certain events, such as royal funeral processions, floods, and so on. Much use was made of illustrations that had previously been published in books; as such, these pictures were by no means a "popular" art form. Little by little the illustration was adapted to the text. In a newssheet dating from 1650, the murder of a "nobleman" is described by a picture that simultaneously depicts the crime—an attack on a carriage—and, in the foreground, the punishment of the murderer.

The woodcut was then replaced by copper engraving. Utilizing first the copperplate (beginning in the fifteenth century) and shortly thereafter the technique of etching, it permitted greater finesse of draftsmanship, but unlike wood it could not, for technical reasons, be combined with the text. The eighteenth century witnessed the birth of the stippled engraving and aquatint processes, which permitted a relatively faithful reproduction of original works of art. Lithography was perfected in Germany in 1796, and made its first appearance in France in 1816. As in the case of copper engraving, only isolated plates could be produced by this process.

The revival of the woodcut through the new technique of wood-block engraving, which appeared in England and was introduced into France in 1817, had decisive repercussions. The principal result, from our point of view, was the reunion of illustration and text (which had been divorced by copper engraving and lithography), and the reintegration of the picture into the sequence and life of the narrative, instead of leaving it isolated and literally "out in the margin." The consequences of this development became immediately apparent in the extraordinary progress made by illustration in the 1830's. In *Paul et Virginie,* published with *La Chaumière Indienne* by Curmer in 1838, text and illustration attained a proportion of one to one. This work is more than a comic strip; the illustrations are so copious that they constitute a genuine film with subtitles. We should keep in mind that in this same period Dickens began as a scriptwriter for an illustrator, George Cruikshank, whose fame was sufficient

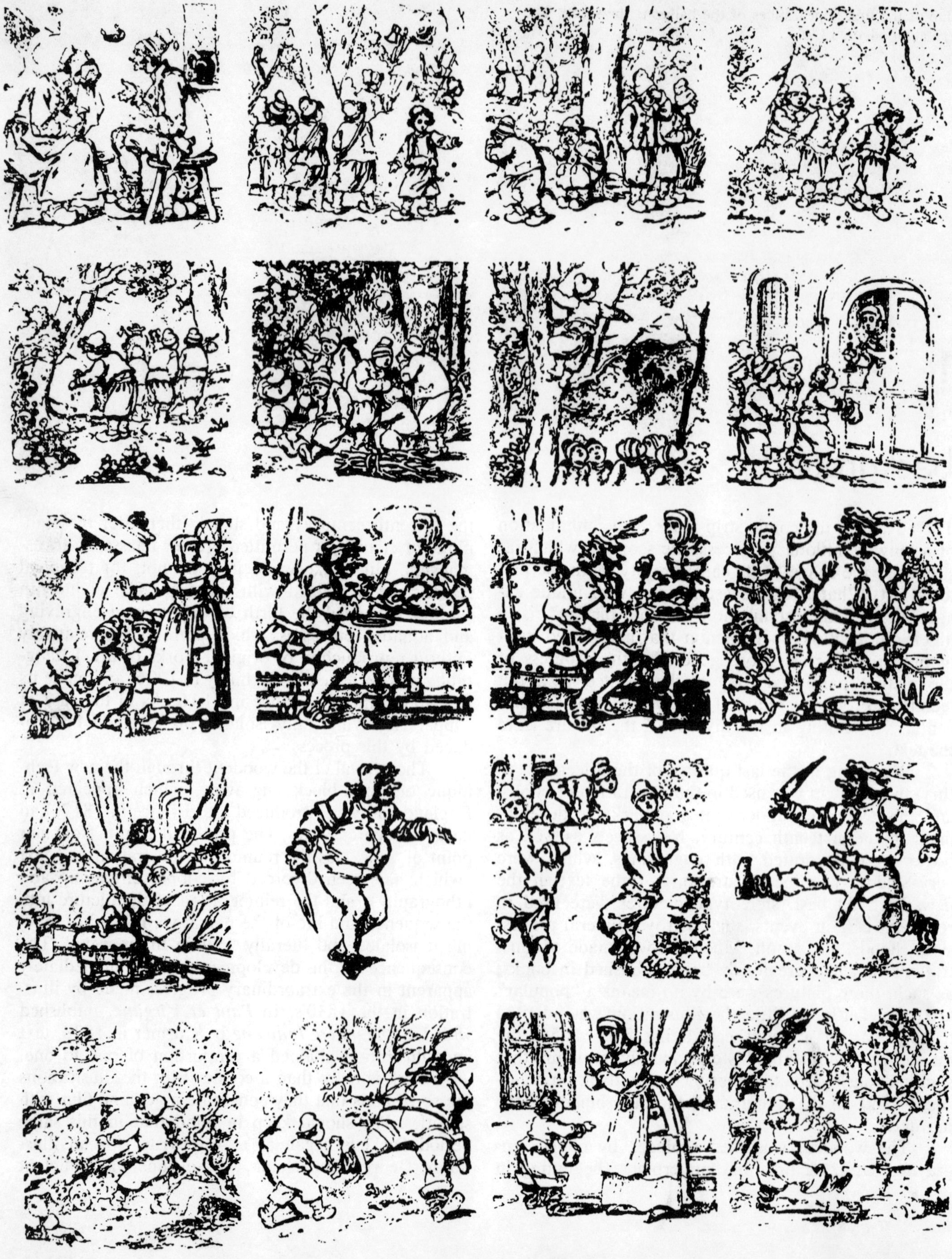

to ensure the success of a book; in France, the immense œuvre of Gustave Doré was a similar case. While the technique of wood engraving permitted the development of the *image d'Epinal,* the latter undoubtedly bears little relationship to the comic strip, the immediate ancestry of which is well known; as we shall see, the forebears of the comic strip link it with the book, the picture album, the poster, and the newspaper, rather than with a pictorial art that was already suffering from obsolescence and archaism.

The illustration triumphed in journalism as rapidly as it had in the book world. In England, France, and Germany appeared numerous magazines with such significant titles as *Le Magasin Pittoresque* (1833), *L'Illustration* (1843), *The Illustrated London News* (1852), *Le Tour du Monde* (1860), *Punch,* and *Der Illustrierte Zeitung.* America had *Frank Leslie's Illustrated* and *Harper's Weekly,* both of which illustrated their Civil War reports with numerous engravings. These magazines had their juvenile counterparts: weekly magazines of a serious nature, illustrated like books. Such were, for instance, in the United States the *Child's Paper* of the 1850's, in France, the *Magasin d'Education et de Récréation, La Semaine des Enfants* and others.

Around 1850 a new impetus was furnished by the process of direct chemical engraving of the drawing onto zinc (zincography, or *guillotage*), then the use of a photographic intermediary reproducing the drawing and applied onto the zinc (line photoengraving, invented in 1873).

Color printing, which had been achieved in copper engraving at the beginning of the eighteenth century by J.-C. Leblon, had fallen into disuse. It was revived by color lithography, a laborious process, but one that gave pleasing results. Chromolithography enriched the world of the picture with a proliferation of labels, decorated with descriptive scenes evocative of a given product; it provided the first impetus for the colored poster and fashion design, which were to influence the comic strip. The other milestone was the perfection of the trichromatic process, of which the American comic strip is the direct descendant. In the same period, the poster became a genuine art form, attracting major artists and creating a vigorous style that was to exercise a powerful influence on the comic strip. Like the latter, the poster "veiled with humor the ferocity of the battles in the struggle for life" (R. Salanon).

The illustration was now firmly established everywhere. To mention only one example, the illustrated Christmas card was born in England around 1866, spread to the United States after 1875, and quickly reached an astronomical rate of circulation. The illustration acquired certain characteristics that were to influence the comic strip; in the England of Dickens, for example, it joined hands with caricature. Moreover, the illustrations in storybooks presented anthropomorphic (or at least costumed) animals whose descendants are immediately obvious. Thanks to photoengraving, the pen, which until now had not been widely used, became a fashionable technique; it was the instrument of Caran d'Ache (Emmanuel Poiré) and of T.-A. Steinlen, and was to become that of the cartoonists.

A radically different process, that of photography, had been developing since 1822, and it was destined to multiply the presence of the image and make the color black the basis for a new esthetics. The first photograph appeared in a newspaper in England in 1880. In 1895 the movie achieved the recomposition of movement based on its image-by-image photographic analysis, thus continuing the purely graphic processes by which Emile Reynaud had achieved the same result, fifteen years earlier, with his praxinoscope. The comic strip appeared at approximately the same time—1889 in France, 1897 in the United States. The animated cartoon, the movie, and the comic strip were born simultaneously; although each appeared independently of the other two, they embodied in three related forms the single deep-seated trend underlying the entire nineteenth century.

The picture-story of "Le Petit Poucet" (Tom Thumb).

SLUMBERLAND CLOSED. WILL BE OPEN AGAIN NEXT SUNDAY M.
I TOLD YOU TO HURRY. NOW. YOU ARE LOCKED OUT. I WILL SEE YOU AGAIN NEXT WEEK
IF YOU HADN'T STOPPED TO TALK TO THOSE WOOD NYMPHS WE'D NOT BE LOCKED OUT. NOW. WE'VE GOT TO WAIT A WEEK
NEMO! NEMO! IF YOU WANT TO GO TO SUNDAY SCHOOL, YOU HAD BETTER GET UP. DO YOU HEAR ME, NEMO, EH?

Winsor McCay, "Little Nemo": The Gate of Slumberland (1906). Little Nemo's dream world is embellished with an astonishing *fin de siècle* architecture. With the permission of Mr. Woody Gelman.

2

the origins of the comic strip

Before being perfected in the United States in its present form, the birth of the comic strip was foreshadowed in Europe by a profusion of picture-stories, either silent or illustrating a text, often very skillful productions by highly talented illustrators, and widely disseminated through newspapers and books. The line of descent linking these picture-stories with the comic strip is indisputable—undoubtedly more so than the influence of the *image d'Epinal*. The two principal names connected with these stories are those of Töpffer and Wilhelm Busch. Töpffer directly influenced Christophe, thereby presiding over the birth of the French comic strip, while the influence of Busch led to the invention by Hearst and Dirks of the first American comic strip.

Rodolphe Töpffer (1799–1846), writer and artist, a native of Geneva and a professor at the university of that city, wrote not only novels but also picture-stories that are richly imaginative. His adventures of Mr. Vieuxbois, Mr. Cryptogame, and Mr. Jabot, which were collected in 1846–1847 under the title *Histoires en Estampes,* enjoyed a great success, and their originality won high praise from Goethe. The narrative is entirely pictorial; there is a short text under the extremely numerous pictures, which are separated by simple vertical lines.

Toward the end of Töpffer's life, the picture-story again came into vogue, with Adolf Schrödter's *Herr Piepmeyer* (1848) and the *Monsieur Réac* (1848–1849) of Nadar Félix Tournachon). Between 1860 and 1870 it developed rapidly in Germany, thanks to F. Steub (1844–1903) and particularly Wilhelm Busch (1832–1908). Busch, in truth, was not so close as Töpffer to the comic strip, and his dubious humor was heavy and savage—a far cry from Töpffer's imaginativeness. Busch illustrated his own satirical or moralizing poems, the most famous of which, "Max und Moritz," recounts the pranks and terrible death of two young scamps. "Max und Moritz" was to play a major role (inspirational rather than technical) in the development of the American comic strip.

In the 1880's the silent picture-story invaded French magazines. Caran d'Ache and Rabier particularly excelled in this genre. Rabier enjoyed a long career as a specialist in picture books of comic animals for younger readers. Most of his work remained on the borderline of the comic strip.

Then Georges Colomb, who signed his works "Christophe," perfected what was to be for a long time the format of the European picture-story, the final experiment before the birth of the comic strip as it would be created in the United States. The son of the high school principal of Lure (a small town near Belfort, in northeastern France), Christophe entered the Ecole Normale in 1878. His classmates included Jean Jaurès, Henri Bergson, and the future Henri Cardinal Baudrillart, all of whom would be most surprised to find themselves mentioned in this book! A fondness for drawing

12

1

LETZTER STREICH

Max und Moritz, wehe euch!
Jetzt kommt euer letzter Streich!

Wozu müssen auch die beiden
Löcher in die Säcke schneiden?

See, da trägt der Bauer Mecke
Einen seiner Maltersäcke.

(Max and Moritz, alas! This is your last prank!
Why must the two boys cut holes in the sacks?
Look! Here comes Farmer Mecke, carrying
one of his sacks of corn.)

1. Rodolphe Töpffer, "Monsieur Cryptogame."
2. Wilhelm Busch, "Max und Moritz."
3. Benjamin Rabier.

2

UN NID CONFORTABLE

A COMFORTABLE NEST

Tom Brown, "Weary Willie and Tired Tim."

Christophe, "La Famille Fenouillard," Copyright Armand Colin.

Being in need of a change of clothes, Mr. and Mrs. Fenouillard return home. Mrs. Fenouillard would like to break out in bitter complaints, but since her mouth is full of cheese she simply maintains a dignified and solemn calm. The young ladies are wailing in touching harmony.

In the evening, now that she has finished swallowing her cheese, Mrs. Fenouillard is finally able to make a few noises. She tells her husband that from now on she won't listen to him when he tries to tear her away from her home on the pretext of a trip. Thus ends the first trip of this interesting family.

led him to major in natural history. After graduation from the Ecole Normale, he sought to augment his income as a teacher by selling drawings. He too created stories without words, and became a frequent contributor to a children's magazine called the *Petit Français Illustré*. Although he sold his drawings, they were originally created for his son; when the boy learned to read, Christophe introduced a text into his stories. In 1889 he created the tale of the spoiled country outing of Mr. Cornouillet, a Parisian jeweler. Later that year, this character was metamorphosed into a provincial middle-class gentleman named Mr. Fenouillard, in "La Famille Fenouillard à l'Exposition" (The Fenouillard Family Goes to the Fair). So great was its success that Christophe was forced to invent a sequel to the adventures of this conceited and stupid family; in a manner reminiscent of Mr. Perrichon and Jules Verne's *Around the World in 80 Days*, he sent them on a round-the-world trip. In 1893 his drawings were republished in book form.

Christophe preferred to create new characters rather than prolong the adventures of the old ones. Very soon he was running two or three series simultaneously. He began "Les Facéties du Sapeur Camember" (The Pranks of Fireman Camember) in 1890; it continued until 1896. Its hero, "a strange mixture of mischievousness and foolishness," was modeled on the handyman at the Lure high school. In an interview in 1934, Christophe described this gentleman as "a naive type, actually a very handsome man, but one who had never been able to learn to read and write. . . . This illiterate Hercules, who was nevertheless a good fellow, was fond of bombast. From his fruitless years of study with the Brothers, he had retained the memory of the sound of the dictation, which he found noble, and he expressed himself in the most incredible fashion. He was in love with my sister, which we found terribly funny, and he used to make speeches to her which went something like this: 'Miss Marie, comma, I'm very much in love with you, comma, we should get married, period. You wouldn't have to do much, comma, I'd do all the work, semi-colon; I'd saw up the wood, comma, all you'd have to do would be to carry it to the woodshed, period.' Despite his simplicity, he was declared fit for a seven-year tour of duty in the military service."

In 1893 the Fenouillard family was replaced by "L'Idée Fixe du Savant Cosinus" (The Obsession of Dr. Cosinus). This traveler, who never got anywhere, was inspired both by Töpffer's Dr. Festus, who was unaware that he had traveled, and the famous fits of absentmindedness of Paul Painlevé and Henri Poincaré. This was the age of the preoccupied scholar; the absentmindedness of the German historian Mommsen was equally legendary. The prototype of the future Dr. Nimbus was created at this time. In 1894 Christophe conceived the adventures of "Plick et Plock," "domestic gnomes who frequented poorly kept houses." In 1899 he began the adventures of the "Haut et Puissant Seigneur Baron de Cramoisy" (High and Mighty Lord Baron of Cramoisy), the inspiration for which derived from Rabelais, and which was in the nature of a tall tale; he abandoned this series in 1902. He died in 1945, without ever having returned to his abandoned characters; in the meantime he had become deputy director of the botanical laboratory at the Faculty of Science of the University of Paris. Thus a Sorbonne professor bears a large share of the responsibility for the creation of the comic strip.

For a long time thereafter, Christophe's style was far superior to anything produced by his successors in the French comic strip. Almost all his drawings demonstrate a remarkable sequence of movements from one picture to the next. He knew how to divide the narrative into small pictures in order to express a rapid succession of events. He also succeeded in varying the size of the pictures, and in using elongated frames worthy of cinemascope. The story abounds in ingenious narrative devices—as, for example, the progressive assembling of a crowd seen vertically (in the Fenouillard series). In the same series, a nocturnal chase in Japan is a classic of its type; we are struck by the movement of the moon, which from one picture to the next rises higher above the walls. Christophe continually employs an ironic counterpoint between text and picture, in which the brutality of the action stands in constant contradicition to the preciosity of the narrative. This detachment from the action on the part of the narrator sometimes creates a certain atmosphere of intellectual amusement—the only defect (and a minor one) to be found in Christophe's work.

England can also lay claim to the invention of the comic strip, thanks to W. F. Thomas's "Ne'er-do-well Ally Sloper," a picture story of a single hero, with text written under the pictures. This story appeared in 1884 (and thus is undeniably a predecessor of the "Fenouillard" series) and continued, with some interruptions, until 1920. "Ally Sloper" was followed by "Weary Willie and Tired Tim," in 1896; this strip, which followed the same formula of a fairly lengthy text under pictures, was the work of cartoonist Tom Brown, and appeared in *Illustrated Chips*, a children's magazine. Willie was a goateed beanpole, Tim a dark, roly-poly type; both were poor devils full of high spirits, and their imaginations teemed with ingenious tricks. Brown's drawing is precise, with vigorous

A predecessor of the American comic strip: a picture story that appeared in color in the New York *World* on February 25, 1894.

Richard Felton Outcault, "Yellow Kid." Copyright King Features Syndicate, Inc.

Dear Old Alphonse, Gaston and Leon!
They Turn Up

black areas that are excellent for the caricaturing of attitudes and physiognomies.

Around 1880 the United States lagged quite far behind Europe in the field of illustrated literature (as of illustration in general). Since pre–Civil War days American cartoonists had been using the balloon in their work, and stories told by means of rows of pictures were not unknown, but these attempts remained isolated and desultory. America possessed excellent artists like Thomas Nast and Bernhard Gillam, but they generally exercised their talents in the field of political or social satire, and took no interest in the studies being carried on at this time in Europe by Töpffer, Nadar, or Caran d'Ache.

This situation was to change rapidly with the appearance and popularization of humor magazines at the beginning of the 1880's, notably *Puck* (created in 1877 as the American version of the German magazine of the same name, but making increasing use of American material), *Judge* (published for the first time in 1881), and *Life* (which appeared in 1883). This development of the magazines, and the competition that resulted, had a beneficial effect on American artists, who rivaled each other in originality and virtuosity of technique. From 1890 on, the essential elements of the comic strip—narrative by sequence of pictures, continuing characters from one sequence to the next, the inclusion of the dialogue within the picture—were combined in these magazines, and it was already possible to discover in their pages the artists who would later become famous through the comic strip: Richard Outcault, James Swinnerton, Frederick Burr Opper.

The blending of the various elements of the comic strip was hastened by the pitiless struggle between the two magnates of the New York press, Joseph Pulitzer and William Randolph Hearst. This struggle, the vicissitudes of which seem to have been borrowed from the script of some serial movie, was perhaps less bloody but certainly as ferocious as the war then being fought between ranchers and sheep raisers in the American West.

Joseph Pulitzer, an immigrant of Hungarian origin, had purchased the moribund New York *World* in 1883, and had turned it into a prototype of the modern daily paper, with huge headlines, sensational articles, sports columns, numerous illustrations, and so on. But he concentrated his efforts particularly on the Sunday supplement, the format of which he was constantly improving. On April 9, 1893, after several unsuccessful attempts, he produced the *World*'s first color page (he had been preceded by one week by the editors of the New York *Recorder*), thus paving the way for future innovations.

Among the numerous artists who worked for the *World* was Richard Outcault, whose chief contribution to the paper ("Down Hogan's Alley") related the generally unsavory doings of the citizens of a New York slum. One of the principal characters in this series was a bald rascal with enormous ears and simian features, who always wore a huge white shirt. The *World*'s mechanical staff wanted to color this shirt yellow, the only color that had not yet been perfected on their presses. On February 16, 1896, the experiment was tried and was a complete success. The brilliant shirt attracted every eye, and the character, immediately christened the Yellow Kid, was to become the major attraction of the newspaper and contribute to the naming of the sometimes unscrupulous practices of a certain sensationalist style of journalism ("yellow journalism").

The Yellow Kid was not yet a comic strip, but rather its immediate predecessor. In Outcault's chaotic and teeming drawings, we can already discern all the harbingers of a new form, including a permanent cast of characters and the increased use of balloons.

William Randolph Hearst, whom Orson Welles later used as a model for his "Citizen Kane," had come to New York from California in 1895. Having purchased the dying *Morning Journal* from Albert Pulitzer (Joseph's brother), he immediately began competing with the *World*. Hearst, like Pulitzer, was aware of the tremendous sales factor represented by the illustrated Sunday supplements. Not satisfied to use his own artists, he lured away those of his competitors; in this way Richard Outcault went over to the *Journal*, taking the Yellow Kid with him.

New attractions were, however, a constant necessity. On December 12, 1897, on the last page of its Sunday supplement, the New York *Journal* offered its read-

An unusual comic strip on which two artists worked, combining their characters. Frederick Burr Opper and Rudolph Dirks, "The Katzenjammer Kids." Copyright King Features Syndicate, Inc.

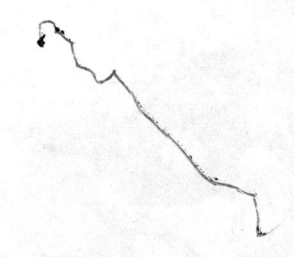

1

"APRIL FOOL!!"

2

AND HER NAME WAS MAUD! By F. OPPER

THAT BOY IS DRAWING SOMETHING ON THAT FENCE

WONDER WHAT IT IS

IS THAT MEANT FOR ME?

HAR, HAR!

3

SAP

CROOK!

EASY, GENTS, IT WAS MY FAULT

ers a new picture series from the pen of a beginner named Rudolph Dirks: "The Katzenjammer Kids." Inspired in part by Wilhelm Busch's "Max und Moritz," the Katzenjammer Kids were the result of a half century of experimentation. Without fully realizing it, Dirks had just given birth to a new artistic method of expression that not until very much later would be given the name of "comic strip."

Situated at first in an undefined country, then in an imaginary African land (perhaps the former German East Africa colony), if not in Polynesia, this strip related in a frenzied style the war to the death carried on by two rascals, Hans and Fritz (the Katzenjammer Kids, more affectionately nicknamed the "Katzies"), against any form of authority, whether parental, educational, or governmental. The mother of the two urchins (die Mama), their adoptive father (der Captain, a former shipwrecked sailor rescued by die Mama), der Inspector (representing the school authorities), are all the butt of a systematic campaign of sabotage that successfully resists spankings, threats, and promises.

Dirks did not use dialogue in the early strips, but very soon his characters were speaking an Anglo-Germanic pidgin, the effect of which was as devastating as the incredible diabolical tricks of Hans and Fritz. "The Katzenjammer Kids" is not a simple strip of comic adventures, but a genuine tale of destruction incarnated in the twin person of Hans and Fritz, for whom, in the Inspector's apt words, "society iss nix." It is this peculiarly diabolical character that, by differentiating it from the hundreds of imitators that later appeared, has undoubtedly contributed to the extraordinary longevity of this strip, the first to appear and the oldest still in existence.

The comic strip, child of commercialism and technology, inadvertently conceived and born by accident, was to grow and proliferate in all directions before anyone even thought of giving it a name.

Side by side with Rudolph Dirks and the inevitable Yellow Kid, and in the chaos of the pages and half-pages of gaudy colors by mediocre artists, this illustrated supplement of December 12, 1897, offered one restful oasis to the eye: "The Little Tiger" of James Swinnerton, the third thoroughbred in the Hearst stable.

Swinnerton, like Hearst, had come to New York from San Francisco, where he had created "Little Bears and Tigers" for the *Chronicle* in 1892. This was not a comic strip, but a series of *images d'Epinal,* peopled with tigers and tame bears who gamboled about and played harmless tricks.

When he came over to the *Journal,* Swinnerton abandoned his bears, and retained only a smart little tiger that gave its name to what had now become, under the influence of "The Katzenjammer Kids," a genuine comic strip, with balloons, a permanent cast of characters, and a continuous story. At first glimpse one is struck by the somewhat quaint appearance of these harmless tigers, but little by little one is won over by the very simple poetry, quiet humor, and mischievous charm of Swinnerton's creations. Unlike most of his contemporaries, Swinnerton cultivated unobtrusiveness. His characters are mischievous without being evil; his landscapes are serene, his anecdotes subtly funny. Swinnerton's style is on a par with his intentions: pretty and a bit too sweet. It has been adopted by many "animal" cartoonists, and can be seen in the early creations of Walt Disney.

In 1905, again for Hearst, Swinnerton created "Little Jimmy." The little boy who bears this name lacks the charm of his animal cousin; in his transition to human state, he seems to have lost his innocence, and the world around him is a little less cheerful, a little more cruel. But the style is still the same: airy, serene, and pleasing to the eye—all qualities that enabled Little Jimmy to pursue his career uninterruptedly into the fifties.

In 1899 one of the most extraordinary and prolific artists of that age in which good artists were so numerous made his debut in the comic-strip world. His name was Frederick Burr Opper, and his first strip was called "Happy Hooligan."

Happy Hooligan is a clown—but a sad clown. His amorphous face, his resigned smile, and the empty can that serves him as a hat plainly stamp him as a

---

1. James Swinnerton, "Little Jimmy." Copyright King Features Syndicate, Inc.

2. F. B. Opper, "And Her Name Was Maud." Copyright King Features Syndicate, Inc.

3. F. B. Opper, "Happy Hooligan." Copyright King Features Syndicate, Inc.

1, 2. Richard F. Outcault, "Buster Brown." Copyright King Features Syndicate, Inc.

victim. He is the quarry of children, the target of hooligans, a goat for all and sundry. His tribulations are as ludicrous as they are pathetic, and while he manages to survive, his ephemeral triumphs are only illusory. In the person of Happy, we can already recognize the tentative outline of the "little man" later made immortal by Chaplin.

Among Opper's numerous other creations, "And Her Name Was Maud!" and "Alphonse and Gaston" (both of which date from 1905) are worthy of special note.

Maud was a mule, a direct descendant of the famous mule of the pope—stubborn, intransigent, and vindictive. The ruses employed by her tormentors to escape their just deserts constitute the plot of this strip. But Maud always has the last word—or rather the last kick.

Alphonse and Gaston are two characters whose ludicrous politeness hampers their every action and leads them into the worst disasters. Their bowing and scraping, their constantly repeated stock phrases of courtesy—"After you, my dear Gaston," "No, after you, my dear Alphonse"—have passed into the language, and have contributed in no small measure to the strange idea many Americans have of the French.

Opper's art is essentially an art of exaggeration. Taking a ludicrous situation as his starting point, he magnifies it to the limit of absurdity and delirium, a practice that marks him as one of the precursors of a typically American form of humor. The imaginativeness of his composition and his caricatural style were to exercise a tremendous influence on the cartoonists of the following generation; this is particularly evident in the works of Milt Gross, Rube Goldberg, and Elzie Segar.

The newspaper war continued. Having left Pulitzer for Hearst, in 1902 Richard Outcault abandoned the *Journal* for the New York *Herald,* for which he created Buster Brown, a carefully dressed, knowing little boy with long blond hair, who is always accompanied by his faithful companion, the bulldog Tige. It would seem that Outcault wanted to depart as much as possible from the Yellow Kid to whom he owed his glory. Buster Brown's pranks, which were never really evil, always ended with an edifying little homily directed at the young reader. In 1906 Outcault returned to the Hearst establishment, and the feats of his characters became more and more conventional. Moreover, Outcault was ill at ease in this style that was not natural to him; his stilted characters lack charm; his style is borrowed; his lack of inspiration is unfortunately only too obvious.

"Buster Brown" nevertheless enjoyed a great success in its early days. But its affectation and sentimentality finally sealed its death warrant (in 1926). In the intervening period, "Buster Brown's" influence on advertising had surpassed that of any other comic strip to date. Buster's wise little face and Tige's jeering snout were used to advertise children's shoes, hats, buttons, and even cigars and whisky! In fact, "Buster Brown" products were sufficiently numerous to permit the establishment of a Buster Brown Museum in New York City (at 119 East Thirty-sixth Street).

Originally comic strips were essentially humorous (whence their early baptism as "comics"), but a great variety of themes were soon developed: the fairy tale, suspense, mythological tales, and even science-fiction appeared one after the other. Some of these creations proved to be ephemeral or premature; others paved the way for renewal and enrichment of the comic-strip genre.

The adventure strip owes its existence to Charles Kahles, the creator of "Sandy Highflyer" (1903) and "Hairbreadth Harry" (1906). Sandy was a fearless lad whose adventures in a balloon were already sowing the seeds of future airplane adventure strips. Unfortunately, his adventures were short-lived—hardly more than a few years. Hairbreadth Harry had a somewhat better fate, since he was still in existence in 1936—thanks, it is true, to the pen of another cartoonist. Harry was a generous boy, a righter of wrongs in the great tradition of the age, constantly busy rescuing some despoiled heiress or mistreated little orphan girl from the clutches of moustachioed scoundrels. Despite the presence of numerous parodical elements in the strip, "Hairbreadth Harry" is nevertheless an excellent adventure series, the vicissitudes of which kept an entire generation of teen-agers breathless.

The style of Kahles, although still caricatural in its depiction of characters, was moving toward greater realism in the suggestion of movement. Moreover, this blend of comical style and realistic action persisted (and still persists) for a long time in numerous adventure-type comic strips, a fact which in no way deprives Kahles of the credit for being the first to introduce suspense into the comic strip.

The Europeans also contributed to the nascent art of the comics. In 1903 the Dutch illustrator and engraver Gustave Verbeck created the series of "The Upside-Downs," which relates the adventures of Little Lady Lovekins and her mentor, Old Man Muffaroo. The drawing is fresh and poetic; the stories are rich in imaginative inventiveness tempered with irony, in the service of an original narrative technique. After

Winsor McCay,
"Little Nemo."

Martian fireworks.

Copyright McCay Company. By permission of Mr. Woody Gelman.

The magician makes Slumberland appear in all its glory for Nemo and his companions.

LITTLE NEMO IN SLUMBERLAND
AW! WAIT! LISTEN! A MINUTE DON'T RUN!
I CANT STOP TO LISTEN TO YOU
YOU SURELY AREN'T GOING TO RUN AWAY FROM ME!
GICK ICK OCK OOCK GEK EK!
I'LL GO AND CALL HELP!
HELP! OH! HELP! HELP! SOME ONE HELP ME! HELP!
I'LL GET SOME ONE TO HELP US!
GOOGLE GEEGLE GIMP IG BUMPLE!
WHO'S... EH! WHO IS CALLING ME? UM SOME ONE IS CALLING ME!
ICE CREAM
TOYS
IT'S ME, NEMO, CALLING YOU! WHAT ARE YOU YELLING HELP FOR? GO TO SLEEP!
WINSOR McCAY

reading the strip, it need only be turned upside down for the uninterrupted continuation of the action. In his use of this method, Verbeck demonstrated an incredible technical virtuosity that foreshadowed the work of Salvador Dali.

Verbeck is also the author of another series, "The Terrors of the Tiny Tads" (also in the old *Herald*), which is less exceptional in its narrative technique but quite nightmarish in atmosphere. In two rows of pictures, each captioned with a short verse, four more or less childlike, tiny characters are seen traveling in a dangerous country peopled by creatures that are hybrids either of various animals or of animals and objects. These creatures illustrate the combination words invented by Verbeck in his text, following the well-known principle in which, for example, "trolley car" and "caribou" give the trolleycaribou, a huge quadruped with windows. The wildcaterpillar, a cross between a caterpillar and a wildcat, frequent forests. The text, which forms an uninterrupted poem, cannot be translated (one could find equivalents in other languages, but the animals would not correspond with Verbeck's drawings). The precursors of this series are to be found in the nonsense rhymes of the English poet Edward Lear, with his jumblies, the boat trips of the owl and the pussy cat, and the Dong with a luminous nose. In contrast to Lear's works, however, "The Terrors of the Tiny Tads" is terrifying rather than whimsical.

In 1906 Lyonel Feininger, the German who was later to become a famous painter, introduced several series, the best known of which was "The Kin-der-Kids" —a skinny kid and his buddy, a boy with a balloon-like silhouette. The Kin-der-Kids travel around the world in a series of adventures that are sometimes comical, at other times fantastic. Feininger's style, full of ease and quiet confidence, is beautifully adapted to portray the somewhat disquieting and yet comic ambiance that forms the setting for his characters' adventures. Feininger's already nascent esthetic preoccupations are evident throughout the entire strip; in the geometrical precision of certain landscape elements, as in the deliberate exaggeration of movement, we cannot fail to recognize the elements of the developing cubist and expressionist movements.

The greatest innovator of the age, however, was Winsor McCay. His wonderful "Little Nemo in Slumberland," a masterpiece of elegance, simplicity, and poetry, was created in 1905 and interrupted in 1911; re-created in 1924, it finally disappeared forever in 1927. Its plot is very simple: each night Little Nemo is carried in dream to Slumberland, and each morning he is brought back to the daily reality by the harsh shock of awakening. The sudden fall of the conclusion, which some readers found disagreeable, was perhaps intended by McCay as a protective screen against possible criticism by narrow rationalists, or even as a barrier against his own somnambulistic tendencies. However, this abrupt conclusion in no way impedes what we might call the ineluctable development of the plot. On each of his nocturnal rambles, Little Nemo penetrates a little more deeply into the dream. One after another he meets those who are to be his companions and guides: Flip, the green, grimacing dwarf who involves him in increasingly dangerous escapades; Impy the cannibal, Slivers the dog, Dr. Pill, and the Princess and her father, King Morpheus. Under McCay's pen, Little Nemo undertakes a genuine methodological exploration of the dream; little by little he reveals to us its logic, its language, and its mythical landscapes. Under their influence Little Nemo changes imperceptibly; the timid, wonderstruck little boy becomes more assured, and grows in his own esteem as he enters into increasingly close intimacy with his

Winsor McCay, "Little Nemo." With the permission of Mr. Woody Gelman.

"The principal factor in my success has been an absolute desire to draw constantly. I never decided to be an artist. Simply, I couldn't stop myself from drawing. I drew for my own pleasure. I never wanted to know whether or not someone liked my drawings. I have never kept one of my drawings. I drew on walls, the school blackboard, old bits of paper, the walls of barns. Today I'm still as fond of drawing as when I was a kid—and that's a long time ago—but, surprising as it may seem, I never thought about the money I would receive for my drawings. I simply drew and drew."

WINSOR MCCAY, letter to Clare Briggs.

THE UPSIDE-DOWNS OF LITTLE LADY LOVEKINS AND OLD MAN MUFFAROO

They try to catch a big fat bird.	The bird runs; they chase him,	But he gets away. Then they proceed, and
Lovekins rescues a little, long-haired boy.	And Muffaroo helps him across the river.	The little boy is glad to be safe on shore.

Gustave Verbeck, "The Upside-Downs." Copyright the Rajah Press.

Gustave Verbeck, "The Terror of the Tiny Tads."

—His Falconductor takes the fares, five acorns each a ride.
The Tiny Tads have paid for theirs—we see them all inside.

—And now they climb up mountains to the dizziest of heights,
Then down again in valleys where they see most wondrous sights.

universe. Ultimately, Little Nemo becomes ruler of his dream when he learns to be master of its powers and to interpret its laws.

In treatment and style, McCay's work is related to the best Art Nouveau. By the detailed imaginativeness of his composition, his fairy-tale landscapes, his grandiose architectural constructions, and the persistence of his dream motifs, he belongs within the great intellectual and esthetic current leading from Brueghel to the surrealists.

George McManus, a young artist in search of his personal style, already had a number of comic strips to his credit, including such humorous creations as "Snoozer," "Alma and Oliver," and "The Merry Marcelene," and a skillful depiction of a bum named Panhandle Pete. He found his style with "The Newlyweds," the story of a young couple and their insufferable child. This being a period of interest in creatures of primitive reactions, the Newlyweds' baby is a nasty little creature who is continually bawling and whose parents would do anything to make him happy. Father is a droll individual; Mother is an elegant woman, always impeccably dressed (in the style of circa 1900) despite the destructive maneuvers of the baby. McManus was now almost completely in possession of the astonishing precision of line that he was to achieve several years later.

For a long while the principal pictorial series were reserved exclusively for the Sunday supplements of the major daily newspapers. Reviving an unsuccessful 1903 attempt of Clare Briggs, on November 15, 1907, Bud Fisher created the first genuine daily comic strip, "Mr. A. Mutt." This strip related the rather unsavory doings of a racetrack sharpie, always ending with a tip for the morrow's races. In 1908, in an insane asylum, Mutt made the acquaintance of his buddy, Jeff of the eternally bewildered expression, and the strip received its definitive title of "Mutt and Jeff."

Fisher's style is quite insipid, and his characters' jokes hardly rise above the traveling-salesman level—which fact may possibly account for the immense popularity this strip always has enjoyed and continues to enjoy today. By becoming daily, the American comic strip increased its range and influence tenfold, and increasingly acquired the appearance of a genuine social phenomenon.

However, the artists continued their experiments. It was at this time that a bond was established between those two equally despised art forms, the comics and the movies. In 1909 Winsor McCay created the first animated cartoon of real merit ("Gertie the Dinosaur"), while Harry Hershfield satirized the serial movies of the day in "Desperate Desmond" (1910). On this year the first age of the American comic strip drew to a close.

It had been a great age, filled with astonishing innovations, exciting experiments, and daring attempts. This period of 1900–1910 is considered by some to be the golden age of the comic strip. In any event it was the golden age of the cartoonists, who were not yet laboring under the difficulties nowadays imposed upon them and who were able to give free rein to their originality, talent, and imagination. Today we are able to discern, in their unorganized efforts and the confusion of their experiments, the first elements of what was to become a monumental creative ensemble.

Now that we have observed the rapid development of the comic strip in the United States, if we return to Europe we find that it is already outmoded and at a standstill, and is clinging to the formula that it invented: that of the picture illustrating a text beneath it. The comic strip in Europe had remained at the children's magazine stage. This is not to say that the European series of that period were lacking in interest or talent. Those that deserve to be remembered, however, are few in number.

According to a survey by F. E. Barcus in one American city, the number of comic-strip titles almost tripled in ten years, rising from 65 in the period 1900–1904 to 165 in 1905–1909, a figure that was never again reached. Before 1910 the casts of characters were permanent, but the titles changed each week; in effect, in these cases the series was called after the name of its principal characters. Toward 1910 permanent titles came into general use, with varying subtitles. Until around 1925 there were many short-lived series, marking the experimental phase of the comic strip.

1. George McManus, "The Newlyweds." Copyright King Features Syndicate, Inc.

THE GENTLEMAN IN BLACK

1. It appeared around the curve in the track, spitting, puffing, grumbling, and terribly filthy. This didn't offend Bécassine in the least. She climbed into an open car into which about twenty people were crowded. Most of them were peasant women returning home from the market at Dinard.

2. A conversation began. "Everything was terribly expensive at the market," said a young woman.

3. "The cost-of-living crisis," said a gentleman dressed entirely in black.

4. His neighbor remarked: "Butter wasn't to be had even for the price of its weight in gold. What are we supposed to cook with?"

5. "The butter crisis," declared the gentleman in black.

6. Another lady added: "And how are we supposed to cook? I've been looking for coal for eight days. Impossible to find it. And yet I saw mountains of it, the other week, on the docks at Saint-Malo. What are they doing with it?"

7. "The coal crisis . . . the transportation crisis . . ." said the gentleman in black. "Ladies, our age will be known to history as the age of crises."

8. He was interrupted by the ticket agent.

9. Upon seeing him, with a single movement all the women and even the gentleman took money out of their pockets—some 5-franc bills, others 10 francs, others 20 francs.

10. "It's always the same story," sighed the ticket agent. "Where am I supposed to get change? I don't have a single sou in my moneybag."

11. "The change crisis!" said the gentleman in black, becoming more and more solemn and gloomy.

2. H. C. Fisher, "Mutt and Jeff." Copyright Bell Syndicate.

LE MONSIEUR NOIR

Il apparaissait au tournant de la route, crachant, soufflant et geignant, sale à faire frémir. Ce détail n'offusqua nullement Bécassine. Elle monta dans une baladeuse ouverte, où étaient empilées une vingtaine de personnes, pour la plupart paysannes revenant du marché de Dinard.

La conversation s'engagea. « Tout était hors de prix au marché, » fit une jeune femme.

« — La crise de la vie chère, » prononça un monsieur tout de noir vêtu.

Sa voisine dit : « Même au poids de l'or on n'aurait pu avoir du beurre. Alors, avec quoi qu'on fera la soupe ? »

« — La crise du beurre, » articula le monsieur noir.

Une dame reprit : « Et comment la faire cuire, la soupe ? Voilà huit jours que je cours pour avoir du charbon. Pas moyen d'en obtenir. Pourtant, j'en ai vu des montagnes, l'autre semaine, sur les quais de Saint-Malo. Qu'est-ce qu'on en fait ? »

« — Crise du charbon... Crise des transports, opina le monsieur noir... Mesdames, l'époque que nous vivons portera dans l'histoire le nom d'époque des crises. »

Il fut interrompu par l'entrée de l'employé qui venait recevoir les places.

A sa vue, d'un seul mouvement, toutes les femmes et le monsieur lui-même sortirent de leur poche des billets, qui de 5 francs, qui de 10 francs, qui de 20 francs.

« — Toujours la même chose, gémit le receveur ; où voulez-vous que je prenne de quoi vous rendre ? Je n'ai pas un sou, pas un franc, rien de rien dans ma sacoche. »

« — La crise de la monnaie ! » dit le monsieur noir, de plus en plus solennel et lugubre.

J. P. Pinchon and Caumery, "Bécassine." Copyright Ed. Gauthier-Languereau.

Louis Forton, "Les Pieds-Nickelés." Copyright S.P.E.

The news that the famous Pieds-Nickelés gang had finally fallen into the hands of the police had spread among the crowd like a trail of gunpowder. An indescribable mob pressed close to the winding-drum of the balloon in order to get a better view of the famous bandits. From the nacelle, Croquignol, Ribouldingue, and Filochard looked down, without the slightest enthusiasm, at the crowd of rubbernecks for whom their arrest was one more attraction among the other attractions of the festival.

With all his colleagues on hand, Mirette gave the order to have the balloon brought down. "We're sunk, fellas," sighed Ribouldingue. "Before five minutes have passed the cops will have collared us."

The nacelle came down very slowly, and soon it was only about a hundred yards above the earth. The Pieds-Nickelés saw the two policemen, who were greeting their arrival with their most mocking smiles, and the words, "Okay, you guys, this time we've got you for good!"

"Not yet, you idiots," sneered Filochard, when the balloon was only fifty yards up. And taking from his pocket an enormous cutlass, he abruptly cut the cable holding the captive balloon. A roar of mingled surprise and stupefaction burst from twenty thousand mouths. The nacelle, no longer held by a cable, had leaped . . .

. . . with a bound to a great height. Hanging joyfully over the nacelle, the three buddies waved their hats, crying, "So long, Cops! It's our turn to make fun of you mugs, you melon-heads! See you again soon, you simpletons!"

Attilio Mussino, "Bilbolbul." Copyright Corriere dei Piccoli.

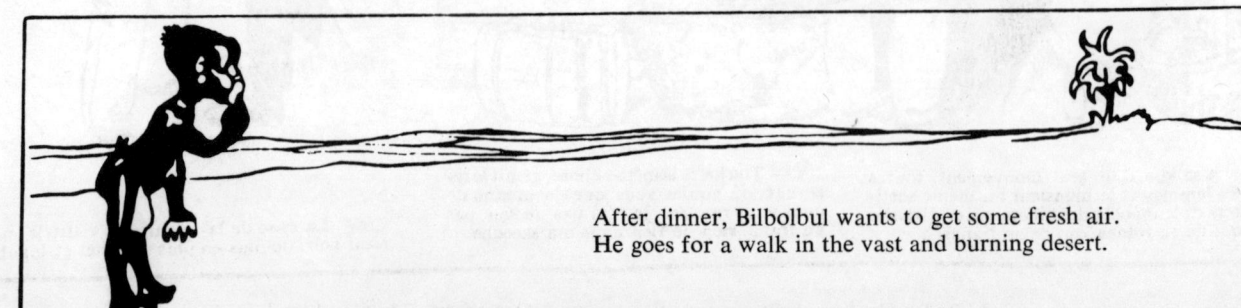

After dinner, Bilbolbul wants to get some fresh air.
He goes for a walk in the vast and burning desert.

In 1905 the painter Jean-Pierre Pinchon improvised a little story for use as a filler in the magazine *La Semaine de Suzette*. Its heroine was a rather stupid young girl from Brittany who had several mishaps in Paris. The readers clamored for the continuation of the story, and so "Bécassine" was born. Pinchon did the drawing for the strip, while the text came from the pen of "Caumery" (Maurice Languereau, editor of *La Semaine de Suzette*). Bécassine remained faithful to the theme of the little story from which she had been born: the adventures of the young Breton housemaid (whose real name was Annaïk Labornez), who was not so much stupid as boundlessly naïve and completely devoted to her mistress, a kindly lady of Junoesque proportions. Out of good nature and a desire to please, Bécassine continually commits stupid blunders, and is continually being forgiven for the same reasons. The Bretons never particularly enjoyed this famous comic strip.

As regards its technique, "Bécassine" alternates between the old-fashioned comic strip and the profusely illustrated novel. Pinchon rarely frames his illustrations, which are very numerous and interlarded with a continuing text. On the other hand, he makes great use of the diaphragm, the small round picture used to draw attention to a point, depict the thoughts of the characters, provide a close-up, or pick out the essential aspects of a background. Pinchon, a professional artist, was a realist and a remarkable chronicler of French life. Everything can be found in his work: the old railroads, the street scenes, the statues of the park at Versailles buried under sandbags during the war, Art Nouveau bathrooms, cubism, provincial drawing rooms, and fashions, which he was the first to introduce into the comic strip. Following the example set by Christophe, the text is written in an excellent literary style tinged with irony.

"Bécassine" was soon followed by a comic strip the heroes of which were neither honest nor devoted nor forgiven. Its creator, Louis Forton, was almost a live version of Mutt: a pillar of racetrack society, who came to the comic strip by accident. In 1908 he created one of the classics of the French comic strip: "La Bande des Pieds-Nickelés" (The Nickel-Plated-Feet Gang). This story of three buddies—burglars, swindlers, and thieves—who possess inexhaustible and more or less effective imaginations excels particularly by its script, which is carried to extraordinary lengths by Forton's inventiveness and by the gallery of characters—dupes, ugly women, conceited bourgeois, female battle-axes—who march through the strip. The draftsmanship is terrible. In technique the strip remains faithful to the system of the continuing text beneath the picture, complemented, however, by a few balloons; we find in it the first onomatopoeia, and even several instances of the "voice-off." The "Pieds-Nickelés" appeared in a children's magazine, but by its subject, its disillusioned and mocking moral tone, and particularly its political allusions, it was certainly an adult series. Forton was the first, and indeed the only, person (not even excepting Al Capp) to use well-known figures in his plot under their real names. He jibed at Déroulède and Jaurès, and assassinated Camille Pelletan, whom he depicted as shabby, covered with dandruff, and "mixed up with hydrotherapy for quite some time." The slang used in the text was a reaction against the literary trend represented by Christophe and Pinchon, and the depiction of the underworld a reaction against the provincial upper classes of "Bécassine."

Italian comic-strip production began in 1909 in the *Corriere dei Piccoli* with "Bilbolbul," a little Negro boy who was able to change his appearance. This character, a creation of Attilio Mussino, had endless mishaps in an imaginary Africa. Mussino systematically exploited figures of speech by depicting them literally: Bilbolbul "had winged feet," became "white with fear" or "green with rage"; things "caught his eye," and he "burst with pride." Instead of balloons, "Bilbolbul" had doggerel verses under its pictures—the distinctive signature of the Italian comic strip.

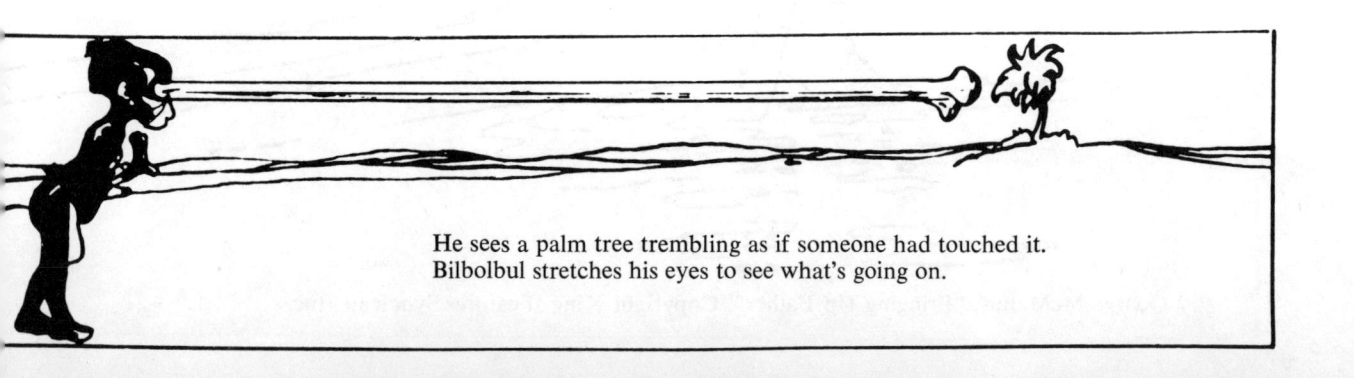

He sees a palm tree trembling as if someone had touched it.
Bilbolbul stretches his eyes to see what's going on.

George McManus, "Bringing Up Father." Copyright King Features Syndicate, Inc.

3
period of adjustment: 1910–1928

Within the growing variety of themes and the astonishing diversity of styles that characterized the American comic strip in 1910, two opposing intellectual currents were already coming to light among the cartoonists. One group, which might be called the "entertainers," saw in the comic strip only an amusement. The other group, the "thinkers," wished to "intellectualize" the comics, and attempt to explore all their possibilities, both formal and narrative. The latter tendency, which we have already encountered in Winsor McCay, found its best representative in the person of George Herriman.

Herriman's strip "Krazy Kat" utilized the most basic possible plot: Krazy is in love with the mouse Ignatz. The latter, exasperated by Krazy Kat's attentions, bombards the cat with bricks. Offissa B. Pupp, the dog and guardian of law and order, is only too happy to collar Ignatz and fling him into jail. Each episode is simply a variation on this theme, and the brick is the instrument of the fate that links the three elements of the eternal triangle. The action, rich in suggestions and symbols, is bathed in an atmosphere of uncertainty and strangeness. Landscapes and objects are constantly changing and being transformed: a rock becomes a battleship; a mountain takes on the appearance of a cathedral; space loses its continuity; and strange shapes arise out of the void; language acquires an autonomous logic, and loses all intelligibility. The protagonists, witnesses of this cosmic disorder, show neither surprise nor curiosity, but tirelessly repeat the same ritual and absurd gestures. It is impossible not to recognize in this strip the methods of surrealism, adapted to the comic strip.

Created in 1911 under the title of "Krazy Kat and Ignatz" (it was christened "Krazy Kat" in 1913), "Krazy Kat" continued without interruption until the death of George Herriman in 1944.

After ten years, another cat came to join Krazy: Pat Sullivan's "Felix the Cat." A newcomer from the animated cartoon, he brought to the comic strip the poetry of its strange landscapes, its flights into the world of the dream, the melancholy of deserted forests and roads in which the skinny black cat wanders under the low-hanging full moon. "Felix the Cat" is full of sadness. Felix is the cat who walks alone; he is not surrounded by the friendly world of that Coconino County in which Krazy lives. Solitude, hunger, cold, and darkness are the themes of his life. Even when he escapes to fairyland, or goes on dangerous sidereal excursions, he always encounters indifference and the big hobnailed shoes that eject him.

Milt Gross and Rube Goldberg must be included among the artists who were then carrying on experiments with the language of the comic strip similar to those of Herriman. These two artists have much in common: a parodical, exaggerated style and a comic imagination for which they are indebted to Frederick Opper, a strong penchant for absurd situations, the effect of which is to precipitate a chain reaction, a tendency to utilize language for aggressive purposes. Even their careers present strange similarities in the number of occupations carried on, often simultaneously, only a small number of which were devoted to the comic strip. Their contribution, however, is by no means negligible.

"Count Screwloose of Toulouse," created by Milt

"KRAZY KAT"
Registered U. S. Patent Office
BUT, MY DEAR KRAZY - A BLUE MOON - NOT A BLUE MOON - - -
YETZ, OFFISSA PUPP - A BLUE MOON - IGNATZ SAID POTZA TIBBLY, WEN THE BLUE MOON CAME UP HE'D BE HERE - AN' HE SAID I SHOULD WAIT.
IN THAT CASE, HE WILL NEVER BE HERE AND YOU WILL BE WAITING A LONG, LONG TIME - - -
YET YOU DO EDMIT THAT A MOON WILL COME UP - -
OH, I DO, INDEED - BUT NOT A BLUE MOON - NO-NO- NO NOT A BLUE MOON - - -
BUT IGNATZ WAS SO SHOE ONE WOULD - AN' WHOM ARE I TO DOT HIS WOID? L'IL BLUE MOON BIMS.
HAA-HAAA A - BEHOLD - THE MOON RISING ALL AGOLD - ERE IT SETS 'T WILL HAVE TURNED TO SILVER - BUT BLUE NEVER
SIT YOU THERE IF YOU MUST, MY FAIR FRAIL FRIEND - UNTIL THAT BLUE MOON POKES IT'S FACE OVER YON MESA - I WILL GO SEEK THE MALEFACTOR WHO CHOUSED YOU.
HE DINT SAY RED, HE DINT SAY GRIN, HE DINT SAY PING - HE SAID BLUE - BEE-ELL-OO-OO-OO BLUE.
2-6
HERRIMAN

1. G. Herriman, "Krazy Kat." Copyright King Features Syndicate, Inc.
Having been fooled by Ignatz, Krazy, "a vagabond, and an explorer of those regions of illusion that only the winds cross by day and the moonbeams reveal by night" (in Herriman's own words), is waiting for the blue moon to rise.
2, 3, 4. Pat Sullivan, "Felix the Cat." Copyright King Features Syndicate, Inc. Even in fairyland, Felix finds cold, indifference, and absurdity.

1. Rube Goldberg, "Boob McNutt." Copyright McNaught Syndicate and Rube Goldberg.

2. Elzie Segar, "Thimble Theatre."
Copyright King Features Syndicate, Inc.

3. Milt Gross, "Banana Oil." Copyright New York World.

Gross in 1919, presents a series of variations on the theme of the madman who escapes from the asylum. Upon contact with the outer world and its divagations, he has only one desire: to return as quickly as possible to the establishment he has left. Boob McNutt, created in 1918 by Rube Goldberg in the series of the same name, is the classic innocent, the butt of the machinations of a world possessed by perversion and madness. Only the stupidity of the character enables him to escape from his adversaries, whose evil but too logical minds are continually circumvented by Boob's completely irrational thinking. The sometimes bitter spirit and frenzied imagination of Gross and Goldberg foreshadowed the grating humor and eccentricities of the Marx Brothers.

Elzie Segar's "Thimble Theatre," which began its long career in 1919, falls between "Krazy Kat" and the creations of Milt Gross and Rube Goldberg. This series tells of the tribulations of a scatterbrained family composed of Olive Oyl, a dull, pretentious old maid; her brother Castor, an irascible idiot; and her mother, Nana; her father, Cole; and her timid and foolish fiancé, Ham Gravy. Segar's humor is verbal rather than visual, and he is a past master in the art of creating inimitable characters whom he then plunges into the most bewildering situations. In 1929, for example, ten years after the beginning of the strip, Olive, Castor, and the entire clan set sail for an African island, accompanied by a magic hen whose power will permit them to blow up the bank of a casino run by a rheumatic and oily character named Fadewell. The stage of the Thimble Theatre was now ready to welcome a newcomer, whose personality and deeds will be covered in more detail in the next chapter.

The Hearst-Pulitzer rivalry continued in the background. In 1912 Rudolph Dirks decided to leave the *Journal* for the *World*, and to take the "Katzies" with him. Hearst was vehemently opposed to this idea, and the case was taken to court, where it was settled in a manner worthy of Solomon: Dirks obtained the right to draw his characters under a new title, while the *Journal* retained the right to the same characters and to the original title. The result of this precedent-making decision was, starting in 1913, two different versions of the same comic strip!

At first Dirks called his new series "Hans and Fritz," but when America entered the war in 1917 against the Germans he rechristened it "The Captain and the Kids," which title it still bears today. To replace Dirks, the *Journal* called upon Harold Knerr, an artist with a great humorous talent. Knerr brought to the strip a better graphic organization, but faithfully preserved its diabolical inspiration, frenzied rhythm, and incomparable speech. This was one of the cases of artistic mimesis of which examples can sometimes be found in the history of the comic strip. During the First World War the strip was rechristened "The Shenanigan Kids," and its protagonists became Irishmen, despite their Teutonic jargon! But the strip quickly regained its original title shortly after the war.

It is rather difficult to decide upon the merits of each of the rival cartoonists. Knerr was perhaps more attentive to detail and composition, while Dirks particularly sought for percussive effect. But the imaginativeness, fun, and ingeniousness are the same in both, and make of this dual comic strip a modern and incomparable comic epic.

The most outstanding comic strip of this period,

"After the everlasting simper of the girly magazines and movies, the hardness of the American comic strip is a relief. It is male and ugly, whereas nearly all the other magazine features of our newspapers are 'sweet femininity' for the delectation of washerwomen. . . . The draughtsmanship itself is hard and angular; the faces and figures are of an intense ugliness, and the strip rejoices in a brutality of color. . . .

"Goldberg's are the most alarming grotesques: the men, who all seem to be made of putty, with floating whiskers and strange knobs on their foreheads, and vast ears and mouths and teeth, are like medieval monsters, like an old lecherous company out of Rabelais; the women are inhumanly fat and ill-favored; the children are little pests; the beautiful women a mockery. The postures and proportions of his people are alike ridiculous. . . . As good is his conception of architecture and interior decoration: his endearingly ugly statues, the hideous lamps set in the middle flight of a balustrade, the tortured figures on which whole edifices rest, the furniture that lacks equilibrium, are all observed phenomena, corresponding fairly to the unhappier efforts of rustic America since simple architecture and good design gave way to suburban developments and manufactured atrocities."

—GILBERT SELDES, "Some Sour Commentators,"
The New Republic, Vol. XLIII, No. 549

40

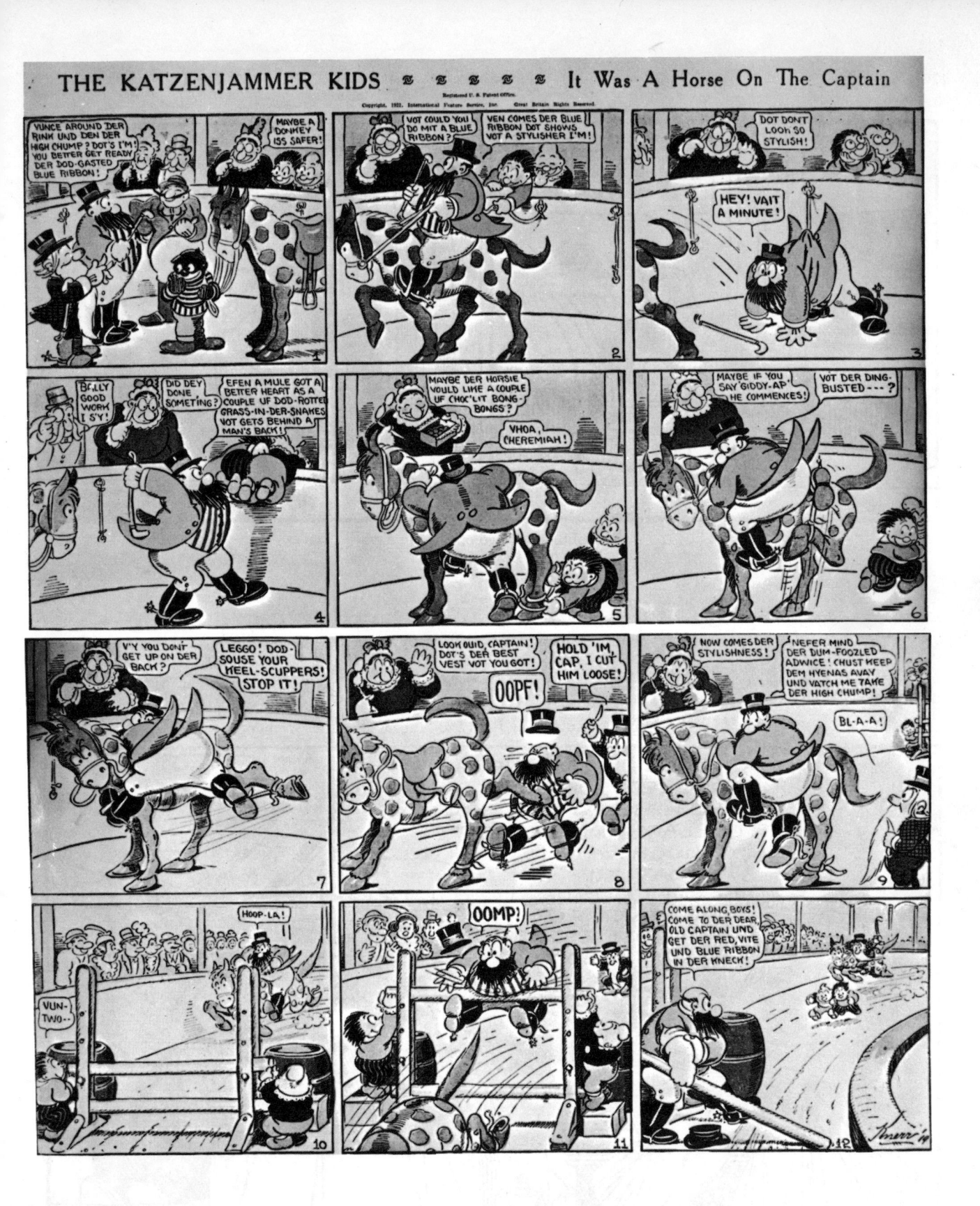

Harold H. Knerr, "The Katzenjammer Kids."

1. A game of golf that won't be peaceful for very long.
2. The Captain, disguised as a cow, tries to flee.

Copyright King Features Syndicate, Inc.

Solitude for two on a rainy day.

George McManus, "Bringing Up Father." Copyright King Features Syndicate, Inc.

Norah, the daughter of Jiggs and Maggie, in all her splendor.

Cliff Sterrett, "Polly and Her Pals." Copyright King Features Syndicate, Inc.

1. Martin Branner, "Winnie Winkle." Copyright Chicago Tribune—New York News Syndicate, Inc.

2. Sydney Smith, "The Gumps." Copyright Chicago Tribune—New York News Syndicate, Inc.

however, was "Bringing Up Father," begun in 1913 by the pen of the inspired and prolific artist George McManus. A play called *The Rising Generation*, which relates the changes that take place in the life of a workingman who has suddenly become rich, furnished McManus with the principal theme for his series. The family quarrels that pit Jiggs, the former mason who has become a millionaire by winning the sweepstakes, and his wife, Maggie, an ex-washwoman, against each other, arise from their contrasting reactions to this unexpected and sudden wealth. Whereas Maggie, a monster of ugliness, snobbism, and egotism, seeks to forget her social origins and frequent the *beau monde*, Jiggs desires only to meet his buddies at the corner saloon for a game of pinochle and a good plate of corned beef and cabbage.

McManus's wealth of imagination is inexhaustible. The secondary characters, who are appropriately ridiculous, are delineated with a sure hand, and the astonishing setting (a mixture of rococo architecture, Art Nouveau furnishings, and overrefined knickknacks) forms an appropriate backdrop for the flood of gags.*

McManus's vocation, like his inspiration, was essentially theatrical, and "Bringing Up Father" abounds in stage devices. For forty years, until his death in 1954, McManus was to dissect the absurdities, fads, and eccentricities of American society with a cheerful briskness and a good-natured humor reminiscent of Eugène Labiche, while the irresistible rhythm and preposterous rebounds of the plot recall Georges Feydeau. Brought to the stage and screen, and translated into every language, "Bringing Up Father" was the first of the comic strips to achieve international fame.

This renown was to a large extent accelerated by the growth of the syndicate system. The syndicates were distributing agencies that served dozens and sometimes hundreds of publications. The first genuine syndicate, the International News Service, was established by Hearst in 1912; in 1914 this gave birth to King Features Syndicate, which was followed several years later by the Chicago Tribune–Daily News Syndicate, the United Feature Syndicate (a subsidiary of United Press International), and numerous others on a smaller scale.

This new method of distribution assured the dissemination of the comic strips on a scale hitherto unknown, and contributed greatly to the wealth of their authors. However, it also imposed sometimes excessive limitations on the freedom of expression of the cartoonists, who, in their desire to reach the widest possible audience, selected their themes with a view to displeasing no one. This resulted in the proliferation of comic strips dealing with that most bourgeois of all institutions, the family. The best (or worst) example of these family strips is furnished by "The Gumps," which appeared in 1917. In conception, spirit, and style this strip is hopelessly mediocre, and its characters (Andy Gump, the father, a caricature composed of a pipestem body surmounted by a chinless face; Min, the mother; and their offspring) are drawn with a total lack of talent. The dialogue, for the most part a compound of gossip and commonplace remarks, is

---

* In an article published in *Terre d'Images*, Pierre Couperie compares McManus's settings with those used by Orson Welles in *Citizen Kane*. Perhaps both of them used the same model: the castle built to the order of William Randolph Hearst at San Simeon, California. In this regard it is interesting to note that Hearst was George McManus's boss.

The topics of the family, the young girl, and the kids predominated from 1910 to 1929. Older couples—the likable "Nebbs" of Sol Hess, C. Briggs's nagging "Mr. and Mrs.," or H. J. Tuthill's "The Bungle Family"—were eclipsed by "Bringing Up Father." J. Murphy's "Toots and Casper" depicted the young and somewhat irresponsible couple. Romantic or silly young girls formed a rhythmic parade of alliterations: "Tillie the Toiler" (R. Westover), "Syncopating Sue" (C. Jensen), "Flapper Fanny" (G. Parker), "Fritzi Ritz" (L. Whitington followed by E. Bushmiller), "Dumb Dora" (Chic Young), "Pam" (Brewerton), "Betty" (C. A. Voight), and "Boots and Her Buddies" (E. Martin). At the beginning of the thirties, Chic Young's "Blondie" began as a scatterbrained young thing. Godwin's "Connie" was a reaction against this trend; it was also represented in England by the first version of Pett's "Jane." There were few teen-agers—C. Ed's "Harold Teen" and M. Blosser's "Freckles and His Friends." Kids, however, were legion. With the exception of P. Crosby's "Skippy," an enigmatic boy with a blank look, they were everyday boys, not evil geniuses like the Katzenjammer Kids: W. Berndt's "Smitty," Byrnes's "Reg'lar Fellows," A. Carter's "Just Kids," Winner's "Elmer," McNamara's "On Our Block," and so on.

1. Frank King, "Gasoline Alley." Copyright Chicago Tribune—New York News Syndicate, Inc.

2. Frank Willard, "Moon Mullins." Copyright Chicago Tribune—New York News Syndicate, Inc.

3, 4. Harold Gray, "Little Orphan Annie." Copyright Chicago Tribune—New York News Syndicate, Inc.

5. Roy Crane, "Wash Tubbs." Copyright N.E.A.

Billy De Beck, "Barney Google." Copyright King Features Syndicate, Inc.

Ed Wheelan, "Minute Movies." Copyright Ed Wheelan.

sickeningly ordinary, and the plot revolves for the most part around petty financial transactions. This noncomic strip possessed neither humor nor wit, but it nevertheless enjoyed an extraordinary popularity that survived the death of its creator, Sidney Smith, in 1935. "The Gumps" was then taken over by Gus Edson, and ended its long career only in 1959.

A variation on the family theme was provided by those strips that dealt not with the parents but rather with the daughter of the house, her problems, her preoccupations—the "girl strips." "Polly and Her Pals," introduced by Cliff Sterrett in 1912, was the first strip of this type. Polly is a sophisticated, poised young person whose very seductive charms contrast sharply with the caricatural appearance of her parents and suitors. While the plot is quite conventional, the strip possesses undeniable plastic qualities. Cliff Sterrett's very personal style consists of an almost abstract arrangement of blacks and whites, a well-developed style of composition, and a completely modern stylization of line. The strip survived two world wars, and disappeared only when its creator retired in 1958.

Martin Branner's "Winnie Winkle" followed in the same tradition in 1920. The fame of this strip is due particularly to the feats of Perry Winkle, the heroine's brother, who took over the Sunday page, leaving the daily strip to his sister Winnie. While they never achieved the stature of the Katzenjammers, Perry and his friends, the Rinkeydinks, possessed sufficient charm, originality, and freshness to have justly acquired international fame. In France, under the title of "Bicot et les Rantan-plans," their adventures have been enjoyed by an entire generation of Frenchmen.

Soon after its debut in 1919, another family-oriented strip, called "Gasoline Alley," marked an important and fundamental innovation in the comic strip: for the first time, characters in a comic strip grew old along with their readers. Thus Skeezix, who was born in 1921, is today in his forties, and the father of several children. The graphic style of Frank King, the strip's author, is simple, and the plainly optimistic plot enables us particularly to participate in the development of the characters. From this point of view, "Gasoline Alley" can certainly be considered the first *Bildungsroman* in pictures!

One voice was raised in vehement protest against this idyllic depiction of the joys of family life: that of Frank Willard who, in his "Moon Mullins," engaged in a bitter and almost despairing satire of family life. Moon Mullins is a hooligan, his brother Kayo a gallows bird, Uncle Willie a derelict, and the other characters are all on a par with these three. They detest one another, but have neither the courage nor the willpower to escape from the mediocrity that binds them together. Willard's humor has a corrosive effect in its sharp precision of line and the terrible truth of the dialogue, as well as in the merciless logic of the situations. "Moon Mullins," which made its debut in 1923, must be counted among the best of our contemporary "black comedies."

All during the twenties, a tiny, often famished-looking man with gaiters and a melon hat, and accompanied by a caricature of a racehorse, was walking across the United States: Billy De Beck's "Barney Google" (1919). He too encountered the most incredible collection of freaks, false friends, fools, and puffed-up individuals imaginable—the perfect complement of those in "Moon Mullins."

With "Little Orphan Annie," created by Harold Gray in 1924, another innovation was instituted: the introduction of political ideology (in this case, that of the Right) into the comic strip. Orphan Annie, the

---

The proliferation of daily comic strips and serial stories resulted in the gradual appearance of five types of serials:

1. Those which were published only on Sunday: for example, "Katzenjammer Kids." (There was a daily strip, but it was very short-lived.)
2. Black-and-white strips, which appeared only on weekdays. This was usually only a transitory stage; when they were successful, Sunday versions were added.
3. Series that appeared on weekdays and Sundays. The Sunday strip was a sequel to Saturday's episode. Since some of the Sunday readers did not buy the newspaper during the week, they were not interested in this type of strip (which is no longer in existence). Two other types of strips were created for them:
4. Series in which the daily strip was carried over from one day to the next and from Saturday to Monday, and the Sunday strip from one Sunday to the next. The hero thus led a double life, since his black-and-white adventures were completely separate from his color adventures.
5. "Synchronized comics," begun by the Chicago *Tribune*. These were carried from Saturday to Sunday, but also, without repetition or break, from Saturday to Monday and Sunday to Sunday. The story could be read six or seven days a week or only on Sunday. The dividing up of the script was an exercise in virtuosity. "Little Orphan Annie" is an example of this type.

BLIGHTER AND FLEA AT THE FAIR AFTER MIDNIGHT

Panel 1. People gone! We able to eat little white man. Good! Good!

Panel 2. Long, long time we no eat human flesh. S-h-h: No noise! White no need know we eat good.

Panel 3. Me make fire.
Me go kill little white man.

Panel 5. (Noise of siren wailing.)

Panel 6. What that siren?
Me not know.

Panel 10. Luckily no damage was done! Congratulations, fellows! I noticed you were the first to arrive at the scene of the fire!

Alain Saint-Ogan, "Zig et Puce." Copyright Alain Saint-Ogan.

BLIGHTER AND FLEA: A BIG HISTORICAL PARADE

Panel 1. No, we couldn't have stayed with that tooth-puller. It wasn't a real job. But in spite of everything we still haven't a cent in our pockets.
Nonsense! We'll soon solve your problem. But Blighter, look at all those people.

Panel 2. Excuse us, sir, could you tell us what everyone's waiting for?
A historic parade is about to pass by. . . . And later on there'll be a big tournament.

Panel 3. There they are!

Last Panel. Let's go to the tournament, Blighter. Maybe we'll be able to earn a little money.
You're right. . . . Let's follow them!

52

1. Louis Forton, "Bibi Fricotin." Copyright S.P.E.

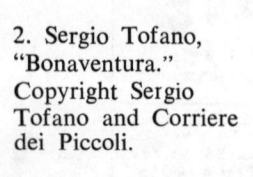

2. Sergio Tofano, "Bonaventura." Copyright Sergio Tofano and Corriere dei Piccoli.

Night is finished, dawn is coming,
And they're still flying through the sky.
What unfortunate far away planet
Is their goal?

heroine of the series, eternally accompanied by her dog Sandy, owes her life solely to the mysterious protection of Daddy Warbucks, a fabulously wealthy and omnipotent captain of industry, the symbolic incarnation of capitalism triumphant. In "Little Orphan Annie," Harold Gray displays a masterly sense of composition and an incontestable evocative power, which unfortunately are spoiled by the rudimentary draftsmanship and frequent insipidity of the story line.

Another novelty was introduced in 1924 by a young artist named Roy Crane, whose strip "Wash Tubbs" marks the definitive debut of the adventure strip. Wash, a pint-sized adventurer—influenced by Barney Google—found a buddy in 1928: a tall chap named Easy, who stole the show from Wash. Crane quickly introduced innovations into his style, using delicate gray shadings and dark blacks, and into the narrative technique, which was rapid and even brutal when required by the plot.

At the beginning of 1929, the American comic strip presented an appearance of stability that in a scant few months was to be radically upset by the introduction of narrative techniques and stylistic procedures of a completely different type. At the origin of these developments (which are dealt with in greater detail in the next chapter) was, in addition to "Wash Tubbs," a series that has unjustly been forgotten: Ed Wheelan's "Minute Movies." Beginning in 1922, this strip utilized the "camera viewpoint" in the treatment of subjects borrowed from adventure novels such as *Ivanhoe* or *Treasure Island*, as well as the close-up in the depiction of the characters, thus paving the way for future innovations.

During this period of adaptation (which in Europe lasted until about 1932), the appearance of the European comic strip was primitive in comparison with the American strip. It was still dominated by a child-oriented imagery with stylized silhouettes, flat tints of bright colors, anthropomorphic animals, and captions beneath the pictures. This style, which in France was represented by Benjamin Rabier and the children of Camo ("Miquette"), reigned supreme in Italy's *Corriere dei Piccoli*, in which Antonio Rubino had since 1909 been employing a geometric stylization and a style of draftsmanship that was simultaneously rigid and mannered, composing pretty pictures very similar to certain advertisements of that day. The style of Sergio Tofano's "Bonaventura" (1917) was more simple and expressive. With his wide white trousers, old-fashioned red coachman's coat, melon hat, and large shoes, Bonaventura is a kind of Charlie Chaplin whose misfortunes all end happily; in the last picture he is always seen receiving a huge sum of money, given him by a grateful citizen to whom he has (usually unintentionally) rendered a service.

In England we find the same general characteristics in another children's series, which appeared in 1914 in *The Rainbow*, an illustrated magazine: H. S. Foxwell's "The Bruin Boys," about several anthropomorphic animals dressed as typical little British boys. The characters created in 1919 by A. B. Payne in the *Daily Mirror* are much more animated: Pip the dog, Squeak the penguin, and soon Wilfred the rabbit, speak and act like human beings (charming ones), and mix with humans, while remaining a dog, rabbit, and penguin. Thanks to its black-and-white drawings, this series, which made considerable use of balloons, already falls within the boundaries of the comic-strip style. Another charming creature was Mary Tourtel's little bear Rupert, the hero of her series "The Adventures of the Little Lost Bear" (1920). The animals in this series, which are completely anthropmorphic, live like young Englishmen in a countryside drawn with a sensitive feeling for landscape. The draftsmanship is delicate and airy.

Side by side with these pictures for very young children, there existed what could pass for the first adventure strips. This phenomenon, which is directly derived from the *image d'Epinal*, was specifically French, and traces of it can still be found today. These stories were drawn in a realistic, often highly detailed, and almost always lifeless style, and were published in short, self-contained episodes totally unconnected with the story following. Especially representative of this type are the "Histoires en Images" and the "Belles Images," as well as the center pages of such newspapers as *Le Cri-Cri* and *Le Petit Illustré*. Their inspiration derived from historical novels, the melodrama, and the popular novel in the tradition of Arnould Galopin and Louis Boussenard.

The First World War, which riveted attention once again on contemporary reality, encouraged realistically drawn, genuine adventure strips. These continued the usual conventions of captions under the pictures and short, unrelated episodes; they were published in newspapers that dispensed martial enthusiasm to young readers (*Les Trois Couleurs, La Jeune France*). They disappeared after the war, and the traditional themes were routinely revived, because no one had realized the appeal of the serial story (although one such story—Forton's "Pieds-Nickelés"—was already in existence). Thus the First World War seems to have had no lasting effect on the French comic strip; the proliferation of sanguinary episodes, the premature failure of the adventure strip, the temporary mobilization of Bécassine (who went to Salonika), and the Pieds-Nickelés (who got as far as the Russian Front), were all transitory phenomena. The triumph of the comic element was more complete than ever.

1. Mary Tourtel, "Rupert."
Copyright Daily Express.

2. H. S. Foxwell, "Tiger Tim."
Copyright from the Rainbow and Fleetway Publications.

3. Austen Bowen Payne, "Pip, Squeak and Wilfred."
Copyright Daily Mirror.

Stories of resourceful youngsters were then fashionable on both sides of the Atlantic. In 1924 Forton created a hero reminiscent of A. Galopin's character Francinet in "Tour du Monde de Deux Gosses" (The Round-the-World Trip of Two Boys) and L. Boussenard's "Gamin de Paris" (Paris Kid). Forton's hero was called Bibi Fricotin, and he first appeared in the October 5th issue (No. 1043) of *Le Petit Illustré*. Bibi is a practical joker and teaser, as malicious as a monkey; but, like Victor Hugo's character Gavroche, he wears his heart on his sleeve. His fundamental goodness is a cause of mistaken judgments, but he more than recoups his losses, and quickly teaches ill-intentioned individuals that his revenge is painful, distressing, and inescapable, for his inventive mind is never lacking in the most surprising tricks. The high point of his career is a long round-the-world tour that would have horrified Lavarède himself, for Bibi travels without a sou in his pocket. Drawn with an agile (and nonchalant) pen, Bibi travels his road, to the accompaniment of beatings, through a festival of pranks and hoaxes, opposing a constant good humor to fate and the stupid evil of human beings.

"Bibi Fricotin" always utilized the continuous text in captions under the pictures, with an occasional balloon. The credit for the creation of the first genuine comic strip in France goes to another artist, Alain Saint-Ogan, who was to reign supreme over the French comic strip for almost twenty years and whose creations were to become known even outside Europe. He came to the comic strip from journalism in 1925, the year in which he created his principal characters, Zig and Puce (Blighter and Flea). These two young boys, one big, red-haired, and unkempt, the other thin, with pasted-down hair, were joined in 1926 by their mascot, the famous penguin Alfred, and the trio roamed the world in a long series of adventures, trying to reach an inaccessible America, which, according to the legends of the day, was the kingdom of millionaires and kidnappers.

Saint-Ogan's style was at first very angular, "decorative," and more or less influenced by cubism, but it gradually softened, without thereby losing the powerful individuality that makes its characters' attitudes unforgettable. The exclusive use of the balloon, a strong sense of effective pictorial narration with a variegated rhythm, and ingenious devices in the organization of its panels made "Zig et Puce" a milestone in the French comic strip, and mark a departure from the archaism in which it had become bogged down. Even this series, however, was not completely free of archaism in its early stages. Saint-Ogan, still under the influence of the "picture-story" tradition, began by drawing panels, each of which was a unit and could be read independently; this resulted in a certain incoherence in the narrative. Faced with the unexpected success of "Zig et Puce" (which was appearing in an adult newspaper, the *Dimanche Illustré*), the events in the story, which had originally been planned for about ten strips, were increased to thirty or forty, permitting numerous rebounds in the story. Saint-Ogan often introduces real-life settings into his pictures; with his funerals, crowd scenes, and street scenes, he is a very humorous observer of French life. His only rival was a young artist, one of his admirers, who in 1929 created another youngster, "Tintin," whom we shall meet again in the following chapter.

However, it was in an English newspaper, the *Daily Sketch*, in 1921, that the first daily comic strip (and the first for adults) in Europe was born. This was J. Millar Watt's "Pop," a fat, small, bald man in frock coat and top hat, who later acquired a confederate, the Colonel, a man twice as big as he. The humor, the skillfulness of the hatched drawing, and the frequent use of white backgrounds that concentrate interest on the characters ranged "Pop" among the best strips in the world, and beginning in 1929 it was published in the United States (in the New York *Sun*).

The comic strip was now making its appearance in various places throughout the world, including Spain ("Macaco" by R. G. López, 1911), Finland ("Pekka Puupää," by Fogeli), and Argentina (Arthur Lanteri's "Raúl"). But in the course of the thirties, an astonishing revival of the American comic strip was for all practical purposes to smother the growing competition.

Having discovered the comics only around 1918, a worthy lady who was something of a bluestocking did not view them as approvingly as did G. Seldes. Her complaints are typical:

"Good drawing in the comics is a mere accident." (Further on, she adds, "Some series are the more annoying because of the cleverness of the drawings.") "The very essence of this humor is its reassuring freedom from any artistic or intellectual nonsense. . . . One asks in dismay what is the use of art schools all over the country, of art lectures and art clubs, of docents in the museums, and critics in the press, of endless chatter about art and bringing it to the people, if the people's eyes are to be debauched and diseased weekly, if not daily, by these raw, crude, discordant washes and messes of the cheapest colored ink. . . . Inequality in our sense of humor would be a danger to democracy . . . nobody should laugh unless the feeblest minded can laugh with him."
—ELIZABETH R. PENNEL, "Our Tragic Comics," *North American Review,* No. 771 (February, 1920), pp. 252, 253, 258.

14

Harold Foster, "Prince Valiant." King Features Syndicate, Inc.

4

the upheaval of the thirties

In contrast to the rather dull interlude of the preceding decade, the period of the thirties witnessed an intense creative activity. The most striking phenomenon produced by this surge of creativity was the definitive establishment of the adventure strips, which were to pursue a resolutely independent course.

The first genuinely modern strip appeared at the beginning of 1929: "Tarzan," with drawings by Harold Foster. This hero of Edgar Rice Burroughs profited greatly by the transformation of his adventures into comic-strip form, in which he was not subjected to the mutilations inflicted on him by the movies. Harold Foster followed Burroughs's original plot quite faithfully, but its adaptation to pictorial form forced him to adopt certain stylistic innovations from the cinema: down shots and up shots, close-ups, backlighting. (It is worth noting that Foster never used the balloon, but rather a direct narrative incorporated into the picture.) Foster's style, rather timid in the early strips, gradually became more powerful, and ultimately achieved a graphic classicism that combined elegance with grandeur. Under the pen of this incomparable artist, Tarzan attained the most noble and most serene of his incarnations.

From its very first day of publication, "Tarzan" enjoyed a tremendous success. In 1936, however, this popularity was endangered by Foster's departure. United Features Syndicate, which distributed the strip, then called on an inexperienced but highly talented artist named Burne Hogarth.

Hogarth's style, at first an imitation of his predecessor's work, quickly changed and acquired an abundance of concepts and reminiscences. Into "Tarzan" Hogarth poured his entire artistic culture, his admiration for Michelangelo and the great baroque artists, his affinities for German expressionism, his knowledge of Far Eastern art. The plot, which no longer owes anything to Burroughs's creation, is thoroughly permeated with a tragic element that can be read in these faces tormented with passion or hatred.

In his desire to blend form and content into a single visual manifestation, Hogarth developed the art of composition to a high degree of exactitude, not for the sake of an arbitrary virtuosity, but in answer to more elemental requirements of subject and plot. Each of these pages forms a vast panorama that could stand alone but that, when considered as part of the whole, step by step reveals a disturbing universe of strange forms, twisted branches, ominous foliage, and needle peaks, into which Tarzan penetrates as if onto a battlefield. The force that sustains the cohesion of this antropomorphic world is movement, which is present even in the trembling of vines and the play of muscles. Hogarth's "Tarzan," the creation of a rare genius, marks one of the supreme moments of the comic strip.

The birthday of "Tarzan"—January 7, 1929—was also the birthday of a second comic strip destined to alter the content of the comics: "Buck Rogers." In this series, which was written and adapted by Philip Nowlan from his novel *Armageddon 2419 A.D.*, and drawn by Dick Calkins, we are immediately propelled into the future. Its hero, like Calkins a former United States Air Force lieutenant, is transported into the twenty-fifth century, where he battles his mortal enemy and rival, "Killer Kane," on land and sea, and in space. Kane's dream is to conquer the entire world and lure away from Buck Rogers his sweetheart, the tender, trembling Wilma. This strip already contains the complete panoply characteristic of the science-fiction genre: space rockets, death-ray guns, and interplanetary expeditions. Calkins's style is outmoded and old-fashioned, and the adventures invented by Nowlan are quite insipid and unimaginative. But however outdated it may seem today, this strip was the first to handle science-fiction themes in an interesting manner, and it was quite influential.

The success of "Tarzan" and "Buck Rogers" convinced the syndicates that the old formats no longer sufficed to hold the reader's attention and that suspense and action together constituted the wave of the future.

58

1

1, 2. Harold Foster's "Tarzan." Copyright U.F.S. In the early pictures the drawing is still very much in the style of 1925. Foster's "Tarzan" later developed a powerful style that some consider the apogee of his work.

2

Opposite:
3, 4. Burne Hogarth's "Tarzan." Copyright U.F.S. At first influenced by Foster's style, Hogarth soon introduced into "Tarzan" his own visions of jungles, lost kingdoms, and titanic explosions.

3

As Fang is about to throw the stick of dynamite at Tarzan and Luling, it explodes in his hands. The whole palace blows up.

Tarzan swims desperately before the oncoming tidal wave.

4

1. Clarence Gray and William Ritt, "Brick Bradford." Copyright King Features Syndicate, Inc.

2. Lieutenant Dick Calkins and Phil Nowlan, "Buck Rogers." Copyright National Newspaper Syndicate.

Thus in 1931 the Chicago Tribune Syndicate encouraged Chester Gould to create a police-adventure strip. Dick Tracy, the hero of the strip of the same name, is a detective in an anonymous city easily recognizable as Chicago. Scrupulously honest, and of unshakable integrity, neither his enemies' attempts at corruption nor the entreaties of his eternal sweetheart, Tess Trueheart, nor the fatherly admonitions of his superior, "Chief" Brandon, can shake his sense of duty. Assisted by his faithful subordinate, Pat Patton, and his adopted son Junior, he is the terror of gangsters, swindlers, spies, and other would-be troublemakers. Gould's style is exaggerated, almost caricatural, and his one-dimensional drawings with their flat black masses are diagrams rather than compositions. Dick Tracy, with his eagle beak and square chin, and his assistants are not very appealing, and are sadly lacking in humor. On the other hand, the scripts are far from mediocre, and sometimes they are even excellent. The outstanding quality of this strip, however, is the minute realism of its details and a certain aura of fatalism that emanates from the often brutal development of the plot.

Until now, King Features Syndicate had seemingly remained aloof from this tremendous change in the comic strip. Actually, however, it was perfecting in the silence of its studios the details of the counterattack. Thus during the month of January, 1934, and separated by intervals of a few days, three new comic strips were born: "Secret Agent X-9," a police-adventure strip; "Jungle Jim," an exotic adventure strip; and "Flash Gordon," a futuristic strip. All three were the achievement of one artist: Alexander (Alex) Raymond (1909–1956).

Of all the great comic-strip creators, Alex Raymond unquestionably possessed the most versatile talent. Other artists surpassed him in creative power or boldness of style, others in the development of the plot or in accuracy of dialogue, but none possessed as varied an array of talents—talents that enabled him to master all the various types of strips at which he tried his hand.

"Secret Agent X-9," the answer to "Dick Tracy," was the product of Raymond's collaboration with the American novelist Dashiell Hammett. X-9 is an FBI agent. In his struggle against crime, he is not satisfied merely to fight criminals; he mingles with them, borrows their habits, jargon, and even their methods. More than a guardian of law and order, X-9 is the implacable, harassing enemy of crime. The fact that he possesses no known name, only a number, and that he always works alone, further heighten his mystery.

For his part, "Jungle Jim" Bradley is a wild-animal hunter and explorer, whose deeds range from Africa to the Far East. Accompanied by his faithful Hindu servant Kolu, and aided by his equally faithful companion, the seductive Lil, he overcomes his enemies—shifty traders, international agitators, pirates of every description—in action-packed and highly imaginative adventures. This strip came extremely close to being the equal of "Tarzan," which it attempted to rival.

In "Flash Gordon" three earthlings—Flash, his sweetheart Dale, and Professor Zarkov—arrive on the planet Mongo, and soon find themselves at odds with Emperor Ming the Merciless. In this strip, which has an epic rather than a science-fiction quality, Raymond gives free rein to his apocalyptic imagination. Amid grandiose landscapes and visionary architecture, and in the most diversified locales (the Kingdom of Shadows, the Undersea City, the Land of the Blue Men), there unfolds a Manichean conflict of gigantic dimensions. While the battle is dubious, its outcome is not uncertain: Flash, the defender of justice, will triumph over Ming, the incarnation of evil. "Flash Gordon" was, if not the best comic strip (others can with equal justice claim this title), at least the most representative of a style and an age.

Raymond's style—precise, clear, and incisive—is perfectly suited to the requirements of the narrative. Between picture and plot there is a perfect unity of style, which Raymond sought to reinforce by abandon-

---

The immediate source of the detective comic strip was obviously the "black" detective story, of American invention. Dashiell Hammett, W. Richard Burnett, James Cain, and Raymond Chandler simultaneously created this new American literary style. (The talent of all four of these authors surpassed its limits.) We may therefore assume that the syndicates were making use of a method already familiar to them. A new type of detective novel was beginning to meet with a certain amount of success, and they very cautiously attempted to adapt it (for example, Chester Gould's "Dick Tracy," Lyman Anderson's "Inspector Wade," Charlie Schmidt's "Radio Patrol," Frank Godwin's "In the Service of the Law"). Commercially the operation was risky, and susceptible of ending in failure. King Features Syndicate called upon the inventor of the genre, Dashiell Hammett, and a young artist, to launch the first "black" comic strip: "X-9"; it was a success. Later comic-strip authors usually avoided its violence and pessimism, here and there borrowing various realistic touches. Ten years passed before the Hollywood producers entrusted to John Huston and Frank Tuttle the creation of Dashiell Hammett's *The Maltese Falcon* and *Blood Money*.

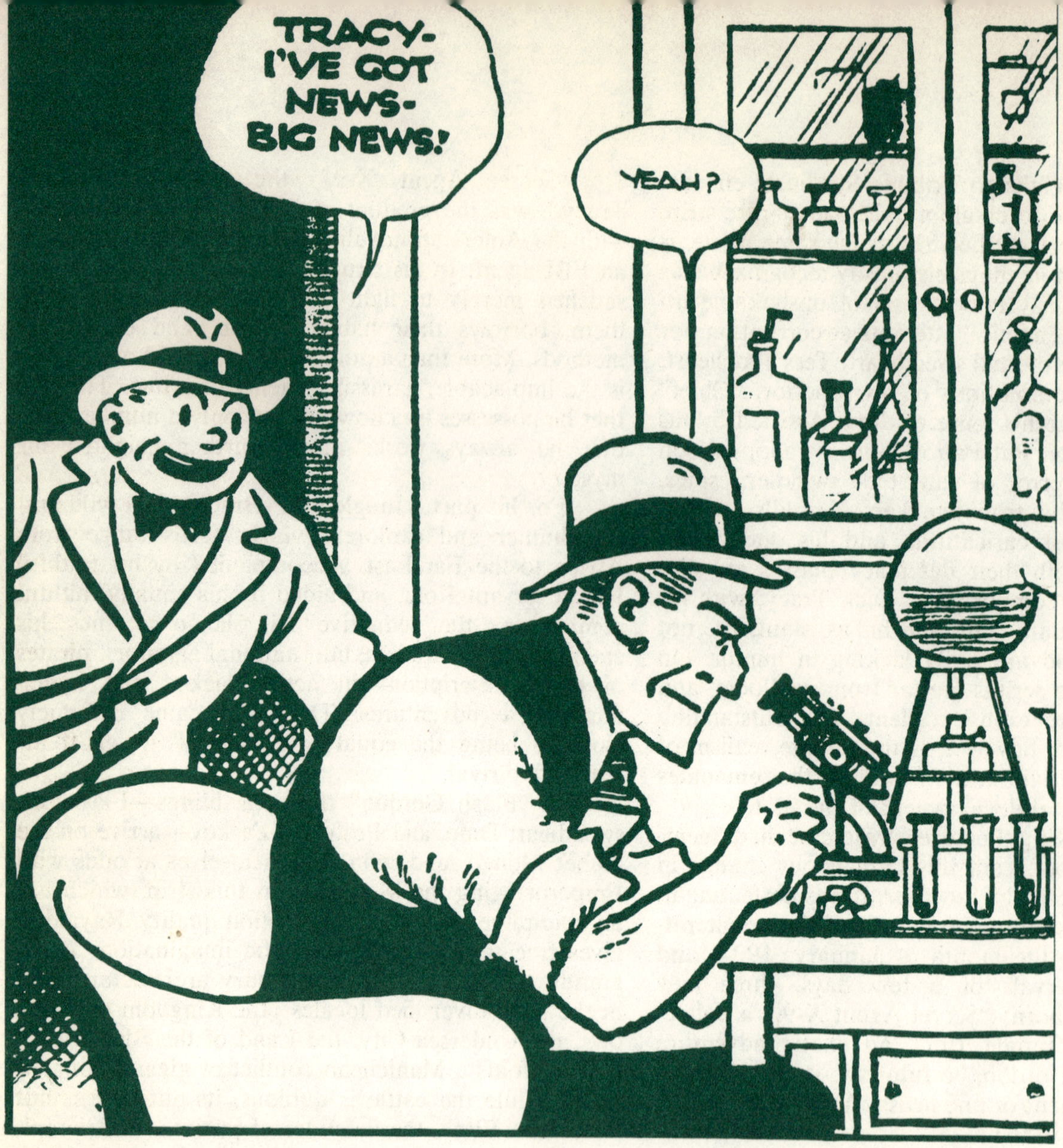

1

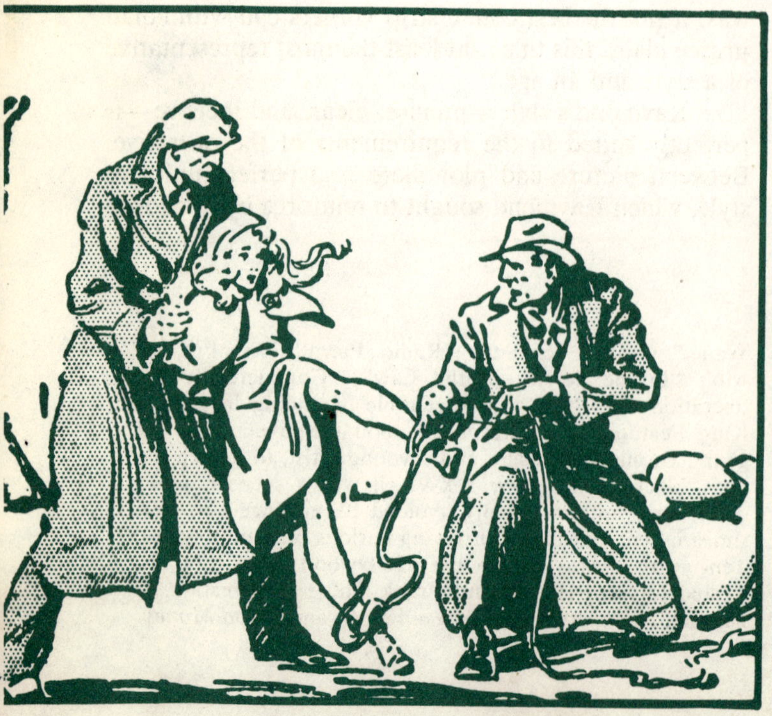

2

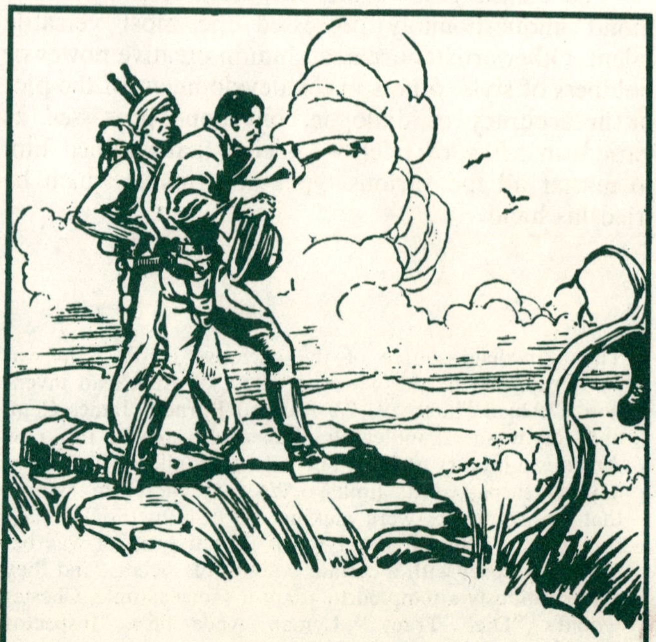

3

ing balloons in favor of a continuous narrative (1938). This was perhaps a mistake, as the strip thereby lost in spontaneity what it gained in homogeneity.

At the end of 1935 Raymond, being completely absorbed in "Jungle Jim" and "Flash Gordon," abandoned "Secret Agent X-9." A bewildering succession of scriptwriters and artists (including Leslie Charteris, the creator of "The Saint") succeeded him; most of them were mediocrities, with the exception of Austin Briggs, to whom we shall later return.

Flash Gordon had been preceded by several months by another space knight: Brick Bradford, born in August, 1933, from the collaboration of William Ritt, the author, and Clarence Gray, the artist. Brick's adventures are sometimes of the crime-solving variety, sometimes fantastic, but he triumphed particularly in the science-fiction genre. He travels through space and time in pursuit of pirate treasure or of a civilization of the future, or penetrates the secrets of the atom. Gray's style—elegant, unambiguous, and devoid of irrelevant detail—and Ritt's imagination, nourished on mythological tales, combined to enfold their hero in a complete setting of futuristic cities and primeval jungles, surveyed by rocket planes and peopled by legendary monsters, and in which Brick's innumerable (and invariably enamored) companions disport themselves. While "Brick Bradford" has neither the grandeur of "Flash Gordon" nor the technical qualities of "Buck Rogers," it radiates a poetry and a festive atmosphere that are very often absent from its two rival strips.

The ardent spirit of the novels of chivalry, already embodied in "Flash Gordon" and "Brick Bradford," found its most perfect champion in the person of Prince Valiant, lovingly brought into the world in 1937 by Harold Foster. Son of the dethroned king of Thule, who has come to seek refuge at King Arthur's Court, Valiant was richly deserving of his name; never did a more noble or more accomplished knight come to sit at the Round Table. For the service of his suzerain and the love of his lady, the tender, shy Aleta, Valiant fights dragons and witches, and checks the pillaging Vikings and the bloodthirsty Huns, and even voyages to Africa and the New World. Foster's style is well suited for the depiction of tournaments and masses of armed men whom he arranges in vast, majestic compositions. Foster represents the classical tradition in the comic strip to a much greater degree than Hogarth, who is too deeply charged with personal preoccupations.

While Foster and Hogarth applied the canons of traditional art to the comic strip, others attempted to find for the comics a style intrinsic to them. The pioneer in this area was Noel Sickles, who in 1934 took over "Scorchy Smith" from the hands of its creator, John Terry. Scorchy, who had first appeared in the late twenties, was an aviator modeled after Charles Lindbergh, who had just conquered the Atlantic a few years previously. While retaining his profession of pilot, Sickles transformed Scorchy into a soldier of fortune ever ready to leap into his plane in order to succor some king threatened by revolutionaries or save an heiress from the hands of her kidnappers. The principal innovation introduced by Sickles was stylistic rather than narrative: the use of the technique of brush drawing, by means of which he obtained quasi-impressionist atmospheric effects.

To a young beginner named Milton Caniff belongs the credit for fusing the cinematographic style, introduced by Harold Foster and perfected by Alex Raymond, and the brilliant draftsmanship of his friend Noel Sickles, into a single esthetic ensemble. His most justly famous creation, "Terry and the Pirates," was begun in October, 1934, and, after the inevitable trial-and-error period, finally found its definitive style. Alternating between the pen and the brush, Caniff became a master in the use of skillful illumination, elaborate chiaroscuro effects, and violent black-and-white contrasts, thereby endowing his narrative with a characteristic atmosphere which it shares with the films of that period.

Caniff, an excellent storyteller, was able to combine an incontestable narrative virtuosity with his graphic qualities. The first episodes do not yet reveal great originality. Terry, a daring and smart lad, and his friend Pat Ryan, an appealing and easygoing adventurer, go off in search of a gold mine somewhere in China. The narrative soon increases in excitement; the characters grow into their true dimensions; and the setting acquires a fascinating authenticity. By 1937 our heroes are fighting the Japanese ("the invaders"). The dialogue, by turns tough, lyrical, or very humorous, possesses literary qualities for which many a dramatic author would envy Caniff. They could also envy him the diversity and appeal of his feminine crea-

---

1. Chester Gould, "Dick Tracy." Copyright Chicago Tribune—New York News Syndicate, Inc.

2. Alex Raymond, "Secret Agent X-9." Copyright King Features Syndicate, Inc.

3. Alex Raymond, "Jungle Jim." Copyright King Features Syndicate, Inc.

1, 2, 3. Alex Raymond, "Flash Gordon." Copyright King Features Syndicate, Inc.

tions: from the voluptuous and implacable Eurasian Dragon Lady, to the shining-haired, golden-hearted adventuress Burma, to Normandie Sandhurst, a tragic heroine *à la* Corneille, torn between her love for Pat Ryan and her duty to her husband, they are all unforgettable.

Caniff's style, a harmonious equilibrium between dialogue and plot, narrative and illustration, has now become the classic comic-strip style.

Among Milton Caniff's many disciples, particular mention should be made of Alfred Andriola, the creator (in 1938) of Charlie Chan. The famous Chinese detective (inspired by the character of Earl Derr Biggers) and his subordinate Kirk Barrow, a likable adventurer in the tradition of Pat Ryan, pursue evildoers to the four corners of the globe in adventures that are full of suspense and unforeseen events. The drawing and dialogues bear a strong resemblance to those of Caniff, but Andriola was able to preserve a very personal style that makes this one of the most attractive strips of the thirties.

When Sickles definitively abandoned Scorchy Smith and the comic strip in 1936, he was succeeded first by Bert Christman, a rather clumsy imitator of his predecessor's style, and then in 1938 by Frank Robbins. Robbins borrowed certain techniques from Caniff, others from Sickles, and blended them into a very personal style. His line is forceful, masculine, and quite heavy; his drawing is done in black masses, and these qualities impart to the strip a gripping reality and presence, while the characters, more humanized and more genuine, also acquire the stamp and personality of their creator.

A great number of other artists adopted the technique introduced by Caniff and Sickles, some of them giving it their personal style, others being satisfied with a slavish imitation of it. A complete new school of artists arose whose intention it was to propagate the "Caniffian" style still more extensively; thanks to their contributions, it became *the* comic-strip style.

One of the best representatives of this new generation of artists was Frank Godwin. He created numerous strips; the outstanding one, "Connie," relates the romantic, mysterious, and fantastic adventures of an enterprising and very spirited young woman. For his carefully finished pictures, Godwin preferred the pen and the grease pencil to the brush. His illustrations, which are composed of a network of fine crosshatchings and a cursive line, are of high artistic quality; his scripts, on the other hand, are vacuous and very often insipid. Only a few episodes in "Connie" are exempt from this criticism.

Ham Fisher's "Joe Palooka," a bastard offspring of the adventure strip, was begun in 1930. The adventures of Joe Palooka, the boxer with iron fists and a heart of gold, his manager, Knobby Walsh, and his sweetheart, the pure Ann Howe ("as good as she is beautiful," as the stock phrase has it), are ridiculously sentimental, but despite (or because of?) its artificiality it enjoyed an unprecedented success.

The first genuine comic book usually defined as an individual magazine, printed in color, about 7½ by 10¼ inches in size—was born in 1933. Entitled *Funnies on Parade*, it was distributed as a promotion stunt by The Procter & Gamble Company. This edition met with great success, which encouraged the Eastern Color Printing Co. to produce, in May, 1934, the first commercial comic book, *Famous Funnies*. At first the comic books merely reproduced the series that appeared in the newspapers. The first original comic book, *New Fun*, appeared in 1935, and contained a variety of humorous stories. But it was the adventure story, for the most part plagiarized from contemporary comic strips, which "made" the comic books. Beginning in January, 1937, *Detective Comics* was completely devoted to the doings of a single hero. Finally Superman arrived—in the June, 1938, issue of *Action Comics*.

Science-fiction was a latecomer to the American comic-strip scene. At first Anglo-French, in 1929 this class of literature nevertheless had behind it a long history in the United States, beginning with the turn-of-the-century novels of L. P. Senarens in the Frank Reade Library. American science-fiction took definite shape between 1911–1912 and 1926. Buck Rogers, the possessor of an entire arsenal of machines, does not reflect the dominant trend, which is represented by the Martian novels of Burroughs, and by the work of Abraham Merritt and H. P. Lovecraft, in which fantasy and poetic adventure completely eclipse the prophetic technological element. Flash Gordon, on the other hand, is related to Burroughs and Merritt: he represents a reversion to the epic. For quite a while technology played only a very small role in this strip, which is actually a novel of chivalry, and also, in its treatment of machines and architecture, superbly prophetic of a new esthetics. Science-fiction strips were never very numerous, but most of the American series made occasional excursions into the genre that were sometimes quite remarkable and lengthy (notably Frank Godwin's "Connie"). In the same period the movie industry produced several important science-fiction films—for example, *The Invisible Man* and *Deluge* (1933), and *The Shape of Things to Come* (1935, script by H. G. Wells).

Harold Foster, "Prince Valiant." Copyright King Features Syndicate, Inc.

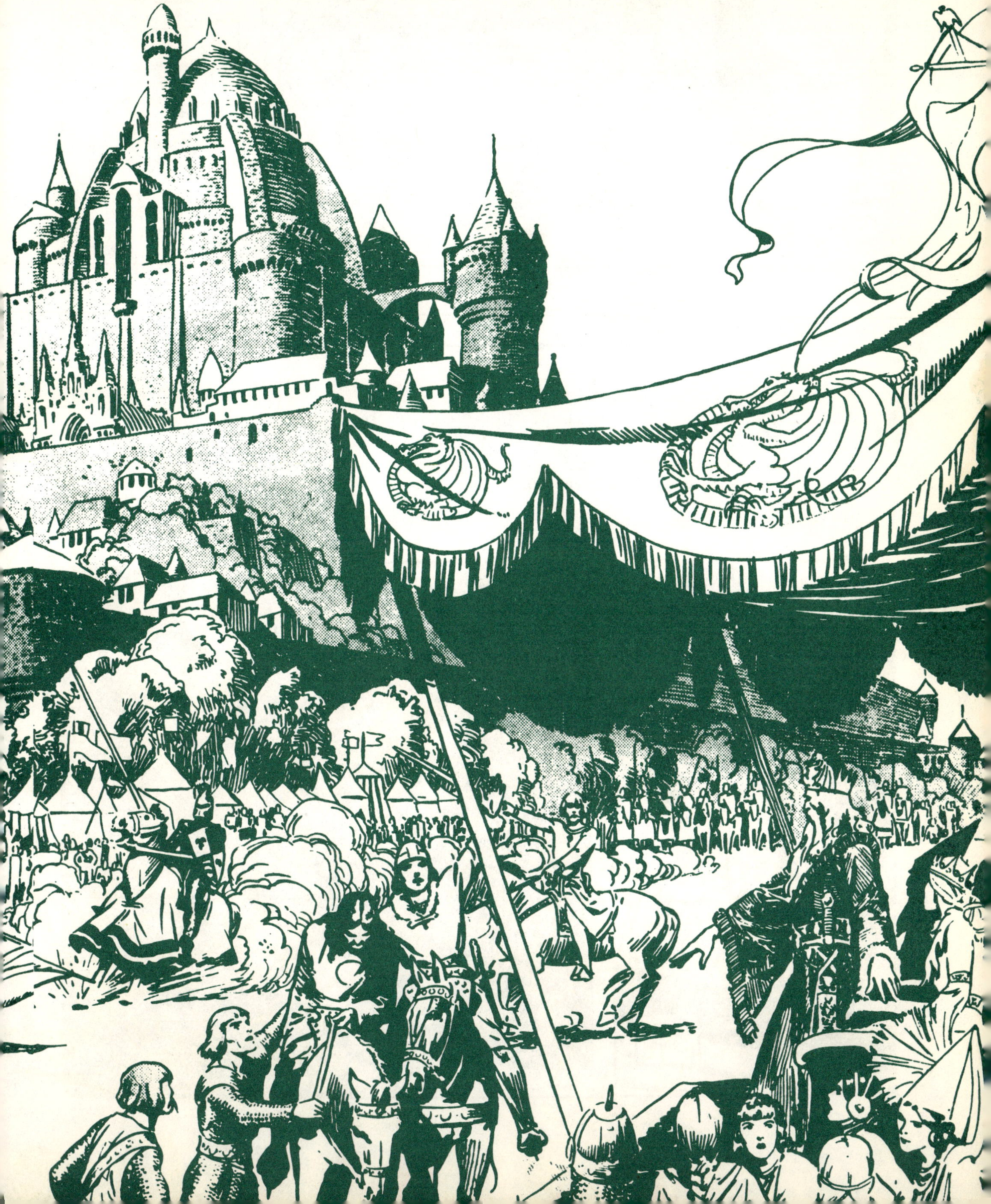

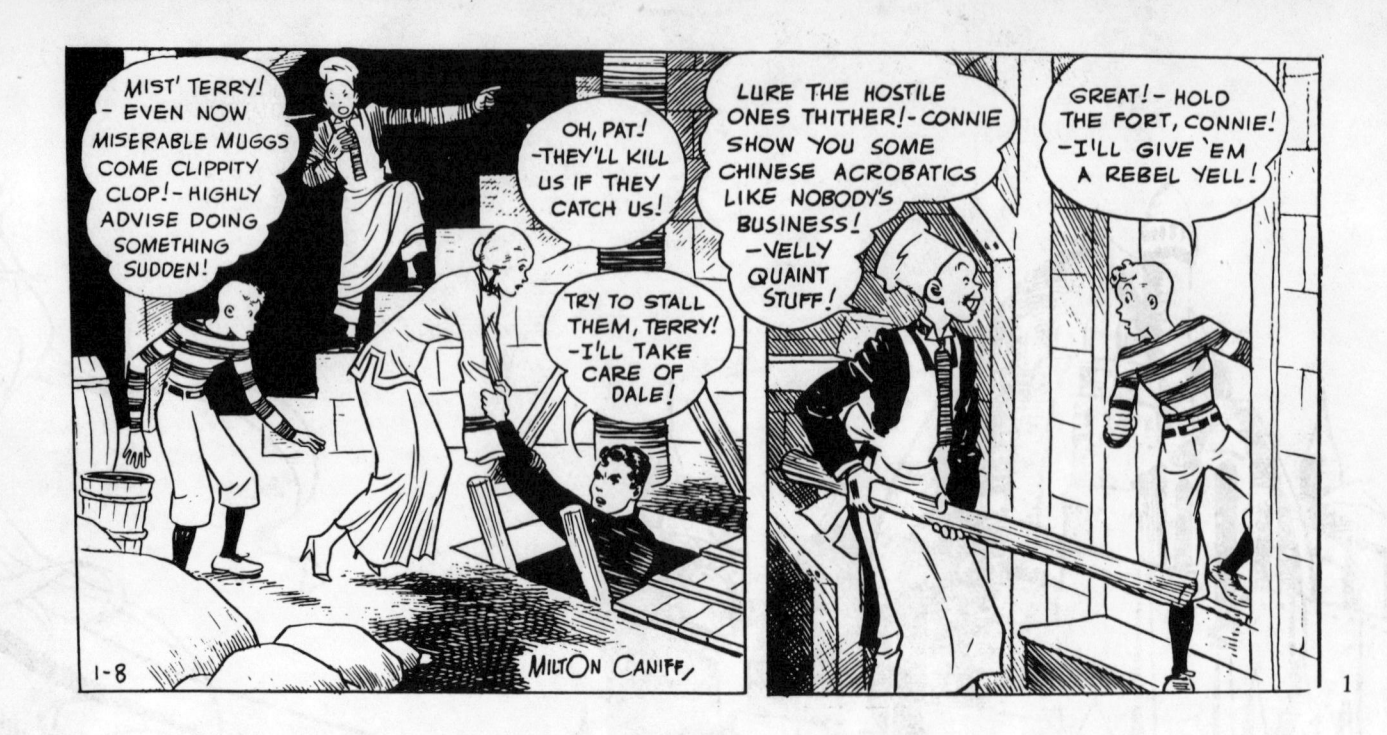

1, 2. Milton Caniff, "Terry and the Pirates." Copyright Chicago Tribune—New York News Syndicate, Inc.

The evolution of Milton Caniff: from the indecision of an almost caricatural style to mastery in the use of blacks and whites.

Superman, the creation of author Jerry Siegel and artist Joe Shuster, is the last survivor from the distant planet Krypton. Endowed with almost unlimited powers, invulnerable, able to fly through the air and pierce walls with his X-ray vision, Superman is the terror of the malefactors of Metropolis, who, for a reason that defies all rational analysis, continue to pit themselves against the Man of Steel instead of going to exercise their talents in less dangerous quarters. Superman's intellectual capacity, however, does not appear superior to that of his enemies, and were it not for his invincibility, he would bear a closer resemblance to Happy Hooligan than to the Superman of Nietzsche. Having taken off his cape and his costume marked with the famous "S," in the guise of the reporter Clark Kent he is the laughingstock of the newspaper; even his young colleague, Lois Lane, with whom he is in love and whom he has saved a thousand times in his guise of Superman, despises him, without recognizing the Man of Steel under his ingenious disguise of suit, hat, and glasses. "Superman" possesses an appropriate story line, style, and dialogue for its hero.

"Superman" enjoyed a tremendous commercial success from its inception, and gave rise to a band of superheroes, each more outlandish than the last. Destined particularly for children, by their unrealism, irrationality, and bad taste, Superman and his fellow were to occasion many passionate controversies, which have not yet died down.

Despite this invasion of the comic strip by adventurers and heroes of all kinds, humor had not lost its rank. At this time Rudolph Dirks launched Hans, Fritz, and the rest of the clan on a long and incredible cruise full of cataclysmic adventures, while Harold Knerr created for the two rascals an antagonist worthy of their talents: Rollo, whose cunning malice and underhanded dealings are equaled only by the diabolical imagination of the "Katzies."

In 1929 Elzie Segar introduced his most original and durable creation: Popeye, the one-eyed sailor with the hypertrophied forearms. Appearing at first in a secondary role, Popeye very soon monopolized the entire stage of the "Thimble Theatre," which presented him as its star. The love of Popeye and the ungracious Olive Oyl soon became part of the plot—a thwarted and stormy love, for Popeye did not lack rivals, whom he succeeded in defeating with the help of spinach. A rough, blunt character, Popeye represents a comic translation of the "natural man" so dear to Rousseau: he can scarcely read, swears in public, is ignorant of good manners, and his bloopers have become famous, but his heart is pure and his generosity boundless.

Around the irascible sailor there ebbs and flows a mirth-provoking band of highly imaginative characters, including Poppa Popeye, the aged (and unworthy) father of the hero; his adopted son, the irresistible Swee'-pea; the Jeep, an animal that always knows (and speaks) the truth; and last, but by no means least, the droll Wimpy, the intellectual sponger whose appetite for hamburgers has become as legendary as Popeye's fondness for spinach. When Segar died in 1938, the strip was taken over first by Tom Sims and Bela Zaboly, then by Bud Sagendorf, but Popeye's poetry, imaginativeness, and salty humor disappeared with his creator.

"Alley Oop," which bears a certain resemblance to Popeye, was created by Vincent Hamlin in 1934. Alley is a caveman, uncivilized and invincible, in the tradition of Popeye, and a doer of innumerable martial feats. Mounted on his faithful dinosaur, he brings order to the Kingdom of Moo, which is declining under the inept rule of King Guzzle. Like Popeye, Alley also has a sweetheart: Oola, a prehistoric version of Mac Sennett's "bathing beauties," and he spends most of his time fighting over her. Hamlin's imagination is unflagging: when he wearies of the prehistoric age, he need only transport our hero, with the help of Professor Wonmug's time machine, to the ages of Cleopatra or the Crusades. The drawing of "Alley Oops" is excellent; its rhythm is lively and brisk; and the hero's adventures are joyously outrageous.

"Blondie," born from the pen of Murat ("Chic")

Air adventure occupied a major position in the comic strip after 1929. It inspired, in addition to "Scorchy Smith," such specialized series as "Skyroads" (Dick Calkins, 1929), followed by "Tailspin Tommy" (Hal Forrest), "Ace Drummond" (drawings by C. Knight, script by E. Rickenbacker, American ace of 1918), F. Miller's "Barney Baxter" and Z. Mosley's "Smilin' Jack." Actually, all the American comic strips included some air adventure: Godwin's heroine Connie was an aviatrix before becoming a reporter, and in "Brick Bradford" and "Wash Tubbs" the plane was the hero's customary method of transportation. Mickey and even Tarzan followed this fashion, which Knerr mocked with the pedal balloon of the Katzenjammer Kids. This style reflects the growth of aviation and the repercussions of the major long-distance flights and international contests, in particular the race from England to Australia (sixty-four planes) in 1934, which is often seen in the comic strips. Its victor, the DH "Comet," was immediately adopted by Barney Baxter. Similarly, the Gee-Bee, a kind of flying barrel and the star of the pylon races, often appears in "Connie," as well as the stratospheric plane, launched by Wiley Post.

1

2

-OMINOUS SCREAM WAFTS ON WIND FROM NEARBY HOUSE —!
Alfred ANDRIOLA

3

4

5

CHARLES FLANDERS

6

1. Frank Godwin, "Connie." Copyright Editor Press.
2. Alfred Andriola, "Charlie Chan." Copyright McNaught Syndicate.
3. Ham Fisher, "Joe Palooka." Copyright McNaught Syndicate.
4. Frank Robbins, "Scorchy Smith." Copyright A.P. News Features.
5. Charles Flanders, "The Lone Ranger." Copyright King Features Syndicate, Inc.
6. Fred Harman, "Red Ryder." Copyright N.E.A.
7. Phil Davis and Lee Falk, "Mandrake the Magician." Copyright King Features Syndicate, Inc.
8. Ray Moore and Lee Falk, "The Phantom." Copyright King Features Syndicate, Inc.
9. Allen Dean, "King of the Royal Mounted." Copyright King Features Syndicate, Inc.
10. Lyman Young, "Tim Tyler's Luck." Copyright King Features Syndicate, Inc.

7   8

9   10

A lineup of Marvel Comics super-heroes. (Among the most famous, one can recognize the Torch, Captain America, and the Hulk.) The Marvel group of super-heroes has dethroned the older comic-book idols such as Superman and Batman, with their down-to-earth characters and campy dialogue. They are currently the craze on campuses throughout the country. Copyright Marvel Comics Group.

Young, occupies a special place between the humorous comic strip and the family strip. The series began in 1930, but acquired its final form in 1933, with the marriage of the heroine Blondie and her rich but clumsy suitor, Dagwood Bumstead. Having disinherited Dagwood, Chic Young then concentrated on depicting the life of a typical (?) American family. Blondie is the boss of the house, and the holder of the purse strings. A devoted wife and affectionate companion, she is constantly obliged to come to the rescue of Dagwood, a husband and father who is full of goodwill but incompetent. The minor characters are just as finely drawn: the two children, Baby Dumpling and Cookie; Dithers, the irascible boss; and the mailman, a confused, blundering individual, are little masterpieces of the genre. The simplicity of this series and its happy, optimistic character, have won for "Blondie" a remarkable international popularity.

Of a vastly different type of humor is "Li'l Abner," created by Al Capp in 1934. This strip presents a savage satire of all aspects of American life and society. Li'l Abner, the hero, is the living symbol of victorious innocence: armed only with his candor and stupidity, he foils the most diabolical plans of his enemies, but finally succumbs to the advances of his girl-friend, Daisy Mae, a semi-nude and artlessly perverse nymph (whom he married in 1952, under pressure of public opinion). His parents are monstrous midgets; the family lives in Dogpatch, a village so deprived that it possesses neither electricity nor running water. Al Capp is not prejudiced; he satirizes with equal pleasure all classes and social groups, and castigates with the same merciless pen all hypocrisies, unscrupulousness, and absurdities, irrespective of whence they come. Among the creators of comic strips, Al Capp enjoys unequaled fame. He has been compared to Rabelais and Swift, and the American novelist John Steinbeck went so far as to write in 1953 that Capp was "the greatest contemporary writer" and that "the Nobel Prize Committee should give him serious consideration."

Behind this brilliant facade, however, the inspiration of the comic-strip authors was already beginning to dry up. To remedy this situation, the syndicates called upon the magazines (Otto Soglow's "Little King" came from *The New Yorker*, and Carl Anderson's "Henry" from the *Saturday Evening Post*), and particularly upon the animated cartoon. Walt Disney's "Mickey Mouse," created in 1928, appeared in comic strip form in 1931. He was soon followed, then supplanted, by "Donald Duck," the cantankerous, jabbering duck.

The variety of the American strip was infinite. Mention should be made of the rough, authentic, and beautiful Western of Fred Harman, "Red Ryder," and two other series, which began very well but then steadily declined thereafter—the Canadian adventures of Allen Dean's "King of the Royal Mounted," a blend of Western and detective story, and Flander's grade-B Western "The Lone Ranger." There were also Bill Holman's eccentric strips, "Smokey Stover" and "Spooky the Cat" (an animal that owes nothing to Felix or Krazy). While "Jungle Jim's" special province was Malaysia and the borders of India, and "Terry's" was China, we must not forget the (very imaginary) Africa of "Tim Tyler's Luck," by Lyman Young (brother of "Blondie's" Chic Young). His two heroes, Tim and Spud, both very young men, were part of a more or less British colonial army regiment whose mission it was to stamp out the trade in slaves and ivory, contraband arms, illegal hunting, and so on. For a long time the draftsmanship of this strip was excellent.

The two heroes created by the scriptwriter Lee Falk are in a class by themselves. In "Mandrake the Magician" (originally drawn by Phil Davis), the opera hat and red-and-black cape of the magician, who is constantly accompanied by an African of Herculean strength named Lothar, are to be found everywhere. Mandrake operates by hypnotism; while gangsters have little chance against him, he has an appropriate adversary in the person of the Cobra, a representative of black magic. This is about the only prolonged manifestation of the fantastic in the comic strip. Lee Falk's other hero, "The Phantom," at first drawn by Ray Moore, is more conventional: a masked judge who rules over faraway jungles, he escapes from the banality of the genre by being not a man but a dynasty established in the seventeenth century. He is the only comic strip hero who is capable of dying.

We should also mention the appearance of the officer-as-hero (beside the aviator, the explorer, the detective, and the journalist), with "Don Winslow of

---

Comic books are individual magazines printed in color. They measure 7½ by 10¼ inches, usually contain three stories, and appear monthly. Thus they are completely different from the daily newspaper with its comic strips. In 1943 their monthly sales amounted to 18,000,000 copies —ten times more than the combined sales of *Life, Reader's Digest*, and *Saturday Evening Post*—and constituted one-third of total magazine sales. Total receipts from retail sales reached $72 million annually. Assembly-line produced (literally) according to stereotyped models, the comic books are tremendous commercial enterprises.

1

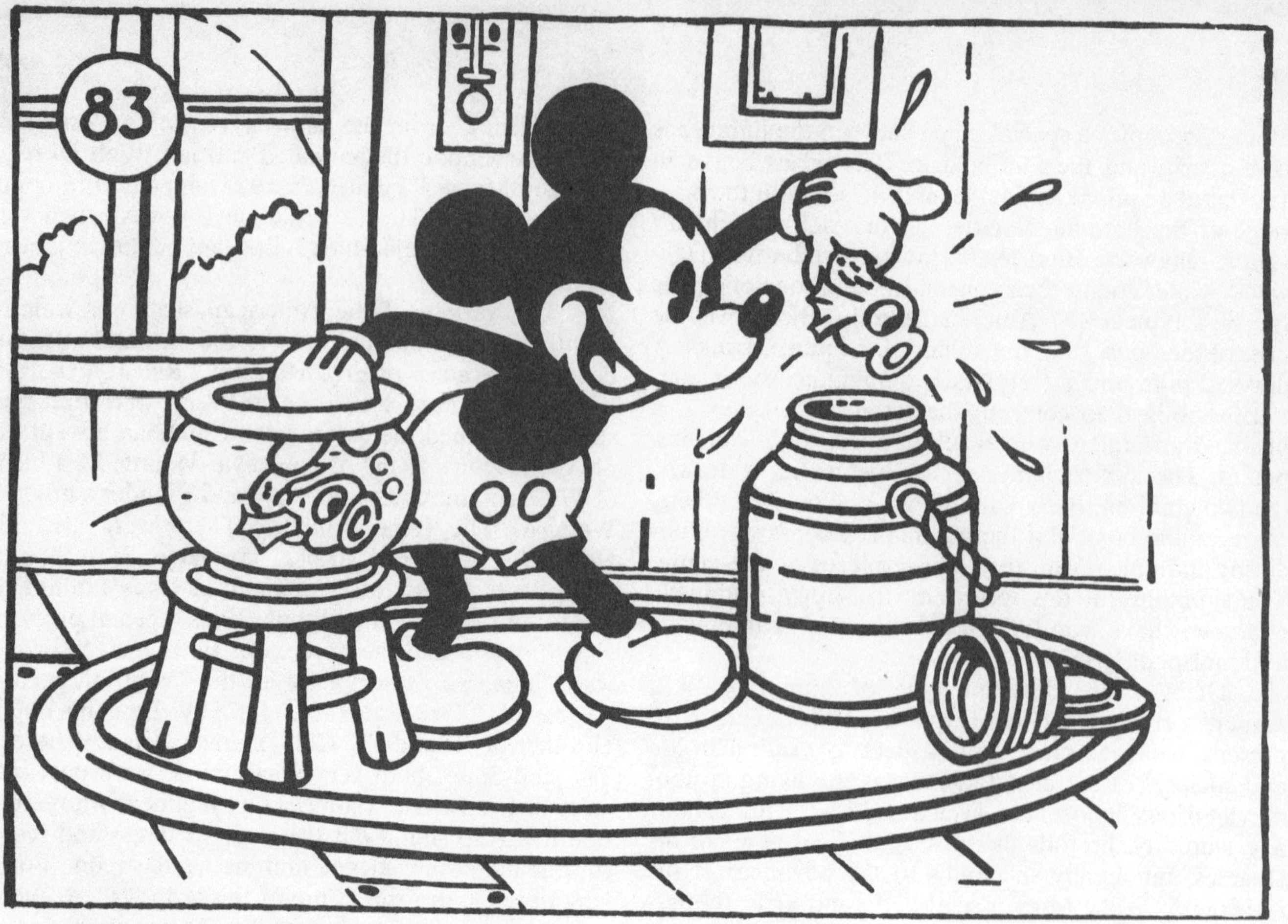

2

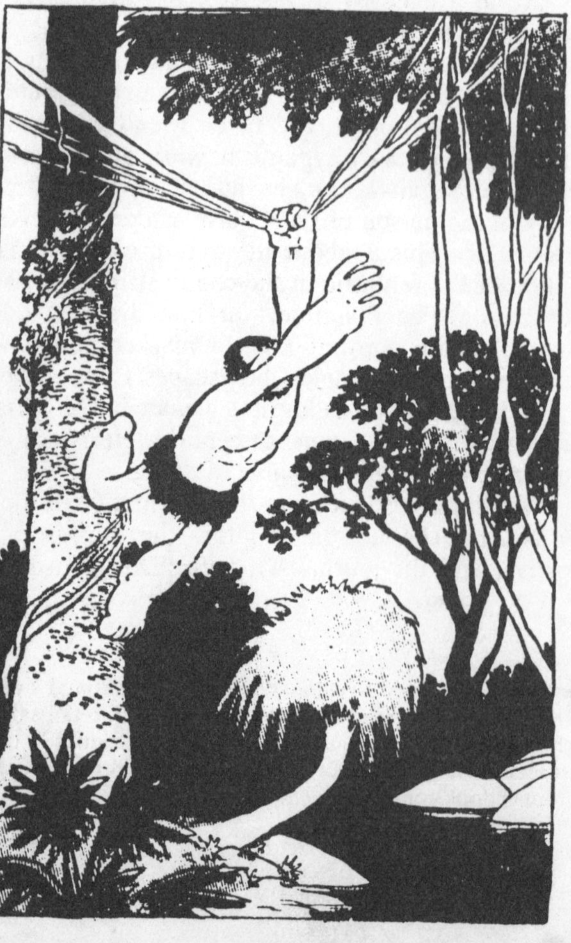

3

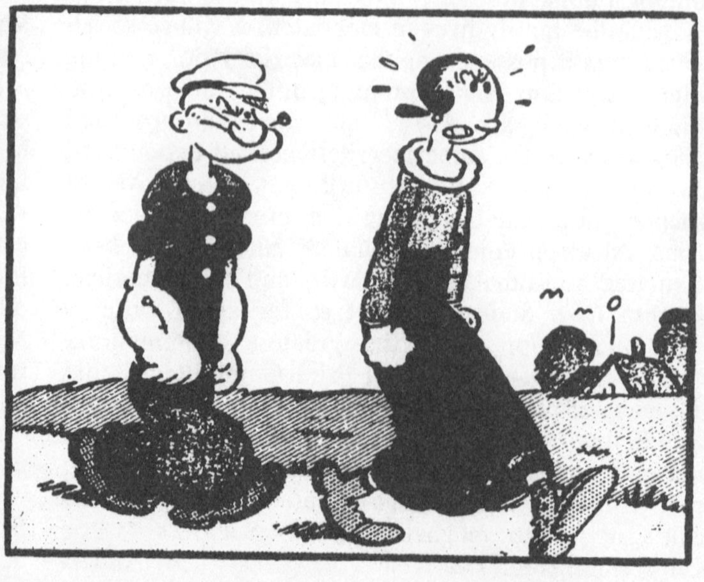

4

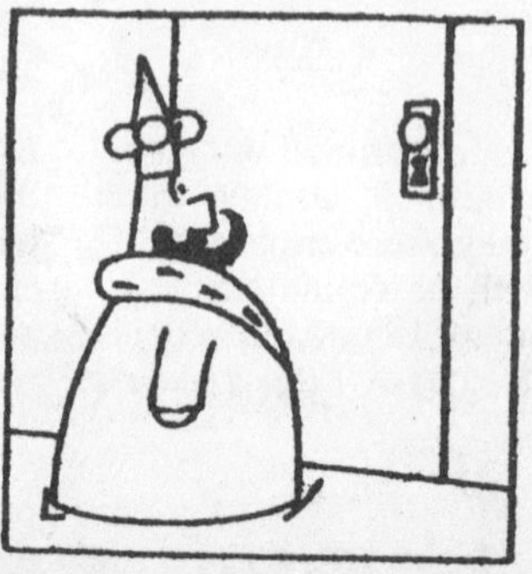

5

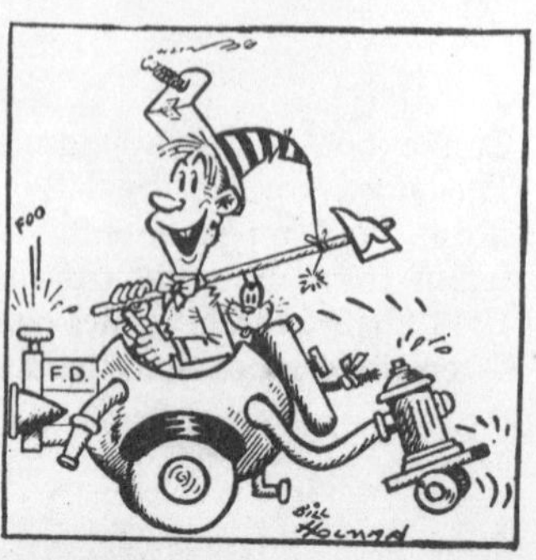

the Navy," written by Lieutenant Commander F. V. Martinek and drawn by L. A. Beroth. There is also the melodrama, an example of which is "Little Annie Rooney," begun by A. Fonsky and then taken over by Darrell McClure. Annie, a fugitive from an orphanage, is forever being hunted down by its directress. After roaming dark roads, Annie is always taken in by kindhearted people, but invariably the orphanage detective discovers her trail after several months and appears at the backyard door. And Annie flees, with her faithful dog, into the night.

In 1940 the American comic strip presented a panorama of impressive dimensions. Its force of expansion was bursting, and the large syndicates inundated Europe with their productions, which the Europeans, faithful to their old habits, poured pell-mell into the children's publications. Brick Bradford became "Luc Bradefer"; Mickey, "Topolino"; Don Winslow, "Bernard Tempête"; "Bringing Up Father," "La Famille Illico"; Flash Gordon, "Guy l'Eclair"; the Katzenjammer Kids, "Pim, Pam, Poum"; Prince Valiant, "Principe Valentino"; Little Jimmy, "Boubou" (unfortunately!); and so on. All the major series were exported, with the exception of "Little Orphan Annie" and "Krazy Kat." The older illustrated magazines were declining, and local production was merely marking time. Badly paid, and for the most part still confined to children's publications, European artists could not rival the Fosters and Raymonds. However, their development had not come to a complete halt. Germany entered on the scene, first with Rudolf Röse's "Witwe Knolle" (The Widow Knolle, 1927), a large woman with a colored nose and a dog named Achilles, and then Erich Ohser's classic, "Vater und Sohn" (Father and Son, 1934), which he signed "E. O. Plauen." This strip was in complete contrast to "Moon Mullins": in it a bald, moustachioed little bourgeois man, full of imagination and tenderness, and his young son, their round faces completely devoid of evil, are observed through the small adventures of their daily life. Mention should also be made of "Die Abenteuer der Fünf Schreckensteiner" (The Adventures of the Five Schreckensteiners), signed "Barlog." Its heroes are three gentlemen of the early seventeenth century. At the stroke of midnight they come to life and step out of the large painting in which they are portrayed, into the gallery of a luxurious residence. Like curious children they launch into modern life, occasionally accompanied by their neighbors from the wall, a beautiful lady in Restoration dress, and a young boy. At one o'clock they all climb back onto the wall, but the owner finds his car in smithereens or stands stupefied before the bronzed faces of his portraits (they spent their hour of liberty under his ultraviolet lamp).

The English comic strip was stagnating; the comic-strip style had not yet come into general use. The adventure series then being created remained faithful to the style of the continuous text under the picture, and were no more than illustrated novels. In France the older series with their outmoded conventions were still very much alive—Benjamin Rabier's animals, Pinchon's "Bécassine," and the "Pieds-Nickelés," which were continued by Forton until his death in 1934, then along the same lines by A. Perré and, after him (an irreversible decline), by A. G. Badert. Alain Saint-Ogan, then at the peak of his activity, led "Zig et Puce" to triumph, and succumbed to the temptation of science-fiction: "Zig et Puce au XXIe siècle" (Blighter and Flea in the 21st Century) abounds in machines and futuristic architecture, and includes a rocket trip to Venus. He created other characters destined to be less succesful: "Prosper l'Ours" (Prosper the Bear, 1933), "Monsieur Poche" (Mister Pocket) and his kangaroo, Salsifi.

A survey of this epoch would not be complete without mention of the artist Le Rallic, whose long career as an illustrator was then exclusively concentrated on the comic strip, and more particularly on the Western and the colonial adventure. While his austere characters all bear a certain resemblance to one another, he is an excellent artist of horses. We should also mention Marijac (Jacques Dumas), the author of competent adventure series, particularly a Western called "Jim Boum" and "Le Chasseur de Monstres"

1. Walt Disney, "Mickey Mouse." Copyright Walt Disney Productions.

2. V. T. Hamlin, "Alley Oop." Copyright N.E.A.

3. Elzie Segar, "Thimble Theatre Starring Popeye." Copyright King Features Syndicate, Inc.

4. Otto Soglow, "The Little King." Copyright King Features Syndicate, Inc.

5. Bill Holman, "Smokey Stover." Copyright Chicago Tribune—New York News Syndicate, Inc.

Numerous artists after Walt Disney have worked on Mickey, gradually changing his features. None have been able to recapture his early charm, when his eyes were simple black circles, before he wore middle-class clothes, and when, always brimming over with optimism, he sauntered about the shabby neighborhoods of the Depression years.

1. Chic Young's "Blondie," February 17, 1933: the marriage of Blondie and Dagwood, culmination of a romance begun in 1930. Blondie was then a typical young scatterbrain.

2. Al Capp, "Li'l Abner." Copyright News Syndicate Co.

3. Erich Ohser, "Vater und Sohn." Copyright Südverlag. GmbH. Konstanz.

(The Monster-Hunter), a story of the Vanished World copiously peopled with dinosaurs. In a completely caricatural style, Mat created boastful southern Frenchmen: "César-Napoléon Rascasse," a combination of Tartarin and Marius, and "Pitchounet," his spiritual heir.

In 1934, after several attempts, a daily comic strip —A. Daix's "Les Aventures du Professeur Nimbus" (The Adventures of Professor Nimbus)—appeared in France twenty-seven years after its appearance in the United States and thirteen years after its debut in Great Britain. Admittedly "Nimbus," which conformed to the archtraditional type of the distracted man, and contained many equally traditional gags, was not the equal of "Vater und Sohn." In 1937 there occurred another milestone in the French comic strip: René Pellos, a well-known sports illustrator, changed over to the comic strip and began a completely adult series called "Futuropolis." At the end of time, a single city, ruled by an implacable and very self-satisfied science, dominates the earth. A revolt by one of its inhabitants gradually spreads until it involves the last unconquered human beings, what remains of the animal kingdom, and finally the planet itself, the convulsions of which end the conflict and pave the way for a regenerated world reunited with nature. This subject is clearly related to criticism of the civilization of the machine and to French science-fiction of the day, which was preoccupied with the end of the world (see Rosny, J. Spitz, and others). This subject was, and still is, an exception in the comic-strip world, and the originality of its style was still more exceptional.

Pellos was the first European artist to bring to the comic strip a knowledge of anatomical drawing. He is a master of muscle and movement; his magnificent, athletic characters, always in action and sometimes grimacing with tension, preceded those of Hogarth, who had not yet completely freed his style of all restraint. Emphasized by a violent and often broken line, the characters of "Futuropolis" leap from the pages. The layout of the panels, unique in the international comic-strip field, reinforces the drawing by its dynamism; it is a disconnected and chaotic layout in which the pictures, separated by circles, lightning flashes, and oblique lines, whirl or burst into a fireworks display that no longer has anything in common with the prim succession of the usual squares and rectangles. The copious but miniscule text is integrated with the pictures and swept up into the chaos. Pellos could rival the best American artists, but his Wagnerian inspiration ("Futuropolis" is a *Götterdämmerung* in which the elements, the sea, the winds, the internal fire, and the thunder participate in the final battle) did not fit into the run-of-the-mill French production. No one knew what to do with his talent, which was employed on humorous series (even on the "Pieds-Nickelés) unworthy of his talent. Another opportunity given him —"Electropolis," in which the earth explodes—was interrupted by the war.

The traditional children's imagery accompanied by doggerel was also being continued in Italy, with Carlo Bisi's "Pampurio" (1929) and Giovanni Manca's "Pier Cloruro de' Lambicchi" (1930). But beginning in 1932, the situation changed rapidly with the arrival of the American strips and the establishment of several newspapers to offer them a home. Imitation created an extensive Italian output; much of it was very mediocre, but there survived several series (for example, Carlo Cossio's "Dick Fulmine," created in 1938, which appeared in France as "Alain la Foudre") that were interesting or successful despite weak draftsmanship and a puerile story line. Rino Albertarelli's Western "Kit Carson" (1937) was already an improvement. Good air-adventure strips came from the pens of the Avai brothers: in "I Moschettieri dell' Aeorporto Z" (The Musketeers of Airport Z), Giacomo depicted the attempts of a small group of aviators and technicians, rich in ideas but poor in material wealth, to create and publicize the perfected models into which they had put their hearts. In the same period Cesare Avai, a remarkable artist, created the character of "Will Sparrow, il Pirata dell'

Exaggerated criticism of the comic strips flourished in both the United States and Europe:

"Sadism, cannibalism, bestiality. Crude eroticism. Torturing, killing, kidnapping. Monsters, madmen, creatures half-brute, half-human. Raw melodrama; tales of crimes and criminals; extravagant exploits in strange lands and on other planets; pirate stories . . . Vulgarity, cheap humor, and cheaper wit. Sentimental stories designed for the general level of a moronic mind. Ugliness of thought and expression. All these, day after day, week after week . . ."

—JOHN K. RYAN, "Are the Comics Moral?", *Forum,* Vol. XCV, No. 5 (May 1936), p. 301.

"These newspapers [those which publish American comic strips] are pouring into the impressionable brains of children the lowest type of pornography, and a taste for murder and the exploits of gangsters . . . the desire to become a spy . . . the desire to participate in a civil war intended to place kings back on their thrones. . . ."(!)

—Georges Sadoul, "Ce Que Lisent Vos Enfants" [What Your Children Are Reading], Paris, 1938.

MAIS UN ÉTRANGE PHÉNOMÈNE SE PRODUIT. TOUTES LES PLANTES ALLONGENT LEURS TENTACULES ET IMMOBILISENT LES APPAREILS.

1. Then a strange thing happens. All the plants stretch out their tentacles and seize the machines firmly in their grasp.
Giovanni Scolari, "Saturno Contro la Terra."

2. He stopped. The deadly voice was still calling to him from far out in space. It was saying: "Rao, why don't you answer? Don't you know that all rebellion is useless? Don't you know that I'm ready to march against you with an entire army of iron?"

He drew himself proudly erect, and started the transmitting waves.

"We accept the combat!" he answered.

3. Marijac, "Le Chasseur de Monstres." Copyright Pierrot.

Il s'interrompit. La voix redoutable l'appelait encore du fond de l'espace. Elle disait :
« Raô, pourquoi ne réponds-tu pas? Ne sais-tu pas que toute révolte est vaine? Ne sais-tu pas que je suis prête à marcher contre toi, avec toute une armée de fer? »
Il se redressa orgueilleusement, mit en action les ondes émettrices :
« Nous acceptons tous le combat! » répondit-il. (A suivre)

2. Pellos, "Futuropolis." Copyright Pellos.

4. Rob Vel, "Spirou." Copyright Ed. Dupuis.

Aria" (Will Sparrow, Pirate of the Air). The possibility of air piracy, a logical sequel to sea piracy, seems to have struck the public imagination in the period between the two wars; the theme is found in America and in Europe, not only in the comic strip but also in the adventure novel (for example, the Bill Barnes series in the United States, which appeared in France as a serial story under the title of *Jacques Barnès*). Cesare Avai is known particularly as the author of the most beautiful of all aviation strips (not even excepting the American strips), "Romano il Legionario," obviously a Fascist strip, with Spain as its locale; it glorified the Aviacion del Tercio, with superb draftsmanship and narrative technique. The artist's point of view whirls with the planes, with close-ups and distance shots, down-shots and up-shots following in rapid succession. Romano is outshone by the real hero of the story—the good-looking fighter biplane Fiat CR 32.

The writer Frederick Pedrocchi wrote the scripts for two epochal science-fiction stories. The first "Saturno Contro la Terra" (Saturn Versus Earth, 1937–1943), drawn by Giovanni Scolari, depicted earthly scientists in a struggle against Saturnian imperialism. Very "Buck Rogers" in style by its use of glass-roofed spaceships and curved wings, and by the liberties it took with science, this strip is of sweeping inventiveness in the continual rebounds of its plot, its monsters, its bizarre devices, and its grandiose war rockets that snake between planets. The other story, "Virus il Mago Della Foresta Morta" (Virus the Magician of the Dead Forest), drawn by Walter Molino, centers upon a classic device of science-fiction of the thirties: a transmitter-duplicator of matter, invented by a frightening scientist whose laboratory is built on quicksand in the middle of a sinister forest.

In 1938 the American strips were banned from Italy. By a phenomenon that was to be repeated in France, far from encouraging home production this event caused it to degenerate, and mediocre imitations of the major American series burgeoned everywhere.

This period witnessed the birth, in Belgium, of what was to become the star performer of the European comic strip: "Tintin," the creation of Georges Remi ("Hergé"), the success of which was to surpass that of "Zig et Puce," but not until after the war. Reviving the physical appearance of his first character, a boy scout of 1923 named Totor, Hergé published the first Tintin episode in 1929, in the weekly supplement of a Brussels daily newspaper, *Le Vingtième Siècle*. In 1930 appeared the first Tintin book, *Tintin au Pays des Soviets* (Tintin in the Land of the Soviets). (There is little likelihood that it will ever be published in Russia!) While the characters were, and always will be, caricatures (in the beginning Tintin bore a particularly strong resemblance to Bécassine), the settings presented an increasingly detailed realism, and the balloons—the weak point of Saint-Ogan, who inserted them anywhere—are clear and rectangular. The general appearance of the strip is carefully finished, orderly, and less whimsical and unrestrained than the style of Saint-Ogan. Whereas the latter was satisfied with combinations of black-white-red or red-brown-blue, Hergé played skillfully with colors, sometimes using cool colors for beautiful night effects, sometimes warm colors in which a scale of browns and beiges predominates. Centered on a single hero—another adolescent, like Bibi Fricotin or Blighter and Flea—accompanied by a friendly dog named Milou, Hergé enlarged his team by adding to it the truculent Captain Haddock, the dizzy Tournesol (Calculus in the English version), and particularly two stupid characters named Dupont and Dupond (in English, Thomson and Thompson) whose blunders and bloopers form the comic counterpoint throughout all the events of the strip.

To date, Hergé has published twenty-one books of Tintin's adventures: *Tintin au Pays des Soviets* (Tintin in the Land of the Soviets—now out of print); *Tintin au Congo* (Tintin in the Congo); *Tintin en Amérique; Les Cigares du Pharaon* (The Pharaoh's Cigars); *Le Lotus Bleu* (The Blue Lotus); *L'Oreille Cassée* (The Broken Ear); *L'Ile Noire* (Black Island); *Le Crabe aux Pinces d'Or* (The Crab with the Golden Claws—which marks the first appearance of Captain Haddock); *L'Étoile Mystérieuse* (The Mysterious Star); *Le Secret de la Licorne* (The Unicorn's Secret*—in which Professor Calculus makes his first appearance); *Le Trésor de Rackham le Rouge* (The Treasure of Rackham the Red); *Les Sept Boules de Cristal* (The Seven Crystal Balls); *Le Temple du Soleil* (The Temple of the Sun); *Tintin au Pays de l'Or Noir* (Tintin in the Land of Black Gold); *Objectif Lune* (Objective: Moon); *On a Marché sur la Lune* (We Walked on the Moon); *L'Affaire Tournesol* (The Calculus Affair); *Coke en Stock* (Coke in Stock); *Tintin au Tibet* (Tintin in Tibet); *Les Bijoux de la Castafiore* (The Jewels of the Castafiore). *Vol 714 pour Sydney* (Flight 714 for Sydney) is now in preparation.

Hergé is also the author of a family series, *Les Aventures de Jo, Zette et Jocko*, of which five books have been published: *Le Testament de Mr. Pump, Destination New York, Le Manitoba Ne Répond Plus* (Manitoba No Longer Answers), *L'Éruption du Karamako*, and *La Vallée des Cobras* (Valley of the Cobras).

A humorous series, the principal characters of which are Quick and Flupke, two urchins of Brussels (ten series have appeared), and a book of satire entitled *Paul et Virginie au Pays des Lapinos* (Paul and Virginia in the Land of the Lapinos), complete this survey of the production of Tintin's creator.

The principal characters in the adventures of Tintin.

Hergé, "Tintin."

A selection from *Tintin au Pays de l'Or Noir* (Tintin in the Land of Black Gold), 1939. This series, interrupted in 1939 by the war, was resumed in 1948.

Balloons (opposite):

1. We've discovered important papers in the radio operator's cabin, sir.
   Oh. yeah?

2. I assure you, Lieutenant, I didn't know these papers were in my cabin.
   The inquiry will decide that. . . . But . . . what's going on?

3. Let go of us! . . . We're from the police! You'll pay for this!
   I'll go even further than that: you'll pay for this!

4. Important papers in their baggage, sir . . . They didn't want to let us examine their belongings. . . . They claim they're from the secret police. . . .
   Oh? . . .

5. Our good faith has been taken advantage of, Admiral! . . . We were given this package by an agent of the Intelligence Service. He said it contained secret documents.
   What's become of this man?

6. He's on board ship, Admiral. . . . Only, it seems that he's suddenly gone insane. . . .
   And as a result we won't be able to learn anything from him!
   Not a bad story, boys—except that *I*'m not crazy!
   Drat! . . . and drat again! I've been following the wrong trail!

10. Boss! He's come! I saw him!
    Who? The one we've been waiting for?

11. Yeah, Boss! . . . But he must have been betrayed! The English have already arrested him.
    We've got to get him out of there at any cost!

12. (The next morning)
    You've been transferred to the Central Prison. . . . Please follow us. . . .

Nous avons trouvé des documents chez l'opérateur de radio, Sir...
Ah! Ah!
Je vous assure, lieutenant, j'ignorais absolument la présence de ces papiers dans ma cabine...
C'est ce que l'enquête établira... Mais... que se passe-t-il?
Lâchez-nous!... Nous sommes de la police et cela vous coû tera cher!...
Je dirai même plus : cela vous coûtera cher!...
Des documents dans leurs bagages, Sir!... Ils ne voulaient pas nous laisser fouiller... Ils prétendent qu'ils sont de la police secrète...
Ah?...
Notre bonne foi a été surprise, amiral!... C'est un agent de l'Intelligence Service qui nous a confié ce paquet en nous disant qu'il contenait des documents secrets.
Qu'est-il devenu, cet individu?
Il est à bord, amiral... Seulement, il paraît qu'il est devenu subitement fou...
Et, par conséquent, nous ne pourrons plus rien en tirer!... Pas mal, votre petite histoire de fou!... Seulement, je ne le suis pas moi, fou!
Zut!... Et encore zut!... J'ai suivi une fausse piste!...
Chef!... Il est arrivé!... Je l'ai vu!...
Qui?... Celui qu'on attendait?...
Oui, chef!... Mais il a dû être trahi!... Les Anglais l'ont déjà arrêté!
Il faut le tirer de là, coûte que coûte!
Le lendemain matin...
Vous êtes transféré à la Prison Centrale... Veuillez nous suivre...
BOUM

Milton Caniff, "Male Call."
Copyright Milton Caniff.

5

the crisis of the forties

Unlike the First World War, which affected the American comic strip only superficially, the Second World War caused a profound and permanent upheaval, not only in the comics but also in the lives of their creators. Before America's entrance into the war, and even before the conflict had officially broken out in Europe, cartoonists had already taken a definite stand on the question. As we saw in the preceding chapter, Milton Caniff's heroes began in 1937 to carry on a crafty guerrilla war against the Japanese, while Secret Agent X-9, under the pen of Austin Briggs, was hunting down a spy network directed by a certain Captain Ludwig, whose name, monocle, shaved neck, and arrogant bearing left hardly any doubt as to his nationality.

After the beginning of hostilities in 1939, the tempo quickened. While the American government declared itself officially neutral, the comic-strip authors scarcely troubled to conceal on which side their sympathies lay. While some comic strip heroes joined the R.A.F., the Canadian Army, or the Foreign Legion in order the fight the "Huns," others who remained behind in the States engaged in an active and sometimes virulent pro-Allied propaganda, often in direct opposition to the newspapers that carried them. In May, 1940, for example, while the publishers of the New York *Mirror* were urging their readers to "keep cool" and to refrain from demanding "an emotionally inspired counterblow," inside the same newspaper Joe Palooka launched a ringing appeal for American intervention. When this intervention finally occurred, on December 8, 1941, the American government found the cartoonists psychologically prepared to contribute their share to the Allied war effort—a share that was to be considerable throughout the war.

The comics, having become propaganda weapons, bolstered the confidence of the G.I.'s and stiffened morale on the home front. In 1941, for example, Joe Palooka joined the army, and his creator, Ham Fisher, became, with the approval of the War Department, one of the most effective spokesmen for the interventionist policy. Joe Palooka's example was enthusiastically followed by other comic-strip heroes, who soon found themselves fighting Japanese or Germans in the most varied theatres of war. Thus we find Jungle Jim engaged in checking the Japanese advance into Burma, Captain Easy foiling enemy intrigues all over the globe, and Scorchy Smith fighting next to the Russians on the Eastern Front, while Dick Tracy, X-9, and Charlie Chan battled spies and saboteurs. Even Tarzan took part in the combat: in 1942 he obliterated a Nazi commando who was just about to establish a secret base in Africa. In the same year Superman demolished the Atlantic Wall in preparation for the Allied invasion—a deed that caused a fuming Goebbels to scream in the middle of a Reichstag meeting, "Superman is a Jew!"

"Terry and the Pirates" reflected more faithfully than any other comic strip the American attitude after the Pearl Harbor attack. The wild adventures of Pat Ryan gradually gave way to the realities of the war. Terry, having finally passed the adolescent stage, became a lieutenant and pilot in the air force, and his commanding officer, Colonel Flip Corkin, moved into the place that until then had been occupied by Pat Ryan, but in a position of greater equality. Without completely abandoning its romantic character, "Terry" became a different type of strip, in which the individual deeds were muted before collective heroism. In his situations, dialogues, and minute details of terrain,

A symbolic battle between Prince Valiant and the Huns.
Harold Foster, "Prince Valiant." Copyright King Features Syndicate, Inc.

weapons, and uniforms, Caniff set himself the task of describing the realities of the war with a dramatic but simple precision of expression that culminated in the famous page of Sunday, October 17, 1943—the first comic strip ever included in the *Congressional Record*.

The war not only changed the character of numerous strips already in existence, but also gave rise to new ones. In 1943 Roy Crane abandoned "Captain Easy" and created "Buz Sawyer." Buz is a pilot in the navy air force, who did for the navy what Terry had done for the air force; that is, he brought the realities of the conflict home to the reader in the States. Together with his comic partner, Roscoe Sweeney, Buz ranged all over the pacific. Crane's dialogues lack the decisiveness of Caniff's, and his adventures are less plausible and more "Hollywoodian." This strip was nevertheless one of the best of the war, surpassed only by "Terry."

Leslie Turner took over "Captain Easy" without appreciably altering either the strip's style or its spirit. Turner's technique is similar to that of his predecessor, with perhaps greater use of solid black areas and a clearer line, but his talent is indisputable.

Frank Robbins's "Johnny Hazard," another "war baby," was born in 1944. Its hero, also a pilot, bears some resemblance to Scorchy Smith, but is more mature and more poised. Johnny's adventures are less extraordinary than Scorchy's, but the strip gains in authenticity what it loses in color. Robbins's line has become lighter and has acquired an ease comparable to that of Caniff, without, however, losing anything of its strongly personal character. After the war Johnny Hazard became a commercial pilot and director of an airline, exercising his talents in the four corners of the world in the rediscovered tradition of Scorchy Smith.

"Johnny Hazard" and "Buz Sawyer" were read chiefly by civilians, but the war also gave birth to strips specially designed for the Armed Forces. Three of these soon began to compete in popularity with the best commercial series: "G.I. Joe," "The Sad Sack," and "Male Call," all created in 1942.

At first entitled "Private Breger," after its author Dave Breger, "G.I. Joe" acquired its definitive title several months later. It was not exactly a comic strip, but rather a series of pictures with a caption under each frame. G.I. Joe is the prototype of the civilian in uniform: well intentioned, decent, and obedient to orders even when he does not understand them. His well-ingrained "civvie" habits, however, turn his best intentions into disasters, and are the despair of the military minds. The thousand incidents in a soldier's life, its duties and the complexities of its discipline, form the content of this appealing series. A harmless satire of military life, "G.I. Joe" enjoyed tremendous success both at the front and at home, and its title has passed into the language as the name for the ordinary American soldier.

"The Sad Sack," created by Sergeant George Baker, is the personification of the poor slob drafted through a stroke of bad luck, a soldier by accident, the perfect goat, persecuted by his buddies, mistreated by his sergeant, and knocked around by the officers. There is something pathetic about this little man, who

Certain American comic-strip heroes were among the first to participate (symbolically) in the ideological campaign against Hitler's Germany. Ed. François remarks that A. Raymond's portrayal of the planet Mongo in "Flash Gordon" changed rapidly in 1937; from a medieval world in which kingdoms are theoretical vassals of Emperor Ming, we move into a totalitarian state with police roundups, government prisons, and military parades, a state in which the emperor (who until then had been an Oriental-style despot, cruel but far from omnipotent) rules absolutely with the support of the secret police and the army. Flash then begins to have a definite objective: the liberation of Mongo with the help of Ming's underground opposition and the small states threatened by him. Similarly, at the same time of the *Anschluss* and the occupation of Bohemia, H. Foster created (in May, 1939) the episode of "Prince Valiant," in which he depicts Europe invaded by the Huns. Prince Valiant leaves Thule in order to combat them; he is soon joined by two other knights of the Round Table, Tristan and Gawain, and they carry on a long guerrilla war in the Tyrolean mountains, teaching the peaceful inhabitants to defend themselves. It is a well-known fact that in Anglo-American slang "the Huns" refers to the Germans. The allusion was so clear that when "Prince Valiant" appeared in France in the unoccupied zone, the "Huns" became the "Patagos," imaginary barbarians.

1. Frank Robbins, "Johnny Hazard." Copyright King Features Syndicate, Inc.

2. Roy Crane, "Buz Sawyer." Copyright King Features Syndicate, Inc.

is always being knocked down and who always gets up again, yet never dreams of cursing anyone, not even his unlucky star. His strange odysseys, his humble resignation, the persistence of the unjust fate that hounds him are reminiscent of the Good Soldier Schweik. Sad Sack, like Schweik, is the victim of external powers unknown to him, and which he does not understand. However meritorious his actions may be, they always rebound. He is blamed for what he does as well as for what he fails to do, and for him the perversity of the world is the only thing that is certain.

Having been requested to produce a strip specially conceived for the G.I.'s, Milton Caniff created "Male Call." Its heroine, Miss Lace, is a pretty, scantily clad, not overly shy girl, whose (quite innocent) relations with soldiers of every rank and every arm constitute the most enduring portion of the plot. Drawn in the best "Caniffian" tradition, Miss Lace enjoyed a richly deserved success with the soldiers, and was to be found in more than one military barracks, pinned to the wall next to photographs of Rita Hayworth and Lana Turner.

Some cartoonists contributed more than their pens and their talents to the war effort. Bert Christman, one of the artists of "Scorchy Smith," joined the navy air force and then the Flying Tigers, the famous unit under the command of Colonel Chennault. On January 23, 1942, he was killed over Burma in an air combat against Japanese planes coming to bomb Rangoon.

In 1944 Alex Raymond was recalled as a captain in the Marines, and served as a public relations officer until the end of the war. After his departure, "Jungle Jim" was drawn by a series of very mediocre artists (one of whom was his brother James Raymond) until its disappearance in 1954. "Flash Gordon" had better luck: his successor was Austin Briggs, who had been drawing the daily adventures of Flash since May, 1940. Briggs was able to sustain the epic inspiration, the exuberant imagination, and the frenzied rhythm that characterized this strip. The line is not always as sure as Raymond's, and the compositions, sometimes too detailed, are less harmonious, but his mastery is nevertheless indisputable. Briggs was unquestionably Raymond's most worthy rival. When he too abandoned the strip in 1948, his place was taken by Mac Raboy, an untalented hack who reduced "Flash Gordon" to the level of the worst comic books.

Not all the comic strips of this period were devoted to martial adventures. In 1942 Alfred Andriola dropped Charlie Chan and created (in 1943) "Kerry Drake," a likable blond-haired detective whose adventures, which are closely related to daily life, are always convincing. The crimes are or could be real; the characters are very picturesque without falling into the exaggeration that characterizes "Dick Tracy"; and the police techniques are scrupulously authentic. The draftsmanship of "Kerry Drake" is more precise and linear than that of "Charlie Chan," while its dialogues are more restrained and have less humor. In his search for realism, Andriola seems unfortunately to have sacrificed the picturesque and imaginative qualities that constituted the charm of his earlier strip.

In contrast to the events of these years, in 1942 there appeared a strip that combined the fantasy of "Little Nemo" with the humor and poetry of "Krazy Kat": Crockett Johnson's "Barnaby." A little boy with an original mind, Barnaby lives in a fantastic universe that parallels the prosaic, drab adult world. He enters the latter in the train of Mr. O'Malley, a talkative, quackish genius whose magic wand is a cigar. The defeats of Mr. O'Malley, who sees his supernatural deeds rebound against him, and the incredulity of Barnaby's parents, the Baxters, furnish the principal plot of the story. An army of legendary creatures—elves, gnomes, sprites—comes to join Barnaby and his inept mentor, notably Launcelot McSnoyd, a cynical, disagreeable hobgoblin; Gus, the timid, eternally terrified ghost; and Gorgon, the talking dog. Johnson's clear, harmonious draftsmanship is very agreeable to the eye; his line is simple; and the action is depicted with great economy. The very stylized settings, and the fact that the balloons are printed rather than lettered heighten the fresh appearance of this strip. The independent Bohemian Crockett Johnson, however, could not long endure being tied to such steady work. He abandoned the strip in 1946; it was revived by Jack Morley and Ted Ferro, but disappeared for good in 1954.

During this period the European comic strip was at the mercy of paper and ink shortages, propaganda, and the memory of the American strips, which were no longer available. The Italian magazines replaced all the American heroes with local imitations: the mouse Topolino (Mickey) became a kid named "Tuffolino," and so on. In the unoccupied zone of France, "Prince Valiant," "The Katzenjammer Kids," Disney's characters, "Connie," and "Popeye" continued until America's entry into the war. But official preference was given to the traditional picture stories devoted to the national heroes, particularly to those who fought against the English: Du Guesclin, Jean Bart, Surcouf, Joan of Arc, and Montcalm perform in small pictures done with execrable draftsmanship and disgraceful

1, 2. Milton Caniff, "Male Call." Copyright Milton Caniff.

3. Milton Caniff, "Terry and the Pirates." Copyright Chicago Tribune—New York News Syndicate, Inc.

3. The famous strip in which Colonel Corkin reminds the recently promoted Terry of his duties to his country, his subordinates, and his predecessors.

Crockett Johnson, "Barnaby." Copyright by Crockett Johnson.

George Baker, "Sad Sack." Copyright Bell Syndicate.

printing. In view of the pressure for a return to the national traditions, the comic strip itself was not favorably regarded, and there was a reversion to the old formula of the children's newspapers: novels, numerous illustrations, and no comic strips. This was the case with, for example, *Sirocco,* the best youth magazine in the Free Zone. In the occupied zone, a Nazi magazine called *Le Téméraire* (1943–44) indoctrinated its readers and, under cover of a club for its subscribers, attempted to sow the seeds of Hitler youth organizations. The comic strip occupied quite an important place in this magazine. Evil men were depicted with hooked noses and weasel faces, and were called Orloff or Venin. In France, as in Italy, many artists were overwhelmed by the recollection of "Flash Gordon" and "Mandrake," and became imitators. The end of the war did not improve the situation. In fact, paradoxically enough, it even precipitated the decline of the American comic strip, a decline that became cruelly apparent after 1946; the humorous strips were no longer so amusing; the adventure strips seemed to have lost their spirit. It is understandable that after a conflict that had cost 30 million human lives, humorists found it a bit difficult to be funny. The adventure-strip authors, for their part, had a still more complex problem: compared with the silent heroism displayed by millions of combatants, famous or anonymous, the exploits of their characters suddenly seemed contemptible, futile, and almost unseemly.

For the cartoonists, as for the great majority of Americans, the return of peace was a period of great disorder and intense intellectual ferment. Thus it is not surprising to see three of the greatest creative spirits of the day—Alex Raymond, Burne Hogarth, and Milton Caniff—almost simultaneously attempt to start the adventure strip on a new path.

The critic Kenneth Rexroth has said that all adventure stories can be reduced to two prototypes: the Iliad and the Odyssey. Alex Raymond, whose "Flash Gordon" was certainly the Achilles of the comic strip, wished to create its Ulysses with "Rip Kirby," which appeared in April, 1946. Like Raymond a former Marine commander, who has become a private detective upon his return to civilian life, Rip Kirby does not depend solely on his physical prowess to resolve the difficult cases handed to him. He likes intellectual pleasures, plays chess, and can enjoy from a connoisseur's viewpoint both the complex harmonies of contemporary music and the heady aroma of a brandy from a good year. His conversation reflects his "gentlemanly" culture, and in his relations with the two rival heroines of the strip—the dark, sensual Pagan Lee and tender, blond Honey Dorian—he is capable of displaying an adroit delicacy. With "Rip Kirby," Alex Raymond deliberately attempted to present the intellectual as hero (in contrast to the trend of contemporary literature). It cannot be denied that the attempt was but an indifferent success—not through lack of talent, but by force of circumstances.

Preceding Raymond's creation by several months, Burne Hogarth's "Drago" appeared in November, 1945. Unlike "Tarzan," its action takes place not in

---

Another cause of difficulties for the comic strip was the reduction of the size of the daily strips in the newspapers. This reduction (by at least one-third) had especially serious consequences for the realistic strips, the adventure series. The characters were stifled, and the artist could not develop the setting and create the space indispensable to illusion. Moreover, since the letters could not be reduced in the same proportions (they would be too small), either the balloon invaded the picture or the dialogue was shortened. Thereafter only thirty-seven words were permitted in a balloon. The cartoonists were unanimous in their denunciation of this restriction:

"While an increasing amount of space is allocated to the comics, the size of each strip is gradually reduced. If I wish to save space for the balloons, I can show only the heads of the characters. Or I can draw them full size, but extremely small" (G. McManus).

"They have almost killed the type of strip I like to draw. There is no longer room for the action or for effects of atmosphere. If the size of the drawings is to be further reduced, I'll give up" (Roy Crane).

1. Burne Hogarth, "Drago." Publishers-Hall Syndicate.

2. Alfred Andriola, "Kerry Drake." Copyright Publishers-Hall Syndicate.

3. Austin Briggs, "Flash Gordon." Copyright King Features Syndicate, Inc.

Africa but in Argentina. However, we quickly rediscover the universe of violent landscapes and sinister shadows so dear to this author. Hogarth's baroque imagination enjoys free play in the opulence of the women's costumes and in the phantasmagorical atmosphere in which this strip is steeped. The heroes of this series—Drago, a younger Tarzan; his comical subordinate, Tabasco; and Baron Zodiac, a sinister Nazi who dreams only of revenge—are all quite conventional, but never before did Hogarth's talent rise to such expressionistic fury. Despite its ephemeral existence (Hogarth abandoned "Drago" at the beginning of 1947 to return to "Tarzan"), this strip remains one of the strangest and most deserving of consideration.

In January, 1947, Milton Caniff created "Steve Canyon." The hero is a former air-force captain who is now director of an airline company perpetually in danger of bankruptcy. This fact obliges Canyon to accept the most dangerous missions, and gets him involved with a host of shifty individuals. With "Steve Canyon," Caniff's style became more tense, troubled, and less elegant, and the characters also displayed this indecision. For a long while Steve alternated between different morphological types before acquiring his present appearance—a testimony to the intellectual and moral preoccupations of the author, as well as a reflection of the uncertainties of the time.

Caniff, Hogarth, and Raymond wished, each in his own way, to begin a revival of the adventure strip, but pressure from a public that desired only an easy escape and intellectual comfort forced them to return to the tested formulas. However, their efforts were not in vain; they opened to others the paths discovered by these artists. In addition, the adventure strip was then experiencing an almost universal decline of standards. The heroes of the great prewar series were aging and becoming middle-class citizens; they seemed to lack inspiration and conviction. Moreover, many artists now abandoned the strips they had created, which thereupon very often fell into the hands of undeserving hacks. The most heartbreaking example is the case of George Wunder, who took over "Terry" on Caniff's departure in 1947; with passionate obstinacy, he seemed to delight in turning the strip into a hideous antithesis of the the "Terry" of the golden age. Unfortunately, he succeeded only too well: the drawings are unsatisfactory; the perspective is wrong; the characters with their equine physiognomies have the stiffness and the behavior of robots; the dialogues are drab and humorless, and the scripts are of a characterless triviality. Despite these glaring defects, this strip has nevertheless lost none of its popularity, which may be due in part to his ability to draw aircraft and other machines.

For a long while those cartoonists who were aware of this problem presented by their public had been attempting to create an association for the protection and defense of their artistic as well as professional interests. Several efforts in this direction had been made before the war, but it was not until January, 1946, with the creation of the National Cartoonists Society (N.C.S.), that they bore fruit. Originally consisting only of its seven founders, today the N.C.S. has more than 500 members, representing not only the comic strip but also the humorous cartoon, magazine illustration, advertising, the animated cartoon, and the comic books. Its first president was Rube Goldberg; in succeeding years this position was occupied by a succession of cartoonists, among whom are to be found some of the greatest comic-strip creators: Milton Caniff, Alex Raymond, Walt Kelly, Mort Walker. Among the numerous activities of the society, special mention should be made of the annual award of the "Reuben" (a statuette representing four ugly gnomes in the process of doing gymnastic exercises—so named in honor of its creator, Reuben "Rube" Goldberg) to the best cartoonist of the year.

Despite these efforts, the American comic strip experienced a slow, steady decline that was not to be checked until the following decade.

In Europe a similar confusion existed. Moreover, the prolonged paper rationing did not encourage illustrated magazines. In France several American series reappeared in irregular order, but they encountered an organized opposition that was a direct continuation of the prohibitions of Vichy and Berlin. The Communists were opposed to the American strips because they were American and because they exalted individualism and the spirit of adventure, both contrary to Marxism; the Right was opposed to them because the strips were American and endangered the national spirit; there was combined opposition from religious sources and the public school system to the excesses of the comic books, with which all the comic strips were more or less sincerely confused. Backing these groups was the opposition of French artists and publishers who, being members of a generation that had been overwhelmed by the Americans, unenthusiastically witnessed the return of these formidable competitors. The Communist Union Patriotique des Organisations de Jeunesse (Patriotic Union of Youth Organizations) prepared, in conjunction with the Catholic Commission d'Etude des Journaux d'Enfants (Committee for the Study of Children's Newspapers), a text which the Communist Party took over and presented for enactment into law; its aim was to prohibit all foreign comic strips. The project, being too extreme, was rejected. The more tactful Catholics re-

1. Alex Raymond, "Rip Kirby." Copyright King Features Syndicate, Inc.

2. Milton Caniff, "Steve Canyon." Copyright Publishers-Hall Syndicate.

3. George Wunder, "Terry and the Pirates." Copyright Chicago Tribune—New York News Syndicate, Inc.

vised their text, which, being more effectively cloaked by moral considerations, was voted into law on July 2, 1949. Since the passage of this law, which established a watchdog committee, the French comic strip has been existing under a shaky protectionism.

In the gray expanse of this uninspired period, in which even a merely competent drawing was a rarity, a few names are worth mentioning. One is the humorist Erik, who was fond of portraying lunatic twosomes like the two mad scientists "Tribacil et Bisulfite," or the two truculent accomplices "Crochemaille et Brisemur" (Crookedstitch and Breakwall), and their medieval tribulations, with epic buffoonery. After a long period of working on "Salvator" (inspired by "Flash Gordon"), Liquois produced a remarkable interplanetary story, "Guerre à la Terre" (War on Earth). Raymond Poïvet, whose career had begun before 1940, appeared as a good science-fiction artist, from "Marc Reynes" to the excellent "Pionniers de l'Espérance" (The Pioneers of the Hope). He also drew the tragic adventures of "Colonel X," a hero of the Resistance movement. René Giffey, faithful to his usual habits, continued the French tradition by devoting himself to the joys of the historico-literary themes of Buffalo Bill's adventures. Marijac ("Les Trois Mousquetaires du Maquis"—The Three Musketeers of the Maquis), Raymond Cazenave ("Le Vampire des Caraïbes"—The Vampire of the Caribbean), and Calvo deserve to be remembered. Le Rallic, still active and well suited to the comic strip, was then turning out the excellent "Pancho Libertas." Lucien Nortier created a Western series, "Sam Billie Bill," for the weekly magazine *Vaillant*.

A generation of talented young artists was appearing, including men like Jean Ache ("Arabelle, la Dernière Sirène"—Arabella, the Last Siren) with Albert Uderzo, who made his debut in 1947 with "Arys Buck," then with "Belloy l'Invulnérable," an athletic, kindhearted hero. The French and Belgian productions (the latter were now experiencing a remarkable development) were gradually combining; in the same period, Spanish artists were coming to work in France, including José Cabrero-Arnal, the author of "Pif le Chien" (Pif the Dog) and "Placid et Muzo."

In Belgium, Edgar P. Jacobs, a collaborator of Hergé, began in 1946 his long series of stories, which are characterized by extreme precision of draftsmanship and solid construction of script. His characters—Professor Mortimer, Francis Blake of the Intelligence Service, and Colonel Olrik—were modeled on three heroes of a science-fiction adventure drawn by Jacobs during the war for the weekly magazine *Bravo;* this little-known series was entitled "Le Rayon 'U'" (The U-Ray). "The Secret of the Espadon," the trio's first adventure, was highly successful, and has since then been republished many times in book form. The story

A French law enacted in 1949 made the corruption of children and young adults by printed material a misdemeanor, and established a commission for the observation and control of publications for children and adolescents. The commission acts only upon already published material (it seemed wise to give up the idea of preventive censorship, in view of the disagreeable memories this would have aroused). The law recognizes the impossibility of defining the misdemeanors in question, but a definition will gradually be outlined by the "qualified individuals" who form the commission (twenty-eight members, including one father and one mother, who are largely symbolical). One clause that would have required that 75 percent of the space of all newspapers be reserved for French authors and artists was abandoned. The cloven hoof was a little too much in evidence, and reprisals were feared. Communists and Catholics mutually attempted to disqualify each other as members, but failed, and joined forces to block the American series. Their local imitations multiplied—Milton Caniff was plagiarized outrageously—with all the defects of ugliness, uncalled-for violence, and poverty of language that were missing in the American strips. By an inexplicable phenomenon, the commission never noticed this, and permitted them to multiply.

1. Accelerating . . . I see the "Flying Fortresses" from afar, circling hopelessly between Boulogne and Calais, not daring to go farther without an escort. Some thirty "Focke-Wolfs" above the Fortresses in single file begin to dive in two's. The mass of bombers is lighted up by a thousand fires from exploding shots reaching their targets, or Colt machine guns, replying. . . .

Calmly, as if at a training session, Mouchotte begins to give orders. An electric shock seems to animate the squadron, and the twelve Spitfires go into action, waver, then drop off to right and left. . . .

"Hello, Turban! . . . six planes at nine o'clock! Above!"

The noise in the earphones deafens my ears. . . . I glance to my left. An avalanche of Focke-Wolfs-190 rushes down out of the sunlight. One of them opens fire. The tracers come within fifteen yards of my wing.

"That's bad!"

I perform a horizontal spin that brings me within a hundred yards of a Focke-Wolf, at which I direct a burst of gunfire. . . .

"Missed!"

2. "Mission accomplished! Successful raid!"

In an apocalyptic vision, the terrible destruction stretching across the steppes and the valleys ravages the country for dozens of miles. The squadron, its mission accomplished, makes a half-turn and heads for its base, while Blake laconically makes his report.

3. On the shore of the lake, the fantastic rodeo begins. Maddened by an invisible presence, the triton dashes against the rocks.

4. This base must be seized at any cost before the last rockets have taken off for their African or Oriental bases. Colonel Veyrac and his kidnappers.
   The group of Martian spheres continues to progress rapidly toward the south. The sky is still clear.

1. Christian Mathelot, "Le Grand Cirque" (The Big Circus), Copyright Flammarion.

2. E. P. Jacobs, "Le Secret de l'Espadon" (The Secret of the Espadon). Copyright Ed. du Lombard.

3. R. Poïvet, "Les Pionniers de l'Espérance" (The Pioneers of the Hope). Copyright Vaillant.

4. A. Liquois, "Guerre à la Terre" (War on Earth). Copyright Coq Hardi.

1. "Wait! He's *eating* them!"
"He doesn't seem to feel any sting!"
"Fantasio, the Marsupilami is an *anteater!*"
"This little animal is definitely one of nature's wonders!"
"Hic!"

2. "The Princess is in a faint. But you have to admit that you're in a good position, my son! Ha! Ha!"
"Don't joke, Cascagnace; the game's not over. The horsemen of Kemberg will surely follow us."

3. The strange duel begins on the platform.

7. Sam faced him again, but his defensive movement was stopped in mid-air, and his face was the picture of amazement. Even more strangely, his assailant also stopped dead in his tracks.

1. Franquin, "Spirou." Copyright Ed. Dupuis.
2. Uderzo, "Arys Buck." Copyright O.K.
3. René Giffey, "Buffalo Bill." Copyright Ed. Mondiales.
4. Morris, "Lucky Luke." Copyright Editions Dupuis.
5. Raymond Cazenave, "Le Capitaine Fantôme." Copyright Coq Hardi.
6. Le Rallic, "Poncho Libertas." Copyright Coq Hardi.
7. Lucien Nortier, "Sam Billie Bill." Copyright Vaillant.
8. Jacques Martin, "Alix l'Intrépide." Copyright Ed. du Lombard.
9. Paul Cuvelier. "Les Aventures de Corentin." Copyright Ed. du Lombard.

6. "Drat! Now they're shooting at me from behind!"

Little Cactus, who is resting his horse, realizes he's surrounded.

8. "I'm not mistaken! That boat is Marsalla's trireme. So it's escaped the pirates."

9. "Give me his mount, and take him back to the house. Keep him in sight until the new moon."
    "Yes, my lord."

1. Half a league away, the convoy is advancing slowly.

2. An exciting fight is about to break out between two trigger-happy guys. All the citizens clear off the street that crosses Ciccitown.
"Run, horse! Every man for himself!"
[Sign on door] Closed for impending shooting.

3. Have pity on a poor man who's missing one leg.
Blind, deaf, and dumb from birth.
"All my friends manage to make people sorry for them. I'm the only one who can't do it. I've got to find a way of stirring up sympathy!"
"Have pity on a man who died while being born."

is still thoroughly permeated with the atmosphere of the last war, but Jacobs presents his vision of a possible international atomic conflict.

In the same period Jacques Martin created the character of Alix the fearless, a young Gaul in the service of Caesar who wanders about the Mediterranean basin in the pursuit of the Greek Arbacès. This series draws upon an enormous fund of information about the Roman age and the ancient East, with the same fondness for subterranean passages and secret societies displayed by Jacobs. Mention should also be made of Paul Cuvelier, the creator of a young eighteenth-century hero named Corentin, and also of Willy Van der Steen, the artist of Bob and Bobette and their innumerable adventures, drawn with typically Belgian humor. At this time the magazine *Tintin,* for which all these artists were working, had an excellent style of presentation (which has since then been somewhat abused).

Franquin, the successor of Gillain, revived a character created by R. Velter before the war—"Spirou," the young groom in red costume—and made him one of the best-known children's comic-strip heroes in Europe. In 1946 Maurice De Bévère ("Morris") began his "Lucky Luke," a very humorous cowboy and the focal point of a series that was to be both an excellent Western and an enjoyable parody. Joseph Gillain was drawing the adventures of "Valhardi," Sirius, "L'Epervier Bleu" (The Blue Sparrow Hawk); Victor Hubinon, "Buck Danny"; and Will, "Tif et Tondu."

But it was Hergé who dominated this era and that of the fifties. Skillfulness of narrative, integrity of execution—in drawing, background information, and finesse of color—and an impeccable and unobtrusive technique, all assured "Tintin" of international success; the editions of the Tintin books rose from 275,000 copies in 1944 to 4,500,000 in 1954.

Italy possessed the strange Jacovitti, a frenzied humorist who displayed a certain sadism, was fond of infirmities, deformities, and mutilations, endowed characters with impossibly bloated faces, put hats on worms, and paved his landscapes with salamis.

It was in England, however, that the most unmistakable signs of evolution were appearing. The *Daily Mirror* opened its pages wide to the adult comic strips (more impossible than ever on the Continent): Jack Monk's "Buck Ryan," an English Rip Kirby; a good science fantasy called "Garth," by Steve Dowling (done entirely in cross-hatching); and lastly Pett's "Jane," which is our best index for determining the progress accomplished during the war. "Jane" had few merits; its rather limp style was well suited to the subject and to the basic range of the plot. Jane, a pretty young woman, lost her skirt in approximately every twelfth picture, and appeared naked at wider intervals. Success crowned this original innovation, with which this survey of the forties may be concluded. We might add that this splendid example has not been forgotten and that the experts now see in its imitation a means of raising the French comic strip to the level of Art.

1. Erik, "Tartol de la Clanche." Copyright Coq Hardi.

2, 3. Jacovitti. The second of the "Cocco Bill" series is especially typical of the artist's exaggerations.

102

6

the regeneration of the comic strip

Toward mid-century, the clouds that had been gradually accumulating over the comics appeared increasingly darker and more alarming. Threatened with artistic sterility, and imprisoned within its own clichés, the American comic strip faced a new and grave danger.

Since their creation, the comics had been the object of numerous attacks. Before the First World War they had been accused of sowing disrespect and insubordination in the minds of children by their glorification of brazen, anarchistic rascals like the Yellow Kid or the Katzenjammer Kids, and of being a waste of time and attention for their young readers. These criticisms led the Boston *Herald,* to abandon its illustrated Sunday supplement in 1908, but the newspaper's publishers quickly reneged on their decision after the loss of numerous readers due to their ill-timed move.

This hostile attitude is summarized in the following definitive condemnation by one infallible "expert":

"I despise the comics . . . because they have no subtlety and certainly no beauty. They oversimplify everything. For a good description they substitute a bad drawing. They reduce the wonders of language to crude monosyllables, and narration to nothing more than a printed film. I detest their lack of style and morals, their appeal to illiteracy, and their bad grammar. I execrate their tiresome harshness, their easy sensations, their imbecilic laughter."

After the Second World War, and with the renewed outbreak of juvenile delinquency, these attacks increased in intensity. Accusing the comic strip of undermining the morals of youth, psychologists, pedagogues, and demagogues of all political colors mounted an all-out assault against it, which culminated in 1954 with the appearance of Dr. Frederic Wertham's book *The Seduction of the Innocents*. Utilizing carefully selected examples, truncated drawings, and sometimes actual falsifications, Dr. Wertham, a psychiatrist by trade, attempted to demonstrate by a specious line of argument and excessive generalization that these comics, guilty of encouraging all the sins and vices of the earth (including some believed to have disappeared from the earth since the destruction of Sodom and Gomorrah) were "the source of all our problems."

Serious studies undertaken by more restrained, less irrationally inclined investigators have since then refuted these arguments and demonstrated that the comic strips exercise on children an influence hardly more dangerous than that of fairy tales or cops-and-robber stories. This mattered little, however: the cartoonists were subjected to a Draconian censorship by the alarmed syndicates. Some artists, like Burne Hogarth, definitively abandoned the comic strip, while others were content to serve up to their readers an inoffensive gruel. These measures simply heightened the crisis and further weakened the already shaky morale of the artists. Never had the American comic strip been so depressed as at the beginning of the fifties, and its detractors were already predicting its approaching demise. However, they were rejoicing too soon, and greatly misjudging its vitality and dynamism.

Following the trail already blazed by George Herriman and Al Capp, and after several false starts, in 1949 an artist named Walt Kelly, formerly of the Walt Disney studios, created "Pogo," which was to revolutionize the style and content of the American comic strip. At first sight, Pogo seems to be a series of little tales, set in the Okefenokee swamplands of Georgia, in which Walt Kelly, "makes use of animals to instruct man," *à la* La Fontaine. This definition, however, becomes increasingly inadequate as we continue reading. To begin with, we are surprised by the Balzacian proliferation of the characters, each of whom is endowed with his own highly individual per-

103

Leonard Starr, "Mary Perkins on Stage." Copyright Chicago Tribune—New York News Syndicate, Inc.

1

I'M GONNA START SOMETHIN' NEW... CAPTURIN' IDEAS.
HOW?

2

We'd like to welcome you good folks to the Okefenokee--Molester Mole, here, is anxious to meet you---

3

WHAT DIFFERMINTS IF WE GOT FOURTEEN (NOT COUNTIN' ONE INVISIBLE) NOMINEES? WE OUTNUMBERS BOTH OTHER CANDIDATES...
WE ARE A SHOE IN
IF ALL OF US IS PRESIDENT, WITH OUR BRAINS, THE COUNTRY IS SAFE.
YEH, WHO WOULD WANT IT?
I DUNNO, IT SEEMS TO ME WE'D BE KINDA MIXED UP...SOMEBODY OUGHT TO BE AT THE HELM.
RIGHT! WE NEED DIRECTION!
WITH THIS CROWD IN CHARGE, THE DIRECTION I'D TAKE WOULD BE TOWARD MEXICO.
8-5

1, 2. Walt Kelly, "Pogo." The favorite strip of the intellectuals, and the one that has justifiably occasioned the greatest number of glosses and commentaries.

3. Pogo the opossum lives and lets live, supported by the friendship of Porky, the misanthropic porcupine, and Albert, the alligator, among the ambitious, idiotic, mediocre and imbecilic malefactors who, in the forms of a bear, a dog, a turtle, or an owl, people the Okefenokee Swamp. Copyright Publishers-Hall Syndicate.

4, 5. Charles M. Schulz, "Peanuts." "Peanuts" breaks with all its precedents: no pranks, no adults. Charlie Brown, the hesitant boy; Schroeder, the virtuoso, who plays Beethoven on a child's piano; the domineering Lucy; Snoopy the dog, who would like to be any animal at all except a dog or a human, are remarkable for their original behavior, which combines adult reactions with childish attitudes. Copyright U.F.S.–U.P.I.

1

sonality. Walt Kelly is extremely eclectic in his choice of sources. Certain characters, like the unmannerly Barnstable or Seminole Sam, the double-dealing, crafty fox, are faithful to popular tradition. Others seem to have been borrowed from the comedy of manners or from the American slapstick film. But Kelly's greatest creations are his own: Doctor Howland Owl, a quack, phony scientist, phony intellectual, a stereotype of the dangerous imbecile; Beauregard, the bloodhound who has no olfactory sense; Porky the porcupine, the Alceste of the Okefenokee; The Skunk, Miss Mam'zell Hepsibah, who is the vamp of the swamp, and lastly the two costars of the troupe: Pogo and Albert (the strip, incidentally was originally called "Pogo and Albert").

Albert the Alligator is the most brilliant personality of the swamp: he is the anarchist, the troublemaker, the poet. When compared with him, Pogo, the rationalistic and humanistic little opossum who opposes the rigor of his dialectical thought to Albert's lyricism, may seem rather drab. In the strictly classical structure of Walt Kelly's universe, Pogo and Albert represent the Protagonist and the Antagonist, the two opposing but indissolubly linked poles of ancient drama.

Walt Kelly, a philosopher even more than an artist, was the first to deal with the great moral, social, and political questions of his age. This won him many enemies (including Senator Joseph McCarthy, whom he attacked violently in 1952, depicting him in the guise of a jackal), but it also won him the respect and admiration of the intellectuals, thereby contributing to the rehabilitation of the comic strip.

Kelly very soon found a kindred spirit in the person of Charles Schulz, who penetrated still deeper into intellectual analysis (oriented more particularly toward psychology and metaphysics) with his "Peanuts," created in 1950. His heroes are not animals but preschool-age children, "led" by Charlie Brown, whose faith in human nature (and in that of his little comrades) is always cruelly deceived. His chief tormentor is a scowling, cynical little girl, a real child shrew, named Lucy van Pelt. Linus, Lucy's brother, is a precocious, delicate intellectual whose nerves give way with the loss of the blanket he always carries around with him to reassure himself. Schroeder, whose greatest pleasure is to play Beethoven on his toy piano; the dirty Pig-Pen, and several others complete this childish team, to which must be added Snoopy, the hedonistic young puppy who is very pleased with living.

These children who reason and act like adults, the situations in which comedy is only a veil thrown over latent sadness, the cruelty that is hidden under laughter, endow "Peanuts" with a bitter-sweet character and a subtle ambiguity that is sometimes disconcerting. In each of his strips, Schulz is not satisfied merely to amuse us; he propounds a lesson, in the tradition of the medieval morality plays. There is in Schulz the artist a cry of despair at the human condition that is almost Kirkegaardian in accent but that is tempered by the theological fervor of Schulz, the lay preacher of the "Church of God," a religious sect in California.

The success of "Peanuts" was instantaneous and even more brilliant than that of "Pogo." By their efforts and talent, Schulz and Kelly endowed the comics with their patent of nobility, and assured the birth and development of the intellectual comic strip.

Mell Lazarus used the same point of departure as Schulz for his strip, "Miss Peach," which appeared in 1957. His heroes—Marcia, an enterprising and aggressive girl; the coquette Francine, the uncouth Arthur, the pusillanimous Ira—are all children, all pupils at the Kelly School. In contrast to "Peanuts," adults play a role in this strip; but Miss Peach, the teacher with angelic patience; Mr. Grimmis, the principal; and their colleagues exist only to serve, by their ignorance, stupidity, or narrow-mindedness, as a foil for the sophistication, superior knowledge, and irresistible *savoir-faire* of their turbulent, macrocephalic children.

1. Johnny Hart, "B.C." Another star of the sophisticated humor strip, set in the middle of a desert and containing a talking rock, several live flowers, an anteater, two dinosaurs, a stock of ants, a turtle and a bird who are inseparable companions, and a handful of cavemen who are closer to the Beatnik type than to the vigorously truculent Alley Oop. Copyright Publishers-Hall Syndicate.

2. J. Hart and Brant Parker, "The Wizard of Id." Copyright Publishers-Hall Syndicate.

1, 2. Jules Feiffer, "Feiffer." Copyright Jules Feiffer.

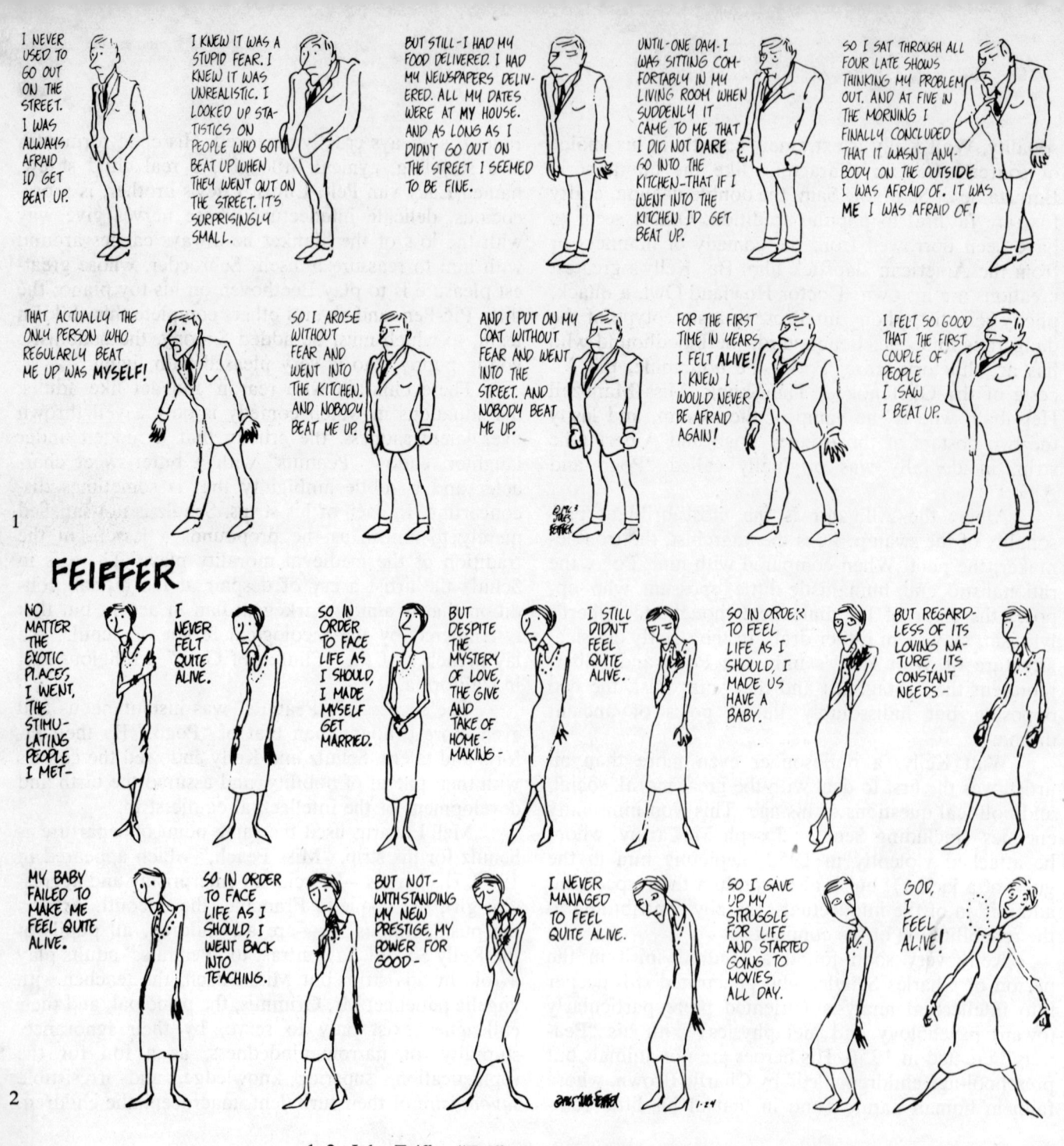

3. Mell Lazarus, "Miss Peach." Copyright Publishers-Hall Syndicate.

At the Kelly School, the children teach the teachers. And that, Mell Lazarus seems to be saying to us with a wink, is no worse.

Once they had tasted heady intellectual pleasures, nothing could stop the cartoonists. In 1958 appeared Johnny Hart's "B.C.," which presents us with an incredible assortment of prehistoric men who spend most of their time on subtle speculations about the world's progress and the future of civilization. Their discussions are often fuzzy, for aside from B.C., the apparent "hero" of this series and a model "average caveman" such as an institute of public opinion might have imagined him, the strip is peopled by such creatures as a dirty one-legged poet, a suavely charming inventor, a rhetorician of the absurd, and a clumsy sophist who gets caught in his own traps, to say nothing of an existentialist anteater and a dinosaur with humanitarian aspirations. (Despite this abundance of talents, however, the world is in no better shape.) The strip is studded with mirth-provoking adventures, burlesque antics, and ingenious devices that make it a masterpiece of light comedy as well as an irrepressible parody of our modern society.

Very similar to "B.C." is the new and equally remarkable "Wizard of Id" (1964), for which Brant Parker does the drawing and Johnny Hart the scripts. In his castle in the middle of a sketchy, desert-like landscape, rules a tiny, blasé, nasty king, the image of complacency and egocentricity, who is humiliated by his small size. He is attended by a magician of dubious achievements and a timid, crafty knight, and his subjects are cheating, arrogant louts. Everyone despises himself and everyone else, and only the disillusioned magician and the constantly intoxicated jester are occasionally human.

In 1956 the comic strip found its first antihero in the person of Bernard Mergendeiler, a pathetic wreck devoured by tics and complexes. His creator was Jules Feiffer, author of the strip entitled simply "Feiffer." Feiffer's universe is the blackest and most depressing ever depicted by the comic strip. Drifting young men, neurotic young women, lovers who are strangers to each other, introduce us to a dehumanized world in which all communication and exchange of ideas are impossible, in which nothing happens and nothing is done. Like robots, the protagonists come and pour out, in plaintive, toneless voices, the account of their disappointments, the sum of their misfortunes. The atrocious repetition and the terrible uniformity of these confessions finish by creating a vortex in which people, language, and concepts are swallowed up and annihilated. A parody of a parody, "Feiffer" can claim unchallenged the title of "anticomic strip."

In addition to their intellectual bias, these strips that we have called "intellectual" present a remarkable esthetic unity. Their creators' affinities lie not with the easy models of the novel and the cinema, but with the most exacting of all methods of artistic expression: the theatre. There are no telescoped planes, long speeches, or panoramic spaces in these strips. The characters are presented in full view, at eye level; we know only what they wish to tell us about themselves, and the only space we are permitted to see is that defined within the rectangle of the picture. The settings are simple backdrops, and their style reflects the intentions or minds of their authors. Very optimistically exuberant in "Pogo," they are refined and stylized in "Peanuts" and "B.C.," and disappear completely in "Feiffer," whose protagonists continue their interminable soliloquies in a world that is empty, in the likeness of their solitude.

These avant-garde strips were joined by others. "The Strange World of Mr. Mum," by Irving Phillips, introduces us into an impersonal and dehumanized world; Frank O'Neal indulges in a sometimes grating satire of our civilization in "Short Ribs," and in "Still Life" Jerry Robinson, using only inanimate objects, offers an acerbic commentary on contemporary customs.

Side by side with these series that deal with the most thorny problems under a mask of humor and fantasy, this period witnessed the birth of a flood of strips that under their realistic exteriors reflect a deliberately restricted and conventional view of the world. "Mary Worth" is an example of this type.

Born in 1932 as "Apple Mary," this strip experienced strange vicissitudes. In the beginning, under the pen of Martha Orr, its creator, it had a popular quality that harmonized well with the climate of the Great Depression. In 1940 Martha Orr abandoned the strip, which was revived under the new title of "Mary Worth's Family" by Allen Saunders (scriptwriter) and Dale Connor (the artist), under the combined pseudonym of "Dale Allen." The series received its definitive title and character in 1947, with the departure of Dale Connor and his replacement by Ken Ernst, who contributed to "Mary Worth" its undeniable graphic qualities. Under this brilliant new garment, however, the rags and threadbare fabric of the good old melodrama are easily recognizable. This is not the fault either of Allen Saunders, whose scripts and dialogues are often excellent and imaginative, or of Ken Ernst, one of the best representatives of the modern school of illustration, but results from the inevitable limitations of this type of story.

This formula enjoyed great success, and encour-

1. Stan Drake, "The Heart of Juliet Jones." Copyright King Features Syndicate, Inc.

2. Alex Kotzky, "Apartment 3-G." Copyright Publishers-Hall Syndicate.

3. Bradley and Edgington, "Rex Morgan, M.D." Copyright Publishers-Hall Syndicate.

aged the Publishers Newspaper Syndicate (a subsidiary of Marshall Field Enterprises, created in the forties), its distributor, to specialize in this "soap opera" type of strip. The chief practitioner of soap operas is incontestably Dr. Nicholas Dallis, a former psychiatrist turned scriptwriter.

"Rex Morgan, M.D.," which relates the tear-jerking adventures of a young doctor, was his first work (1948); it was followed in 1952 by "Judge Parker," an account of the cases of conscience that may confront a scrupulous judge, and in 1962 by "Apartment 3-G," which depicts the sentimental adventures of three young women who share an apartment.

While the draftsmanship of Marvin Bradley, Frank Edgington (the artist of "Rex Morgan"), and Dan Heilman (the illustrator of "Judge Parker"), who was recently replaced by A. Ledoux, is competent but rather commonplace (moreover the styles of these artists strongly resemble one another), special praise should be given to the artist of "Apartment 3-G," Alex Kotzky, whose brilliant, sophisticated style reflects a very appealing exuberance, freshness, and *joie de vivre*.

A noteworthy contribution to the sentimental genre was made by Stan Drake in 1953, with his creation (for King Features Syndicate) of "The Heart of Juliet Jones." The romantic adventures of the heroine Juliet, a sometimes deceitful old maid, and her younger sister Eve (a very appropriate name) are guaranteed to move even the hardest hearts. Drake's style is sure, penetrating, and appealing, and his scripts are no more absurd than any other of the same ink.

It would be an injustice to include "On Stage," the strip created by Leonard Starr in 1957, among the soap operas; while its situations are similar, it differs from them in style and spirit. Mary Perkins, the heroine of the series, is an actress, and this gives Starr an opportunity to depict theatre surroundings, which he does with a very sure pen. The atmosphere, settings, and characters are faithfully depicted, but their realism does not exclude either poetry or romanticism. Starr's line is vibrant, incisive, and authoritative, and his style, which successfully combines Milton Caniff's expressionist vigor with the classic elegance of Alex Raymond, is easily recognizable. Starr excels in depicting even the most fleeting emotions, revealing gestures, and furtive expressions, as well as vast urban panoramas of peaceful mountain landscapes. The imagination and originality of the scripts, the accuracy of the

After an early trial-and-error period, "Steve Canyon" acquired its definitive form with the outbreak of the Korean war. Having reenlisted for this occasion, Steve becomes a lieutenant-colonel in the air force reconnaissance service, which carries him to every place where the Cold War is raging: Turkey, Greece, Formosa, Vietnam. These adventures are separated by more peaceful interludes, the heroine of which is Steve's ward, Poteet Canyon. Caniff's style has evolved toward a more nervous and more impressionistic draftsmanship.

Buz Sawyer, now parted from his buddy Roscoe Sweeney (who reigns supreme over the Sunday strip), is continuing his career in the navy air force and in the C.I.A. Realizing the interruption caused by the introduction of family scenes, Crane has caused Buz's wife to disappear, and has returned to the true adventure strip. He has maintained his high standard of excellence in the use of blacks and doubletone paper.

Frank Robbins has remained faithful to the freewheeling adventure. "Johnny Hazard" is graying at the temples, but he is still a dashing bachelor. Remaining on the outskirts of international events, he has more liberty of action, and even makes forays into science-fiction—a James Bond before James Bond. In accordance with the time-honored (and excellent) tradition, his adventures are uninterrupted. Robbins's draftsmanship has become more elegant, while remaining perhaps the most vigorous to be found. His very spirited narrative technique is also among the best in the comic strip.

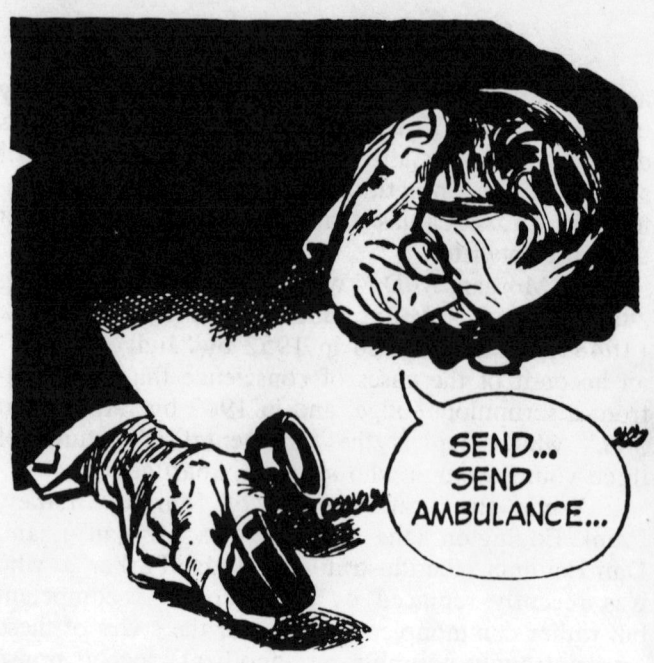

1. John Prentice, "Rip Kirby." Copyright King Features Syndicate, Inc.

2. Leonard Starr, "Mary Perkins on Stage." Copyright Chicago Tribune—New York News Syndicate, Inc.

dialogues, and the authenticity of the situations make "On Stage" one of the best of the contemporary comic strips.

During the forties and fifties, the traditional humor and adventure strips were seriously affected by the death or retirement of many cartoonists; the adventure strip in particular suffered heavily from these losses. Burne Hogarth (who had gone into other activities), and Clarence Gray and Frank Godwin (having abandoned "Connie," the latter had just created "Rusty Riley"), both of whom had succumbed to illnesses, were succeeded by inferior scribblers who caused "Tarzan" and "Brick Bradford" to founder in mediocrity. Only "Rip Kirby" escaped the general leveling. Upon the accidental death of the latter's creator in 1956, the strip was taken over by John Prentice, who proved a worthy successor to Alex Raymond. Prentice's style has a clarity, vigor, and precision that are especially suitable for this series, as are his restrained compositions of alternating masses, elaborate chiaroscuros, and daring visual effects.

No good adventure series was created during this period, with the possible exception of "Steve Roper," drawn by William Overgard for a script by Allen Saunders. In this case, however, we cannot speak of an original creation. Begun in 1937 under the title of "The Great Gusto," and later called "Chief Wahoo," the strip acquired its present title and appearance only at the beginning of the fifties. We should also note the comeback of "Secret Agent X-9," excellently drawn since January, 1967, by the talented Al Williamson under the title "Secret Agent Corrigan."

The ranks of the humor strip were also decimated. Harold Knerr, who died in 1949, had left "The Katzenjammer Kids" in the hands of Doc Winner, whence it passed to Joe Musial, who turned it into a paltry anthology of insipidities. After the death of George McManus, "Bringing Up Father" had a slightly better fate in the hands of Hank Fletcher and Vernon Greene (the latter has recently died), who succeeded in giving a competent version of the strip without, however, completely restoring its finesse, spirit, and flavor.

But other strips came to continue the tradition. Mort Walker's "Beetle Bailey" appeared in 1950 and immediately won over the public. Bettle, a shirker and tatterdemalion, his buddy Killer; Sarge, the ferocious sergeant; and the officers, each more incompetent and ludicrous than the next, are the ringleaders in this lighthearted satire of military life, drawn with a spirit, liveliness, and verve that not even Courteline would have repudiated.

With "Dennis the Menace" (1951), Hank Ketcham proved that the kid strip was not yet dead. Although his hero, a tousle-headed, enterprising little boy, does not attain to the stature of the Katzenjammers, he is nevertheless a lively creature whose counterfeit innocence, frankness, and joyous vandalism are a delightful contrast to the docile conformity of the adults, his inept and helpless victims.

Still other humorous strips were born at this time, signaling a vigorous renaissance of the genre. "Mr. Abernathy" (Frank Ridgeway and Ralston Jones), "Rick O'Shay" (a Western by Stan Lynde), and "Hapless Harry" (George Gately) offer a wide choice ranging from the crudely comic to sophisticated humor.

The American comic strip is now seventy years of age. During these seventy years we have watched it unfold its succession of images and mirages, weave its tapestry of revelations and illusions. Generations of

---

The old humor classics are continuing brilliant careers. Chic Young's "Blondie" is still the model comic strip all over the world (in 1,600 newspapers!). The drollery and humanity of this couple, whose children are now teenagers, cannot help making them favorites everywhere. The Sunday strips are often full of a lunatic, hectic humor (a neighborhood riot, invasion by the police and firemen) worthy of Mack Sennett's films.

"Moon Mullins," continued by Ferd Johnson, is less nasty but as enjoyable as ever, and remains one of the best series.

Highest honors must go to Rudolph Dirks, who has been active since the days of Hearst and Pulitzer; he has found his best collaborator in his son John. For the past ten years "The Captain and the Kids" has enjoyed renewed youth. By giving the twins a permanent adversary, the odious Rollo, Knerr has permanently confined them within the comic genre, awe-inspiring in his hands but mediocre in those of his successors. With Dirks, Hans and Fritz are less terrible, more freewheeling. They make lengthy incursions into humorous science-fantasy, in which the Isle of the Lost World, the parallel universe of flat people, the Venus rocket, and the soluble diamond are classics. After seventy years of existence, Dirk's characters are once again in the front ranks. It is unfortunate that they do not enjoy the circulation they deserve.

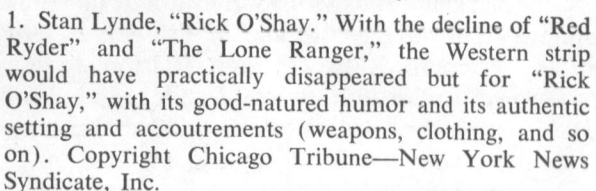

1. Stan Lynde, "Rick O'Shay." With the decline of "Red Ryder" and "The Lone Ranger," the Western strip would have practically disappeared but for "Rick O'Shay," with its good-natured humor and its authentic setting and accoutrements (weapons, clothing, and so on). Copyright Chicago Tribune—New York News Syndicate, Inc.

2. Hank Ketcham, "Dennis the Menace." The comic kids of the earlier tradition—the Katzenjammers, Perry Winkle, Buster Brown—exploited the adult world for their own profit. Dennis, who is even younger, is unaware of it. He is the quintessence of the exasperating child. Copyright Publishers-Hall Syndicate.

3. Mort Walker, "Beetle Bailey." This series would have been inconceivable before the war, when military service was unknown in the United States. Hopefully, Beetle and his buddies—Killer the seducer, Plato the intellectual, and Cosmo the profiteer, under Sarge's bawling, good-natured authority—have a long life still ahead of them. Copyright King Features Syndicate, Inc.

artists have succeeded each other, each bringing to the comic strip its own style, vision, and preconceptions. The various types of strips have been regenerated in cycles and temporary vogues; their fortunes have experienced the strangest fluctuations. Only yesterday the comics were being denigrated and attacked on all sides; today they are arousing an extraordinary passion and interest. Psychologists are analyzing them, sociologists are dissecting them, painters are trying to capture their spirit and indispensability ("Pop Art," for example, attempts to treat the comic strip as a constituent element of the contemporary landscape.) A criticism that was for a long time narrow-minded is gradually awakening to the realization that the American comic strip is not an incoherent series of pictures, but the most authentic form of the dreams, hopes, splendors, and miseries of our century.

During its American renaissance, the comic strip has been developing brilliantly in the rest of the world. In every country a national product is appearing: "Max" (known in France as "Max l'Explorateur"), by the Belgian Bara, Lars Jansson's "Mumintrollet" in Sweden, "Far til Fyra," by Enghelm and Hast, and small family-type humor strips. Germany is lagging, with several series that are interesting but have old-fashioned draftsmanship, such as Roland Kohlsaat's "Jimmy das Gummipferd" (Jimmy the Rubber Horse). In contrast, the expansion of the English adult comic strip is astonishing. Next to the traditional series (children's stories like D. Collins's "The Perishers," young couples like Jack Dunkley's "The Larks" or "The Gambols," by Dobs and Barry Appleby; office-typist series like Leslie Caswell's "Better or Worse," cockney stories like Smythe's "Andy Capp") there exists an ensemble of impressive graphic quality, usually obtained by the cross-hatch style, which disappeared in the United States with Godwin's death. There are Westerns ("Wes Slade," by G. Stokes, and H. Bishop's "Gun Law"), adventure and espionage strips (Peter O'Donnel's "Modesty Blaise"), detective and romantic adventure (D. Wright's "Carol Day"), exotic adventure (Frank Bellamy's "Frazer"), and science-fiction (Keith Watson's "Dan Dare" and Sydney Jordan's "Jeff Hawke"), which have replaced American series no longer in existence. And while "Jane" is dead, the English have retained and enriched its tradition with Maz's "Jane, Daughter of Jane," done in a much more "pinup" style, and Jim Holdaway's "Romeo Brown."

The Latin countries are now heard from and are producing artists whose graphic style is perhaps the most beautiful on the contemporary scene. Several American syndicates have been able to secure the cooperation of South American artists, especially Argentinians. The best known is José-Luis Salinas, the author (for King Features Syndicate) of a remarkable Western called "Cisco Kid," which is characterized by suppleness of line and a brilliant hatching technique. Less well known, but nevertheless an extraordinary artist (even surpassing Salinas, whose characters are sometimes rather overfinished), is Arturo del Castillo. He too is the author of a Western "Randall," the hero of which is a tall, relaxed fellow. Its style carries the technique of the Western almost to perfection. Landscapes, horses, and characters rise out of hatchings and dark blacks that give to the pictures an astonishingly rich texture. The backgrounds are sometimes handled in an abstract manner, with blobs of ink or perpendicular hatchings crossed by oblique lines, as in Villon's work. Del Castillo's narrative technique is worthy of his graphic genius. His lyrical desert rides, fights, night rounds in city streets, are classics, without ever giving an impression, however, of a sophistication sought after at the expense of other qualities.

Another remarkable artist is the Portuguese, Etchevery-Quello (he signs his strips "ETC"), who works in Italy for the French newspaper *Vaillant*. He has done numerous series for this paper, the most beautiful of which was "Les Aventures de Ragnar le Viking" (1956–1966). Thanks to a different and equally competent style, he need not fear to be compared with Harold Foster's "Prince Valiant."

In Italy, the frenzied Jacovitti exhausted his extravagant style with the adventures of "Cocco Bill," but talented artists are also appearing: Hugo Pratt (now living in Argentina), who draws, among other strips, "L'Ombra" (The Shadow), about a masked but very attractive judge; M. Uggeri ("Avventure di Capitan Coviello"), and especially Dino Battaglia and Guido Crepax. Battaglia, the author of numerous series ("Ivanoe," "La Pista dei Quattro" [The Path of the Four], a Western, and so on.), in which he demonstrates a strong feeling for action and space, is particularly brilliant in science-fiction ("I Cinque Della Selena" —The Five of the Selena), in which his disquieting draftsmanship, skillfully imprecise and shot through with mists, excels in suggesting other worlds and existences beyond our dimensions. In the magazine *Linus*, Crepax draws "Neutron," in a very precise, purely black-and-white style very different from the cursive and impressionistic style common to Battaglia, Uggeri, and Pratt. He has deliberately (and very successfully) made it a sophisticated and extremely bizarre strip in which he performs painstaking experiments in narrative technique, notably by sometimes fragmenting the action to an extreme degree.

116

1. Sydney Jordan, "Jeff Hawke." Copyright London Express Features.

2. Ernest Ratcliff, "Lindy." Copyright Evening News.

3. Maz, "Jane, Daughter of Jane." Copyright Daily Mirror.

4. David Wright, "Carol Day." Copyright Daily Mail.

5. Peter O'Donnel and Jim Holdaway, "Modesty Blaise." Copyright Evening Standard.

OH, LORD, I HOPE THAT'S GOT RID OF HIM FOR THE NIGHT—
4

YOU'VE GOT THOSE KNIVES ON YOU! AND SHE'S GOT A GUN!
MARJ... YOU'RE GETTING UNDER OUR FEET
5

Crepax, "Neutron." Copyright Crepax/Figure.

It must be admitted that the Franco-Belgian comic strip, still too highly specialized in children's and young adults' strips (in which field, moreover, it is the leader), possesses no artist of the stature of Del Castillo, Jordan, Wright, Starr, and Crepax—unless it is simply that the routinism of the publishers and the public, and the low pay, prevent them from appearing. This idea would seem to be supported by the example of Paul Gillon, whose strip "13, rue de l'Espoir" (13 Hope Street) is adult and of good quality but makes no innovations in relation to the American strips, which created this type. On the other hand, Gillon is remarkable in "Les Naufragés du Temps" (The Shipwrecked Men of Time, which appeared in the short-lived newspaper *Chou-Chou*), as is Gigi in "Scarlet Dream." The French newspapers *Coq Hardi* and *Vaillant* sometimes published remarkable stories, but their drawing was, unfortunately, inferior to the scripts. However, Marijac's "Jim Boum" and "Les Trois Mousquetaires du Maquis" (The Three Musketeers of the Maquis), "Nasdine Hodja" (drawn originally by Bastard, then by Le Guen), and Gillon's "Capitaine Cormoran" and "Fils de Chine" (Son of China) are worthy of mention.

It was in *Vaillant* and *Caméra* that Jean-Claude Forest made his debut. The furor created by his "Barbarella" should not be permitted to obscure its weaknesses. Forest is a wonderful cover illustrator, but he has not adapted to the comic strip. Interest is too exclusively concentrated on large poetic or sensual pictures framed by a filler of small, too often neglected, pictures. The linear style is suitable neither for black and white nor for color; despite the elegance of line, the picture is white and hollow, and does not allow even the slightest enlargement. The plates lack a coherent organization, whether from a plastic or narrative point of view. Its quality resides in several large pictures, which fact reveals the temperament of a first-class illustrator who has strayed into the comic strip. His latest efforts to tighten up his style indicate that Forest is aware of this.

We should also keep in mind the persistence of the traditional historico-romantic picture-stories of famous love affairs and crimes, brought up to date by the addition of a few nude scenes, which decorate (?) the pages of various daily newspapers in the form of a vertical grisaille. These serialized illustrated novels, which do not belong to the comic strip, aroused some zestful kidding from John Crosby, a columnist for the former New York *Herald Tribune*:

"The French comics are passionately French. There is one called 'Famous Love Affairs.' In its latest episode, Richelieu, at the Court of Louis XIII, had an affair with the wife of a banker. He said, 'I appeared, I pleased, I was loved, and I loved, seduced by charms which I have never found in any other woman.' If only Dick Tracy talked like that! And you'll notice that this isn't small-fry stuff, like Dagwood...."

The Franco-Belgian production for young adults is of excellent quality. It could be reproached at most

Captions (opposite):

1. Profiting by the incident, Neutron quickly dashes down the path . . .

3. . . . which is suddenly barred by two creatures who resemble his previous assailants.

4. Surprised by the lack of hostility in the behavior of these strange men, he agrees to follow them . . .

5. . . . and begins another very long descent. . . .

Among the contemporary strips, mention should be made of Jay Irving's "Pottsy." Pottsy is a tubby policeman, full of imagination and mischievousness and sometimes even poetry—obviously a rather unconventional type. "Hi and Lois" (script by Mort Walker, drawing by Dik Browne) is about a couple, their children and their baby. The latter is the star of the strip; although he does not speak, this does not prevent him from thinking, and his thoughts are depicted in bubble balloons. "Dondi," a children's story drawn from their eye level, was created by Gus Edson and Irwin Hasen, while Harry Haenigsen's "Penny" and Lee Holley's "Ponytail" depict the difficult but charming teenager. John Cullen Murphy launched "Big Ben Bolt," a college-educated boxer who, however, has long since retired from the ring; the strip is now a detective-type strip. "Connie," the reporter-aviatrix-astronaut of the thirties, has disappeared, to be replaced by Dale Messick's sticky "Brenda Starr," also a journalist but of a soap-opera type —the strip could almost be called "Glycerine Alley." "Hagen, Fagin and O'Toole," by Brinkerhoff and Bowen, the story of a charming trio formed by a Great Dane, a Siamese cat, and a parrot, was unfortunately short-lived.

Arturo del Castillo, "Randall."

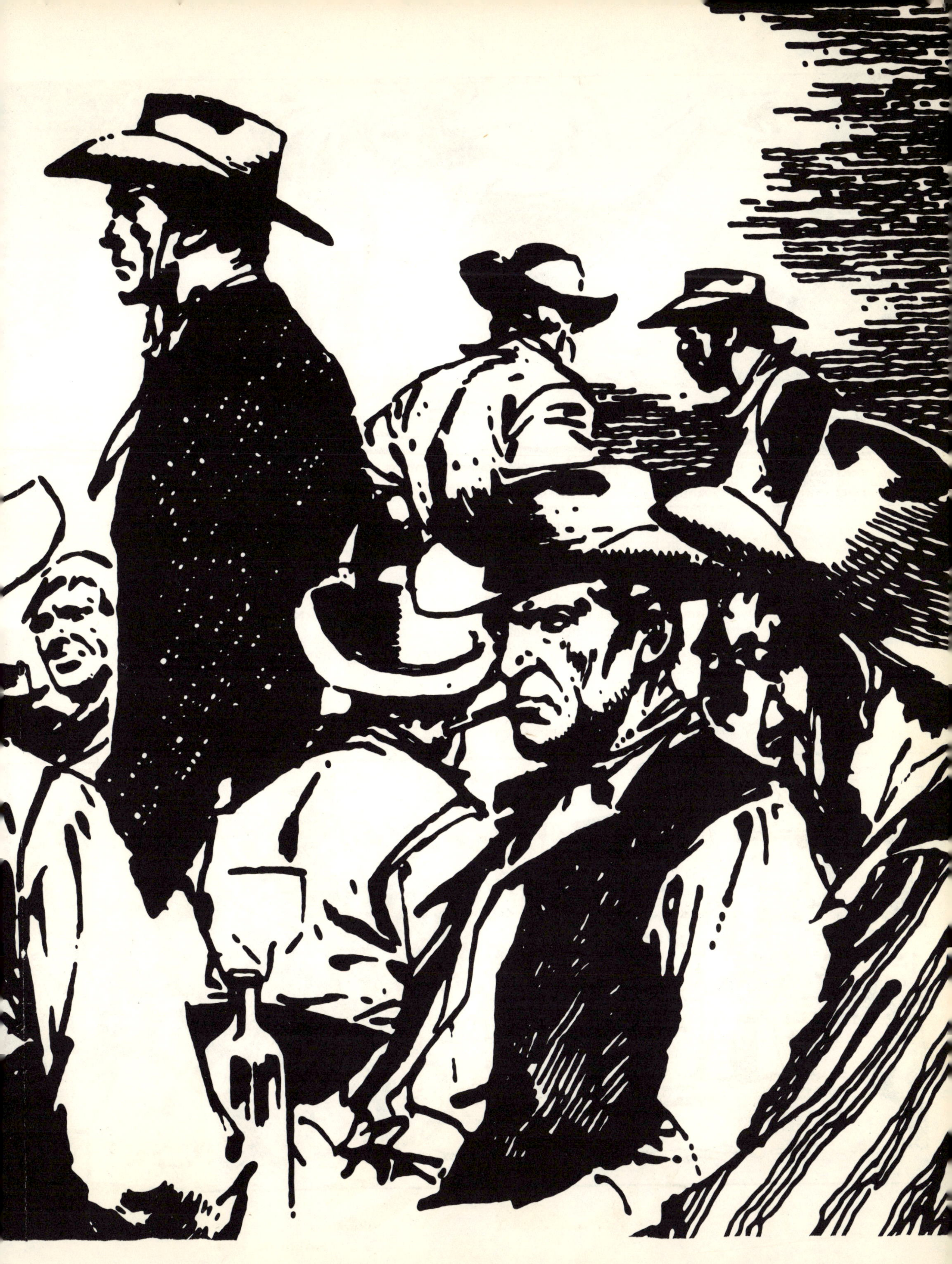

TANDIS QUE LES VIKINGS FERMENT LEURS YEUX AVEUGLÉS, UNE VOIX PROFONDE S'ÉLÈVE DES EAUX, UNE VOIX QUI FAIT RÉSONNER LE CIEL ET L'OCÉAN ET SEMBLE CONTENIR TOUS LES CRIS ANGOISSANTS DE LA TEMPÊTE :
— OUVREZ LES YEUX, HOMMES TÉMÉRAIRES, ET REGARDEZ LE FILS DE FORNJOT, LE FRÈRE DU VENT ET DU FEU ! JE SUIS AEGIR, LE DIEU DES MERS. TREMBLEZ, VOUS QUI M'AVEZ OFFENSÉ EN ME JETANT AUX PIEDS LES ARMES QUE LES ELFES NOIRS ONT TOUCHÉES. RIEN DE CE QUI APPARTIENT A LA TERRE NE DOIT SOUILLER MON ROYAUME !

1. While the Vikings close their blinded eyes, a deep voice surges from the waters, a voice that makes the sky and the ocean resound and that seems to contain all the anguished cries of the storm:

"Open your eyes, rash men, and look at the son of Fornjot, brother of the wind and the fire! I am Aegir, the God of the Oceans. Tremble, O ye who have offended me by throwing at my feet the weapons touched by the black elves. Nothing belonging to the earth should be permitted to befoul my kingdom."

E.T.C., "La Harpe d'Or." Copyright Vaillant.

2. José Luis Salinas, "Cisco Kid." Copyright King Features Syndicate, Inc.

with a certain hardness of line, a tendency to introduce caricatural characters into realistic series (which undermines their authenticity), and the rapid debasement of certain styles, resulting from the fact that the badly paid artists are obliged to take on more strips than they can properly handle.

Morris, the father of the cheerful "Lucky Luke," entrusted the script to René Goscinny, after having originally done it himself. His style has clearly improved; although somewhat clumsy at the beginning, even then it demonstrated constant experimentation with effects of framing and perspective; his style has become stronger, and has acquired great assurance. In addition to his layouts, which are inspired by film techniques, Morris draws his themes from the movies and the history of the Far West, depicting Judge Roy Bean, Billy the Kid, or Calamity Jane. Like many other artists, he has enriched his original cast by adding to it Ran Tan Plan, the most stupid dog in the world (a parody on the Rin-Tin-Tin of third-grade American Westerns), and by giving Lucky as opponents the four Dalton brothers, bandits of diminishing size but of equally evil intentions.

Franquin turned "Spirou" into a rival of "Tintin." Like the latter a serious teen-ager, Spirou is contrasted with his friend Fantasio, whose name alone suffices to define his character. They were at first accompanied by a squirrel, Spip; his role gradually declined, and he was supplanted by the Marsupilami, a mythical yellow-spotted animal with an interminably long tail—a worthy successor to "Popeye's" Jeep, and one of the successes of the contemporary comic strip. This little world was enlarged by the addition of the Count of Champignac, a lovable, extravagant, but authentic scientific genius, a breeder of dinosaurs, and a savage enemy of evil men who wish to enslave the world. The group was gradually joined (and then abandoned) by the eternally weary figure of Gaston Lagaffe, a gentle lunatic and incorrigible jack-of-all-trades who carries his personal (and not always stupid) logic into a world the conformity of which sickens him.

Jijé (Joseph Gillain), Franquin's predecessor on "Spirou," is particularly known for "Jean Valhardi" (a likable adventurer who is half secret agent, half knight-errant) and "Jerry Spring." The latter is the protagonist of a good Western, in which he is accompanied by a round, jovial Mexican named Pancho, a Sancho Panza minus that character's ridiculousness and cowardice. Most of the artists on the magazine *Spirou* have been influenced by Jijé.

Since 1964 Jijé's rival Gir (Giraud) has been producing an excellent serious Western, "Fort Navajo," certainly the best of its kind since Fred Harman's "Red Ryder." In this strip there is no attempt at embellishment; the characters are presented with their good qualities and their faults: the hero, Lieutenant Blueberry, with his Belmondo face, and his fondness for fighting but also for poker and whisky; his old friend Jimmy MacClure, a confirmed drunkard with a clown's face, but a courageous man and a faithful friend.

Tilleux has revived the Anglo-Saxon private-detective tradition by creating the character of a young lawyer, Gil Jourdan, who carries out difficult investigations, accompanied by the extraordinary Libellule, a reformed burglar whom he has made his assistant, and the grotesque, solemn, but efficient Inspector Crouton. A sense of humor, good layout, and excellent night effects endow this strip with a certain appeal.

Since 1959 Albert Uderzo (drawing) and René Goscinny (scriptwriter) have been giving a novel twist to the French tradition of the historical comic strip: Vercingetorix has become "Asterix." Based on the theme of the little man and the big man, which he had already utilized, Uderzo has constructed this Gallic story, which does not aspire to the heights of graphic art but is worth reading for its rudimentary but comical folklore, its very individualized characters, its collection of gags (from balloons written in hieroglyphics to anachronisms, as spontaneous as they are humorous), and its ingenious turns of dialogue. Uderzo, who was already the creator of the Redskin Oompah-Pah, is also the author of the only good contemporary air-adventure strip, "Michel Tanguy," a carefully researched, minutely realistic strip not lacking in humor. Its overworked author has recently surrendered "Michel Tanguy" to Jijé.

The most authentic success, however, is to be found in the legendary and poetic domaine ruled by Peyo and Raymond Macherot. Raymond Macherot enchants us with his evocation of the country inhabited

---

In the course of the past few years, the comic strip has inspired a certain school of painting, being one of the sources of Pop Art (so called because it is neither popular nor artistic). The Pop artists copy the most mediocre pictures of the comics.

Recently Pop Art in turn inspired a comic book, G. Pellaert's *Jodelle*—a rather amusing *divertissement* but one without a future, because it is stamped with the "mechanical" character inherited from Pop Art (which itself has already died out in its birthplace).

1. "I think we'll be seeing each other again soon, Black Jake...."

Joseph Gillain, "Jerry Spring." Copyright Editions Dupuis.

2. Gillon, "Les Naufragés du Temps" (The Shipwrecked People of Time). Copyright Editions Dargaud.

3. "O.K.! I believe you.... But in that case some pretty funny things are going on here, Jimmy! And that worries me!"

J. Giraud (Gir), "Le Cheval de Fer" (The Iron Horse). Copyright Editions Dargaud.

4. "Don't ask questions! Quick, take this.... Be careful; it's not an hourglass. Wait until you're alone to turn it over."

J. C. Forest, "Bébé Cyanure" (Baby Cyanide). Copyright Editions Dargaud.

1. "Particule and her kidnapper are behind that fence!"

    Macherot, "Chlorophylle." Copyright Editions Dargaud.

2. That morning, in the village of the Schtroumpfs: "Hey there, you two! Go schtroumpf me some nuts!"

    "Yes, Chief Schtroumpf!"

    Peyo, "Les Schtroumpfs." Copyright Editions Dupuis.

3. "They're better built than the Romans, don't you think, Asterix?"
    "Yes, less organized, but tougher. Besides, they're not afraid."

    R. Goscinny and A. Uderzo, "Asterix et les Normands." Copyright Editions Dargaud.

by the Dormouse Chlorophylle, his friend Minimum, the otter Torpille (torpedo), and their enemy, the black rat Anthracite. Originally animals living in a world of human beings, these characters were soon allotted a special world from which human beings have disappeared but have left behind their attributes, ranging from clothes to armies, and including cities and automobiles. The draftsmanship changed at the same time; the characters became as far removed from animals as Mickey is from a real mouse. Macherot is the poet of the countryside, of Mediterranean coastlines, of the streets and peaceful suburbs of small cities. The landscapes are at ground level; the ponds have archipelagoes, and, in the eyes of the tiny animals, the city rises like a chain of mountains on the horizon of wastelands.

Having located the character of Johan in a distant medieval age, Peyo gave him a companion in Pirlouit, a kind of medieval and extremely comical Bibi Fricotin: whimsical, harum-scarum, bad-tempered, and droll. In the course of their mythical adventures—Moon Rock, the Fountain of the Gods, the War of the Seven Fountains—they discovered the now famous little people, the Schtroumpfs, who later became the heroes of an independent series. The Schtroumpfs, blue goblins with white bonnets, are the appealing descendants of all the gnomes of European folklore. In the center of an imaginary country between the mountains and the river Schtroumpf are squeezed the mushroom-shaped houses of their village. Here they lead a usually carefree life, quickly forgetting the mishaps that Peyo invents for them. All identical in appearance, the Schtroumpfs have their individual personalities: there is the comedian, the gourmand, the lazy man, the importuner, the misanthrope, and so on. Some of their adventures are morality plays, as for example the episode in which one of them discovers demagoguery and succeeds in getting himself elected "Schtroumpfissime" in the absence of the village patriarch. Shortly thereafter he institutes a police force, forced labor, and, unwittingly, civil war. Fortunately, the patriarch returns just in time. The ground-level landscapes, gigantic flowers, and expeditions in autumn woods among the mushrooms and huge dead leaves endow this strip with a genuine poetry. There is nothing comparable in the United States, and in Peyo, Franquin, and Macherot the French-language comic strip possesses three of its most original creative talents.

Edgar Pierre Jacobs continues the story of the adventures of Professor Mortimer, whose most interesting episodes are "Le Mystère de la Grande Pyramide" and "Marque Jaune" (The Yellow Mark). With Jacobs archaeology enters the comic strip—an archaeology that is perhaps sensationalized but may arouse interest in teen-agers.

While continuing the adventures of Alix, Jacques Martin has created the character of Lefranc, the reporter who is constantly matching wits with the gentleman gangster Alex Borg. This series is closely akin to that of Jacobs in its well-developed fondness for detail, but its style is completely different.

We should mention in passing that these strips, specially conceived for color, lose most of their evocative power when printed in black and white.

Meanwhile, a self-confident "Tintin" has been pursuing its career on a steady level of solid craftsmanship. A trip to the moon, a book of exegesis, and a film adaptation mark the high points of its career. That it has been less talked of in recent years is due solely to a certain moderation in self-promotion, for which we may be grateful to Hergé.

Parents have reproached Hergé for creating in "Les Bijoux de la Castafiore" (The Jewels of the Castafiore) a story directed toward adults. The author's satirical verve has never before been so well utilized as in this series (which, moreover, is excellent from all points of view), but the psychology of the characters outweighs the plot. Hergé has corrected this flaw in the new Tintin story, "Vol. 714 pour Sydney" (Flight 714 for Sydney), and has returned to the adventure, a subject his young readers will surely find more interesting.

Some people may find it cause for regret that Hergé has not concentrated on being a storyteller for adults, in the manner of the American masters. His chief talent, however, is that he has been able to create an *œuvre* in which every age group can delight.

WHAT'S THE
DEA, CANIFF?
YOU CAN'T
BREAK UP
CONTINUITY
THIS WAY!
OH YES
I CAN, BOYS!
THIS IS REALLY
SPECIAL...

Milton Caniff, by himself.

7

production and distribution

As we have seen, the production of the comic strips was radically changed by the organization of the syndicates. In the infancy of the American comic strip (as is still the case in France), the artist was the employee of a newspaper, or of a publisher who owned a chain of newspapers, and his strip appeared only in this newspaper; he worked in the newspaper offices, occasionally doing a sports or political drawing. All this has been changed by the syndicates—companies that employ journalists, critics, and columnists and that sell to newspapers editorials, sports articles, recipes, woman's columns, cartoons, and comic strips. The artist is the employee of the syndicate, which owns the title, subject, and characters of the strip.

The statutes governing the comic strip are badly defined. The precedent was established by the Hearst-Dirks case of 1912, which confirmed the rights of the employer but recognized the artist's right to draw his characters under another title. The Hearst-Fisher case of 1913, on the contrary, forbade Hearst to have "Mutt and Jeff" drawn by another cartoonist. Since then nothing has happened to clarify this extremely complicated situation.

Matters have become much more complicated since the passage of the new French law regarding the rights of authors. The artist is bound to the syndicate by a contract, of limited duration and containing various clauses, which guarantees him a fixed salary and a percentage on sales and adaptations for cinema, advertising, and so forth. On the other hand, the syndicate retains the rights to his production, and disposes of it at will. It seems that this type of contract is illegal in France, and repercussions in these matters are international. Meanwhile, the syndicate may withdraw a strip from its creator, as it can name a successor upon his death. (We have seen the succession of artists for "Flash Gordon," "Tarzan," and "The Katzenjammer Kids.") On the other hand, the European publisher who has renamed an American strip that he is publishing is the owner of the new title; he can stop buying the American strips and commission imitations under the same title known to his readers. The French publisher of "Bicot" (the French name for "Winnie Winkle") did just this, and under the title of "Pim, Pam, Poum"—the customary French name for "The Katzenjammer Kids"—several artists are doing imitations of this strip.)

A comic strip may be born in two ways. In the first method, the syndicate decides that it needs a strip of a certain type for its collection. Many series have been created to profit by a fashion launched by a competitor; thus "Dan Dunn" was a double for "Dick Tracy," "Little Annie Rooney" for "Little Orphan Annie," "Flash Gordon" for "Buck Rogers," and so on. In general, the artist who accepts this work imparts to the strip a personal character that quickly obliterates all traces of imitation. The melodramatic atmosphere of "Little Annie Rooney" has nothing in common with the detective-type atmosphere, full of political undertones, of "Little Orphan Annie," although both cases involve an orphan accompanied by a faithful dog.

To create completely original series, some syndicates make surveys to determine what the public ex-

Studio 43: Robert Gigi, Lucien Nortier, R. Poïvet, Christian Gaty. (Photo Serge Sineux.) Lucien Nortier at his worktable.

pects. The best method, however, is to welcome the artist who goes from one syndicate to another with his drawing under his arm, trying to place the series he has conceived. "No survey will ask for a really original strip, a 'Pogo' or a 'Peanuts.'" Sometimes the artist encounters a shortsighted commercial viewpoint: the syndicate may be in search of a proven formula. Al Capp has told of his rebuffs with "Li'l Abner." A comics editor told him: "No one's interested in a country bumpkin. A Jersey family would be better. And then the old mother has to be sweet, not funny. And, for heaven's sake, take that pipe out of her mouth. The young gal's okay, but she doesn't work. She could work in an office in New York, and your Abner in another one. . . ." In short, he should have repeated the time-worn formula of "Tillie the Toiler."

There are special cases: the initial approach may be made by a kind of middleman. Thus "Red Ryder," "King of the Royal Mounted," and "Ozark Ike," the products of a studio of artists, were sold by Stephen Slesinger, the studio's business agent. Some well-known artists offer a strip to a syndicate for distribution only, while they themselves retain ownership of it.

Comic-strip production represents a curious evolution from a modern type of industry, in which the employees work together in a shop under the boss's eye (that is, on the newspaper premises), to a medieval craft guild, in which each person works at home, preferably at the opposite end of the country, the company's role being limited to receiving and selling the products. The comic-book industry, on the other hand, operates on the principle of the assembly line and narrow specialization, with the results that we have seen.

The stages in the production of a comic strip are very clearly defined. First, the complete development of the episode, in narrative or novel form, must be finished. As in the movie, this narrative is divided so that it can be adapted for a sequence of pictures; it becomes a script with dialogues and directions for scenes and settings. For the sake of coherence, the artist may be required to make a map of the areas in which his characters are performing, and some artists do not hestiate to draw up a detailed plan of an imaginary city. In the words of Al Capp:

"To write the continuity of a script is one of the most complicated methods of developing a story. For the author must relate his main script in a series of short episodes—the daily strips—and each one of these short episodes must contain all the elements of a complete story introduction, climax, conclusion—plus the suspense. Everything I know about comic strip narration I learned not only through my own efforts but from the study of two great masters: Chester Gould and Harold Gray."

Once the script has been worked out—either by the artist or by a scriptwriter—the drawing begins. In the case of the Sunday pages this may be done three months before publication. Since the script may have been conceived three months before this, we can understand the problem faced by the authors of comic strips centered upon current events. Caniff's hero Terry, who was operating in China, completely missed the beginning of the war. The lesson hit home. Cartoonists must possess the art of situating their characters in relationship to events.

The comic strips are drawn with India ink on bristol paper, one-quarter or one-third larger than their finished size, sometimes even larger. (Strips 7¾ inches in height, pages nearly 3 feet high, have been drawn by Foster, Hogarth, and Raymond.) This facilitates the work, and the best artists find in these large sizes of activity more congenial to their talent. The balance of the pictures is verified with the help of a mirror, in accordance with the time-honored painters' rule, but some artists who have worked with the animated cartoon (for example, Hank Ketcham, father of "Dennis the Menace") prefer to work with an illuminated drawing board.

Several famous comic strips are today being drawn by the third or fourth generation of cartoonists. "Tarzan" was created by H. Foster. His daily strip, however, which he did not wish to draw, was entrusted to the deplorable Rex Maxon. When Foster abandoned "Tarzan," Burne Hogarth succeeded him; after Hogarth, "Tarzan" became the victim successively of Rubimor, Bob Lubbers, John Celardo, and others. As for "Flash Gordon," his daily strip was given to A. Briggs, who took over the Sunday strips as well when A. Raymond was drafted in 1944. During this period Paul Norris made a comic-book version. When Briggs left, the Sunday strips were taken over by Mac Raboy, the daily strips by Dan Barry. It is the common practice to entrust the Sunday and daily strips to two different artists. Such was the case with "Bringing Up Father" after the death of McManus.

1. Sketch and final version of a cartoon by Burne Hogarth. Note the suppleness of line in the drawing of the sketch, which is lost when the drawing is enclosed within the frame. Copyright U.F.S.

2. Harold Foster's style is different from Hogarth's: the treatment is less free. Foster remains a prisoner of the classic technique of the illustrators. Copyright King Features Syndicate, Inc.

Execution combines pen and brush. The pen reigned supreme until the thirties, when brush drawing gained ground; the latter still dominates today, although the pen is constantly used in a supporting role. The author of "Apartment 3-G," for example, uses the brush for his characters, but finishes them with a flexible pen; he uses a hard pen for the backgrounds and metallic objects. Similarly, Caniff paints in large shadowy masses, then outlines with his pen the lighted contours of the characters. The gray tones are obtained by applying transparent screens of dots or hatchings over the picture; this work is done at the syndicate, before the photoengraving of the strips. With a pale blue wash the artist indicates the areas to be tinted gray.

The techniques of draftsmanship are very standardized. Some authors, however, have recourse to more original methods. Watson, the English artist of "Dan Dare," uses a wash far removed from the "comic strip" style. Frank Bellamy, another Englishman, is a virtuoso in the use of a skillful pointillism reminiscent of lithography. In the United States, Roy Crane was at first one of the few cartoonists to use pencil rubbings on rough-textured paper (in the early years of "Wash Tubbs"). He then introduced the use of Craftint "doubletone" paper (see marginal note), from which he obtains striking results. Various firms, particularly Craftint, place at the disposal of cartoonists a large variety of screens that are transparent or transferable by tracing, which would permit enrichment of the texture of the pictures. Few make use of them, with the exception of several beautiful examples in the work of S. Jordan ("Jeff Hawke") and Al Williamson.

The Sunday strips present a color problem, for which there are several solutions. Authors in whose strips color plays a role tint a photographic reproduction of their drawings with watercolors. But the hue is not everything: there is also the problem of density. By the use of the so-called "Ben Day" method, color printing can apply colors either in a continuous spread or in series of parallel lines or dots, and combine these styles by juxtaposing or superimposing them. A light orange is obtained by superimposing a network of yellow dots and a network of red, light green by a blue network on a solid yellow area, and so on. Approximately eighty combinations of colors and densities are available. Knowing by experience the effects of the various inks, certain artists merely indicate in the appropriate areas on their drawings the colors to be applied, by means of a code which expresses both color and density (for example, "SYDB" indicates Solid Yellow Dots Blue). The color may also be applied at the syndicate. Many humor strips have their colored universe, the stability of which is an important characteristic. Once this universe had been created, the artist's color assistant (or one of the assistants to the syndicate's comics editor) takes full charge of it, without any intervention by the artist.

Production by workshop is the rule in the comic strip. We must remember that most American artists must produce six strips and a color sheet fifty-two weeks a year, in conformity with an inexorable rhythm. Today every artist has at least one assistant; this was already the general practice in the thirties. The division of labor varies considerably. Among authors who have only one assistant, the latter always does the lettering of the balloons. Since the assistant is paid by the artist and not by the syndicate, many artists try to limit themselves to a family workshop. Among others the division of labor is much more highly developed: the author may draw the characters, leaving the background and lettering to his assistant; lettering, background, and color may be handled by three people. In the United States, Philip "Tex" Blaisdell, a comic-strip landscapist, does backgrounds on order for several artists, without being associated with any of them. High quality and discipline assure the efficient functioning of the system.

Specialization seems to be more highly developed in Europe, where a strip has been interrupted when the firm's assistant left to do his military service; the shop's chief was not able to replace him! The best organization has been achieved at the Hergé studio, where one assistant prepares the characters, another does the landscapes, and another the balloons, while two people handle the coloring. There is also a researcher, in

---

Craftint "doubletone" paper is bristol board on which are printed two superimposed, almost invisible networks of lines or points that may be more or less closely spaced, regular or irregular, depending on the type. After the pencil sketch, a yellowish developer is applied with brush or pen, which causes both networks to appear: this is the dark-gray area. Another, colorless developer brings out one of the networks: the light gray. Lastly, the black areas are filled in with India ink. The gray tones of the doubletone having thus been processed in right from the beginning, the picture can be directly photographed for printing. This technique requires considerable discipline, since the artist has at his disposal only a black, a white, and two gray tones. He cannot abuse the intermediate nuances obtained by hatching the dark gray with black and the light gray with white.

1. "DID HE BRING HIS COMPASS?"
"HE COULDN'T FIND IT. PROBABLY HAD BEEN STOLEN. BUT NO MATTER, WE'LL STEER BY THE STARS."

2. "...AND WE ADAPTED TO A SUBTERREANEAN EXISTENCE..."

SAVAGE WORLD

addition to personnel who, in the United States, would be working for the syndicate (that is, to handle administrative duties and commercial use of the characters).

Often there is yet another collaborator: the scriptwriter. Before the war authors did their own scripts. This situation seems to have become exceptional for the authors of continuous strips, although the greatest cartoonists, like Foster or Caniff, protest against this trend. As for the humorists, they may, in "dry" periods, buy an idea from a gag man. Many scriptwriters prefer to remain anonymous; this permits them to dodge the syndicates and to furnish ideas for several artists at once.

The steps in drawing vary from one artist to another. After the rough sketches have been done, it is customary to draw the balloons first. Then comes the pencil drawing, done by the author himself; then the inking (lettering, balloons, faces, bodies, and backgrounds, in that order—this, however, may vary somewhat, as we have already noted). The daily strips are sometimes drawn to a rhythm of one per day, sometimes finished 6 by 6, in several days. Once the drawings have been examined, reread, signed, and sealed, there remains only the trip to the post office.

The artist-author must have a method for finding ideas. If he is a humorist, the author of a daily-life strip, he has a calendar studded with the great milestones of the national life: Christmas, taxes, the opening of the baseball season, vacation, and so on. He must also have on hand a mass of exact information on fashion, weapons, airplanes, automobiles, trees, and so on, carefully filed and kept up to date. (When he worked for a newspaper, its morgue solved this problem for him.) His salary must pay for his assistants, his equipment, the live models some cartoonists use—which explains the heights salaries can reach, at least in the United States.

Upon receiving the drawings, the syndicate's comics editor has an important job to do. Strips and sheets are first reread, to eliminate errors in spelling and punctuation and lapses of taste. He checks the consistency of the drawings (for example, that no door is without a handle, and so on). He is particularly careful to see that the strips will not be offensive to any reader: the syndicate sells not only to newspapers in all parts of the United States but sometimes to dozens of foreign countries. Indecency is forbidden. So the comics editor not only searches for awkward arrangement of lines but also examines the form of the spaces between the characters. Any suggestion of immorality is deleted: when "Boots" had a baby, close attention was paid to the passage of nine months after her marriage. Some newspapers do not like snakes: a very amusing boa that Segar created for "Popeye" had to be rejected. The syndicate bans swear words, which in the beginning were replaced by conventional signs or pseudo-swear words (but now that the public has become accustomed to them they are read as real swear words), and controversial topics such as God, religion, race, and ticklish political questions. However, these subjects are permitted, as can be noted with increasing frequency, when they are handled skillfully or from a point of view that corresponds with the syndicate's opinions. (Most syndicates are neutral, but the Chicago Tribune—New York News Syndicate, being the emanation of a newspaper, has very clear-cut political and social choices.) Cruelty to women, children, and animals is absolutely debarred, as is divorce: "Jiggs never struck Maggie, and will not divorce her" (the reference, of course, is to "Bringing Up Father"). Crime must not pay, or even childish pranks: Buster Brown and the Katzenjammers are always punished. Traditional jokes about dentists, laundrymen who ruin shirts, and children's chemistry sets that blow up have gradually disappeared as a result of furious protests from the groups at which they were directed. One must also keep in mind the foreign clientele. The Mexicans, who are heavy customers, are not happy when a ludicrous or undesirable character is called "Don Alvarado." However, one cannot foresee every possibility. "Mickey" was banned in Yugoslavia in 1937, when the Yugoslavs took offense at an episode that occured in Medioka, an imaginary, quite Balkan country ruled by a playboy king and his assistant, a scheming regent. The Yugoslav monarchy recognized itself in this picture!

After possible correction of a few details, the inspected drawings are photographed and engraved. A sheet of special cardboard is applied under great pressure on the zinc plate of the photograph, and this mold (which in the United States is called a matrix) takes on the imprint of the plate. Each newspaper client of the syndicate receives, two or three weeks in advance,

1. Roy Crane, "Buz Sawyer." A beautiful example of the doubletone technique. Copyright King Features Syndicate, Inc.

2. Al Williamson, "Savage World." The graduated Craftint texture strongly sustains the dramatic structure of this cartoon. Copyright Witzend-Wallace Wood.

3. Frank Bellamy and George Beardmore, "Frazer," showing the influence of lithography. Copyright Editions Dargaud.

3. "Just one!"
"No! I'm having the queen for company, and I want to offer her doughnuts with the tea."

4. "Is it really done for?" "I don't think so!"

5. "Aunt Pim, what will you give us if we get your fire started?"
"Ten lollipops and ten francs to buy ten more!"

6. "Impossible to get out of it—it's solid!!"

the matrices of the series it publishes. Their low price puts them within range of even small newspapers; thus the syndicate ships millions of matrices throughout the whole world. The matrices for the Sunday strips are sent directly to the newspaper if it has the equipment necessary for color printing, or, if not, to the printer that does this work for the paper. From the very beginning some large newspapers had printing contracts with local papers, to which they sold their ready-printed color supplement. Together with the packages of matrices, the client receives samples of all the strips, so that the editorial board can easily check their contents. The matrices are then placed in a circular foundry that makes a curved plate exactly identical, right down to its curve, with that of the syndicate. This permits the plate to be adapted to the cylinders of the rotary presses. When a newspaper buys a new strip, the syndicate sends it a complete advertising campaign designed to pave the way for the appearance of the strip; in it the characters appear and announce their approaching arrival.

The newspaper itself makes a certain number of (necessarily crude) changes. These were particularly frequent during the thirties, in French newspapers that published American series. These newspapers, destined to be read by young readers, deleted pictures, modified the clothing and anatomy of certain feminine characters, and omitted certain objects. For example, all weapons were removed from the last pages of "Scorchy Smith" to appear in France in 1941: we see Scorchy stretch out an empty hand, and ten yards away his adversary crumbles.

Foreign newspapers are serviced in the same fashion as the American ones. The Spanish often receive their strips already translated; for this purpose the syndicate maintains a staff of translators. The latter have their own requirements; one series that used a verse text in its balloons had to give this up, since the Spanish translators were not able to rhyme in their language. Even strips exported to English-speaking countries have to be adapted, since certain Americanisms are not understood in the Commonwealth countries. ("Flash Gordon," for example, became "Speed Gordon" in Australia.)

Thus the history of the comic strip is the history of its methods of distribution, the newspaper being the principal but not the only method; in the newspaper itself, the presentation of the comic strips has varied considerably with the passage of time. This is also an area of total difference between the United States and Europe. The American comic strip is the product of a commercial rivalry, of which the Hearst-Pulitzer conflict was the most conspicuous manifestation. Long before this, however, the newspaper struggle had acquired characteristics that created the milieu in which the comic strip was to develop. In the 1870's certain daily newspapers began to appear on Sundays in order to outdo their competitors. These newspapers then

"The Katzenjammer Kids," originally drawn by Dirks (1), and continued by Knerr (2) after the lawsuit between Dirks and Hearst. When Knerr died, King Features Syndicate continued the series with Winner (3) and, after the latter's death, with Musial (4). In France this series was called "Pim, Pam, Poum." Several artists drew imitations (5–6) under this title, which was applied not only to the authentic Katzenjammer Kids but also to the strip that Dirks continued ("The Captain and the Kids") (7). Copyright King Features Syndicate, Inc.; U.F.S.–U.P.I.

A picturesque example of the alterations that some newspapers with special editorial viewpoints made on comic strips is supplied by a mishap of "Tarzan" in *Russky Golos,* a radical anti-Communist, anticzarist, anticlerical Russian newspaper of New York. Tarzan is the son of a lord: they turned the father into a professor, and his mother's title of "Lady" thus disappeared as well. Tarzan and Jane married in church: feeling that it was impossible to present this episode to its readers, the editorial staff left the picture blank, but inserted a text indicating that they were being married in a civil ceremony. When a disagreeable Russian appeared in the script, the editors made a czarist out of him. The paper immediately received angry letters from its White Russian readers, and thus discovered that they were readers of *Russky Golos,* undoubtedly for the sake of its comic strips! When a second antipathetic Russian came to join the first one in the story, the chauvinistic editors turned him into a Pole. This time there was general approval from Russians of all colors, and letters of congratulation arrived even from the Soviet Union. Another brazen and protracted case of manipulation occurred in the prewar Italian press when, thanks to "free" translation the alterations in a few details of dress, a completely apolitical English serial was transformed into a Fascist strip.

Alex Raymond, "Flash Gordon." Copyright King Features Syndicate, Inc.

Burne Hogarth, "Tarzan." Copyright U.F.S.

battled among themselves by offering increasingly voluminous editions. Pulitzer chose, as his weapons, first copious illustration, then color printing applied to picture-stories. When Hearst attacked, he employed quantity (eight large pages in color as against the four half-size pages of Pulitzer's *World*); then he commissioned the first comic strips. Thus the American public became accustomed to color and generous illustration, and the comic strip quite naturally came to take its place, at the end of a continuous evolution, in the adult press. The orientation already given to the struggle caused the comics to be considered from the very beginning as a major factor in the sale of the newspaper. The fierceness of the competition, the certainty that only by giving the most could one stay in the race, created the paradoxical situation whereby the very troublesome full-page comic, in colors, preceded by ten years the modest black-and-white daily strip. Toward 1900 Sunday newspapers of more than fifty pages, with a "comic supplement" of at least four pages in color, were becoming the general rule.

In France, which was then America's only rival, the comic strip was immediately relegated to the children's newspapers. While the latter sheltered it, they also imprisoned it. Even today this tradition remains the strongest; the French (and even European) comic strip has not known the powerful life and enormous audience of the daily newspaper. In the absence of studies on what was considered to be the role of the picture in the French press during the *Belle Epoque,* we shall refrain from attempting to build up fascinating but unsubstantiated explanations based on factors such as traditional culture and the like. We shall simply note that it is not a question of a technical lag: the United States imports its rotary color presses from France and England.

As we have already noted, the daily comic strip appeared in the United States in 1907 ("Mutt and Jeff"). Here again, reliable statistics are lacking, but it seems that this form of comic spread very slowly, and did not become really well known until after 1920. In 1932 the Baltimore *Sun* had only three comic strips; in 1935 the New York *Herald Tribune* was publishing only two, and in 1940 only one. On the other hand, beginning in the twenties the Hearst papers and the Chicago *Tribune* had seven or eight strips. Their presentation was different from what it is today. The daily strips were scattered throughout the thirty or forty pages of the newspaper, at the top or bottom of the pages, alone or in two's; they frequently exchanged locations. Newspapers like the Chicago *Tribune* retained this arrangement for a long time. But beginning in the twenties another practice came into being, from which the present system has become general: the comic strips were grouped together. Starting in 1920, the New York *American* grouped eight strips on one page. In 1922 still another solution was found: the "American Pictorial," a daily illustrated supplement of photographs and comic strips, in black and white, folded into the paper. In the thirties the now classic device was discovered: one whole page, and the major portion of a second page, were devoted to the comics. Before the forties the comic strips were much larger than they are today: the standard size was 3 to 3½ inches high by 10⅖ to 12⅘ inches long. In place of the usual horizontal layout, the comic-strip page consisted of overlapped horizontal and vertical strips, laid out in squares or (for strips of six or eight pictures) two-column vertical strips.

The Sunday editions were still further removed from the European models. The newspaper consists of ten or twelve sections, each forming a special folio of from six to forty pages differing in presentation, size, and specialty: sports, advertising, news, woman's magazine, and so on. (The size of the Sunday papers is a source of jokes for Americans.) Included in these sections is an eight- or twelve-page comic supplement. Some newspapers also have a children's section (without comics!). Here, too, the presentation has changed. Before the advent of eight- or twelve-page color supplements in the thirties, pages one and four of some newspapers (for example, the old *Herald*) were printed in color, the inside pages in brown or green on white; later came two-color pages (gray and ocher, gray and blue). In the twenties the Chicago *Tribune* was still employing this system almost unchanged. In those happy days each strip occupied a whole page in the newspaper; the pictures were very large, and the stylists—McCay or McManus—obtained striking results. The pictures of "Little Nemo" were sometimes

---

The results of censorship of the comic strip by the newspaper itself:
The appearance of the daily strips presented certain newspapers with a problem. Refusing to appear on Sunday, yet not wishing to let themselves be outdone, they published the Sunday color comics on Saturday. When they also published the Saturday daily strips, both the Sunday and daily strips were published in the same issue, the former in color, the latter in black and white. The readers of these newspapers had two series of comics for the price of one paper. Fearful of the competition, some dailies brought out two comic supplements in color, one on Saturday and one on Sunday.

140

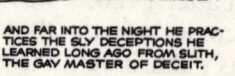

1, 2. Burne Hogarth, "Tarzan." Copyright U.F.S.

3, 4. Harold Foster, "Prince Valiant." Copyright King Features Syndicate, Inc.
Two examples of possible reassembly of a strip (full page and half page). In the "Tarzan" strip, the fifth frame is removed for the half page. In printing jargon this is called a "drop."

5, 6, 7. Johnny Hart, "B.C." Copyright Publishers Newspaper Syndicate. Transformation of a strip into full page, half page, and a third of a page.

1

Time-saving roller socket adjustment

These time-saving new-type Hoe roller sockets are designed for easy and accurate setting of the inking rollers. In recognition of the importance of proper ink roller settings for quality printing results and economy of ink and power consumption, Hoe roller sockets are engineered to provide maximum rigidity as well as convenience and accuracy of adjustment. This assures maximum operational and maintenance efficiency. They are fitted with high capacity SKF ball bearings... lubricated and sealed for life. The roller sockets are in full view, easily accessible and all adjustments can be made with the same wrench.

Hoe engineers are constantly combining creative engineering with mechanical practicality to cut costs, save time. It will pay you to get in touch with Hoe.

R. HOE & CO., INC.
910 East 138th Street, New York 54, N.Y.
BRANCHES BOSTON • CHICAGO • SAN FRANCISCO

2

SUNDAY NEWS — 15¢
NEW YORK'S PICTURE NEWSPAPER

'We're a-Rushin' Right Into...

The New York SUNDAY NEWS With Six Pages of the Best Comics From the Sunday Mirror

Also in This Issue:
PLAY POST POSITION ON PAGE 27

3

THE EXCITING 1962 FALCON FUTURA. Individually contoured front seats, handy personal console, elegant trim, wall-to-wall carpeting. Priced even below some *standard* compacts!

WHAT FORD NEEDS IS A SLOGAN...ONE THAT SUGGESTS HOW MUCH A FALCON GIVES YOU WHILE SAVING YOU LOTS OF MONEY....

HOW ABOUT, "HOW GREEN WAS MY VALUE"?

Peanuts Characters © 1960 United Feature Syndicate, Inc.

Ford Falcon '62
BEST SHAPE ECONOMY'S EVER BEEN IN

4

CHAUSSURES tintin

as large as 8 inches high by 5 inches wide. The crowding together of the comic strips began, though on a modest scale, in the thirties, averaging fourteen series in eight pages.

The changes that have taken place since that time are due to the appearance of half-size newspapers (tabloids) and to the very success of the comic strip. The tabloids were born in England; the first one to appear in the United States was the New York *Daily News* (1919). The formula slowly became more general (there were twelve in 1930, and fifty in 1940). They too had their comic supplement, and during the forties the syndicates had to plan their creations with these clients in mind. Series designed to fill large pages had to be reduced by half. Normal half-page strips became full-page in the tabloids, but had to be made taller. This is simple if the strip has an even number of pictures, but it is not always possible with an odd number. (A large picture can, in certain positions, hinder this operation, and one tall picture that straddles two rows invariably does so.) Solutions were rapidly standardized: the abandonment of unusual page layouts, and insertion in the half-page of an unnecessary picture, usually more narrow, which was eliminated in the process of transformation into full-page form. Thus an almost immutable rhythm was imposed on the artist's story.

Surveys taken in the thirties had demonstrated that the comic strips were a newspaper's principal element of attraction. The papers therefore began accumulating the largest collections possible (sometimes rising as high as forty-five), and this precisely during a period of paper shortage (during the war). This proliferation could be achieved only at the price of a reduction in size. The daily strips acquired their present size ($2\frac{2}{25}$ inches high, sometimes only $1\frac{2}{3}$ inches high, by $7\frac{2}{5}$ inches long) at this time. The practice of removing the frames from the pictures (which since then has become much more widespread) must result from a desire to combat the cramping of the characters. The Sunday supplements were also in trouble: the practice of placing eight series on eight pages (around 1920) has grown today to eighteen, twenty-two, and even twenty-eight series on eight pages—a confusion of clashing styles, a hideous chaos of tiny pictures. "Prince Valiant," which was the last series to appear full-page on large pages, is now reduced to half-page. Moreover, in obedience to the wishes of the misers, the syndicates created a new size: the one-third-page strip, obtained by completely removing the first row of the standard strip (the three-row half-page). This imposes a new curb on the artist: the pictures in the first row must form simply a removable prologue. Some newspapers reduce their strips still more, and place them on one-sixth of the page! Today the comic strip is well presented only in the tabloids, which publish many series in full-page format.

In France the comic strip rarely appeared in large size. The children's newspapers to which it has been confined have traditionally been called "little newspapers." When they published American series, it was often with serious diminutions: great reduction in size; excessive changes in layout requiring the omission of pictures or, on the contrary, their enlargement by the addition of carelessly drawn areas; distortion of the pictures; the necessity of enlarging the balloons, since the concise English language requires less space than its translation; in Italy, the balloons were often

Comic-strip heroes are used in an advertising campaign to praise the advantages of a product.
1. Alley Oop for Hoe.
2. Li'l Abner. Advertising for a comic strip appearing in a newspaper.
3. Peanuts for Ford.
4. Tintin for a line of shoes.

During the thirties the following page types were in use:

1. One strip covering the entire page (for example, "Prince Valiant," "Tarzan").

2. The half-page strip ("Don Winslow," "Smokey Stover," and so on).

3. An entire page given over to one artist, and divided unequally between a "star" strip, covering two-thirds or three-quarters of the surface, and a complementary strip ("companion strip," also known as a "top"). "Jungle Jim" was the "top" for Alex Raymond's page, the star strip being "Flash Gordon." Similarly, "Bringing Up Father," which took up four rows, had a two-row companion strip, "Rosie's Beau." Knerr drew a "top" for "The Katzenjammer Kids": "Dinglehoofer und His Dog Adolph." "Winnie Winkle" was accompanied by a small strip at the bottom of the page: "Looie Blooie."

This type has now almost completely disappeared.

1. A visitor to the exhibition of Burne Hogarth's works, in the Galerie de la Société Française de Photographie, standing in front of a gigantic blowup (11½ feet long) of an original cartoon (4⅔ inches) from "Tarzan." (Photo E. François.)

2. Burne Hogarth, "Tarzan." Copyright U.F.S.–U.P.I.–Ed. Mondiales–U.P.I.

TARZAN GRIMACED AS HE SWAM THROUGH THE NOISOME ODORS RISING FROM THE SLIMY WATER AND FROM THE LOW, MARSHY BANK BEYOND. GREAT, UNBLINKING EYES HUNGRILY WATCHED THE MAN SWIMMING DIRECTLY TOWARD THEM.

omitted and replaced by quatrains under the pictures. The situation has worsened since 1945. In a new edition of "Prince Valiant," gaudy colors made the character hideous; in the Italian version of "Flash Gordon," not a single picture retains the original colors, and not a single page layout by Raymond has been kept (half of the drawings have been omitted and/or redrawn). It is for this reason that studies on the language and esthetics of the comic strip that are based on material published in France are quite naïve.

The dissemination of the comic strip in books is known throughout the world. More specifically American is the custom of turning comic strips into novels; the author himself sometimes does this work (for example, "Flash Gordon in the Caverns of Mongo," by Alex Raymond), but more generally it is done by the employees of Whitman Editions. Comic-strip characters were very soon used in advertising, not only in the United States but also in Europe (for example, Bécassine, the penguin Alfred). Around 1935 it occurred to the police of Waukegan, Illinois, to paint them on stop signs; drivers braked in order to see them better! Some comic-strip heroes are on occasions used in political or sports drawings.

A more widespread form of dissemination is the movie. The animated cartoon very soon took over the Katzenjammer Kids, Jiggs, Krazy Kat, and Mutt and Jeff; in the same period (1917–1918) Emile Cohl did animated cartoons of the Pieds-Nickelés. In the thirties there were very few adventure or detective strips that were not adapted: "Jungle Jim," "Flash Gordon," "Dick Tracy," and others were put on film or have been since then. At this time certain shortcomings of the movie vis-à-vis the comic strip became apparent. There were also radio programs ("Jungle Jim" in particular) and adaptations for television. With forty films (not including televised series), several novels, and even a popularized study, "Blondie" holds the record for adaptations in addition to its record for international distribution. Several musical shows (*You're a Good Man, Charlie Brown*), a ballet (*Krazy Kat* in 1925, with music by John Alden Carpenter), and dramas (*Bringing Up Father* and *Bonaventura*) have been made from comic strips. After a long career as a cartoonist, Rube Goldberg has changed from India ink to bronze, and is now creating "comic sculptures," which extend the comic strip into three dimensions. Lastly, let us mention two special aspects of comic-strip distribution: library collections and exhibitions. Not much can be said in praise of the conservation of comic strips in libraries. In France they are badly filed, badly cared for, and incomplete, because the American newspapers are practically absent from the French libraries. In the United States, newspapers and libraries eagerly microfilmed and then sold their old newspapers by weight. Now they are learning that microfilm lasts for barely twenty years! Moreover, it reproduces color pages very badly, so in any event these are lost. Fortunately, collectors have acquired the newspapers sold.

Exhibitions of comic strips are not a novelty; the first (?) one was held in April, 1922, at the Waldorf-Astoria, in New York. There were several others, notably the "Cavalcade of American Comics," held in New York in 1963. In Paris in 1965–1966, the Société d'Etudes et de Recherches des Littératures Dessinées (Organization for the Study and Research of Pictorial Literature, popularly known as SOCERLID) organized exhibitions ("Ten Million Pictures," "Burne Hogarth," "Milton Caniff") a quite different type: it made use of photographic enlargements and original drawings lent by the authors. This was intended to enable the public really to see the comic strip, to help it distinguish that which is art in the artist from that which is betrayal in the newspaper. Thanks to the quality of the paper and the clarity of the blacks and whites, the photographic enlargement makes it possible to free the comic strip from the small size that stifles it and to exhibit it in the usual dimensions of the works of art to which the public is accustomed. The works of certain artists can be enlarged, without loss of quality, to an extraordinary size (pictures of six inches enlarged to six and a half feet or more). The large size of these pictures and of the original drawings was a revelation that was ultimately to bring the comic strip into the Musée des Arts Décoratifs in the Louvre.

The republishing of comic strips in books was inaugurated in 1893 with the publication of *La Famille Fenouillard*. In the United States, F. A. Stokes collected Buster Brown, the Katzenjammers, and other strips, between 1900 and 1914. In the twenties and thirties appeared the books of Cupples and Leo, almost square in shape, which reproduced "Little Orphan Annie," "Bringing Up Father," and many others. In France, books of the Mickey, Felix, and Tarzan strips, published by Hachette, completely distorted these strips by eliminating balloons (replaced by childish texts under the pictures) and by mutilating or suppressing pictures. A more unusual type was the "Big Little Books" of the thirties, which were almost cubical; they had a picture on the right-hand page, and a continuous text on the left-hand page.

Schulz, "Peanuts." Copyright U.F.S.–U.P.I.

Love is lending your best comic papers

8

the comic-strip audience

The comic-strip audience is both badly known and misjudged. While very thorough investigations by American sociologists have revealed the general features of the situation in the United States, their work has no equivalent in Europe. Even in the United States much remains to be done; there are discrepancies in the results of the surveys, as the reader will notice—we have not attempted to conceal them. On the other hand, the findings concerning this audience clash with prejudices that are so deeply rooted, both in the United States and in Europe, that the results of the investigations have not yet succeeded in seriously weakening them.

The size of the American comic-strip audience is the characteristic least open to debate. The estimates of its number do not always tally with each other. One estimate claims more than 100 million Sunday readers, 90 million of whom are regular readers (that is, read the daily strips); this evaluation seems modest. According to another estimate, four out of five Americans living in a city of over 2,500 inhabitants are assiduous readers of the comic strips. A few million more or less does not alter the major premise that no art form, not even the movie, reaches such an enormous public. To know this public is an essential concern of the syndicates and of certain newspapers; inevitable and legitimate aspects of market research are involved in sociologists' studies. In accordance with the usual preconceptions, the early surveys were conducted with children. In 1923–1924, 5,000 children, both rural and city dwellers in Kansas and Missouri, ranging in age from 8½ to 15½, were given a list of amusements, and were asked to check off those that had occupied them during the preceding week, and to list them in order of importance. In order to reveal seasonal variations the survey was made in November, February, and April; it showed no such variations, and little difference between boys and girls or white children and Negroes. On the other hand, there was a clear-cut distinction between city and country: rural children read the comics less, and more irregularly. The classification showed that the reading of the comic strips headed the list of amusements of all city boys, both white and Negro, of all ages; the same was true of the girls. In the country, reading the comics ranked variously from second to thirteenth place: only once did the comics place first. The survey could not indicate whether rural youngsters lacked newspapers or simply preferred fishing.

If memories and impressions are trustworthy, it seems that the situation was the same in France during the thirties; illustrated magazines were almost completely unknown among the farmers. Moreover, it seems unlikely that the reading habits of boys and girls were as strikingly similar as in the case of the young Americans.

In the course of the thirties the newspapers, alarmed by the economic crisis and the cost of color printing, hesitated to maintain large pages of comics. Then the Gallup Institute discovered that in the eyes of the entire reading public the comic strips were the principal attraction of the newspaper. "Bankers, university presidents, professors, and doctors," proclaimed Gallup, "read the comics as eagerly as truckdrivers and laborers." A more recent survey by the sociologists W. Schramm and D. M. White in a moderately large city in Illinois differs slightly from, without invalidating, the Gallup conclusions. Their conclusions: the reading of the comics reaches a peak during adolescence and gradually drops off after age 15, and more rapidly after age 50; it also decreases in proportion to amount of education and prosperity. But the striking fact is that the percentages denoting interest in the comics are always high, to the eyes of a European.

®beetle bailey
by mort walker
WHEEE! I DON'T HAVE TO DO ANYTHING ON SUNDAY!
WOULDN'T YOU KNOW IT! THE ONE DAY I DON'T HAVE TO DO ANYTHING, I FEEL LIKE DOING SOMETHING!
AH! THE PAPER IS HERE!
HEY, BEETLE! CAN I SEE THE FRONT PAGE?
DIBS ON THE COMICS!
I'LL TAKE THE SPORTS SECTION, BEETLE
I WANT THE EDITORIAL PAGE
ANY RIOT NEWS?
GOOD! HERE'S THE FINANCIAL LISTINGS!
I LIKE THE WOMEN'S SECTION
I'LL TAKE THE MOVIE GUIDE!
GIVE ME THIS PART
GIVE ME THAT!
I NEED THE WANT ADS!
THE GUY WHO SAID NEWSPAPERS HAVE SOMETHING FOR EVERYBODY NEVER LIVED IN A BARRACKS WITH 75 OTHER GUYS!
10-20
MORT WALKER
© King Features Syndicate, Inc., 1963. World rights reserved.

To a non-American it is the size and universality of the phenomenon that are striking, together with the unimportance of the differences between categories of readers, and the fact that the comics always head the list of newspaper features in order of interest. Only women over 60 are genuinely uninterested in the comics (12.1 percent as against 36.5 percent of men in the same age category).

The following surveys, which were carried out with a different sampling, did not tally with these results. It would seem that Schramm and White encountered in Illinois a kind of provincialism. Wishing to define the face of "the American who does not read the comics," E. Robinson and the same Manning White made a survey of the better educated groups, in the belief that this was the natural place to find him. They discovered that the practice of always conducting these surveys among children and illiterates was a mistake, since they supplied only children's and illiterates' answers (a fact that is known but always forgotten). They discovered among educated people a very lively interest in the comic strip, a respect for comic strips as a genre and as a means of expression, and a clear-cut opposition to sweeping condemnations of them.

The same authors then launched (in 1962) a national survey, using a scientifically measured sampling that covered the entire country. Its results are particularly interesting. The reading of the comics reaches a peak between ages 30–39, and then gradually declines. The highest proportion of readers is found in the white-collar class. The comics are closely associated with childhood memories, but more than 50 percent of those interviewed stated that the reading of the comic strips was not an idle pastime but rather a positive pleasure. Hostile answers varied between only 4 percent and 10 percent. As regards the attitude of educated people, the results of the previous survey were confirmed: these people feel they are betraying culture; they are afraid of seeming backward because they believe they are exceptional in their group. They imagine that the greatest reading of the comics is done by quasi-illiterates: "Contrary to the general notions of the adult population about comic strip fans, readers in the most highly educated group are the rule rather than the exception." The lessening of interest after age 40 is more likely to signal a nascent intellectual sclerosis than the flowering of maturity.

At the same time, other surveys confirmed that of all the features in the newspaper the comics are the most widely read (13.2 percent of the total against 8 percent for war news); 58.3 percent of the men and 56.6 percent of the women stated that they particularly read the comic strips. Proportionally they are twice as effective as the sports pages. On the whole, visual forms accompanied by a text constitute one-fifth of the features and claim half of the reading time.

The prime importance of the comic strips in the newspaper was again revealed in the purchase of the

---

Everyone grabs the section of the paper that interests him. The comics page goes to the idiot—a classic joke among cartoonists, who depict the comic-strip enthusiast as a moron.

Mort Walker, "Beetle Bailey." Copyright King Features Syndicate, Inc.

An investigation conducted in Kansas in 1923–1924 showed that the percentage of white boys who read the comics rose from 93 percent to 100 percent between the ages of 8½ and 12½ years; at age 15½, it was still 100 percent. Among Negro boys the percentages were slightly lower, reached their peak sooner (94 per cent between 10½ and 11½ years), and began to drop at 12½ years, falling to 85 percent by age 15½. Among white girls, the percentages were higher than for boys in the younger age groups (8½ to 10½ years), and remained high after that age. Among young Negro girls, interest remained stronger than that of the boys, beginning at age 12½ (97 percent were reading the comics at age 15½, against 85 percent of the boys).

The investigation made by Schramm and White in Illinois indicates that interest in the comics drops from 76.5 percent in the 10–19 age group to 36.5 percent in the 60-and-over group. The latter group, however, does not accord greater attention to the editorials (36 percent) or the news (36.9 percent). The interest of the affluent group versus that of the poorer class is 49.1 percent against 57.3 percent; the interest of those who have gone to high school, contrasted with those who have a grammar-school education, is 46.8 percent against 55.5 percent.

1

GASP!!-??-"FEARLESS FOSDICK" ISN'T IN MY PAPER!!
NOR MINE!!
WHY ISN'T OUR IDEAL IN THE PAPERS ANY MORE?
ACE MAGAZINE

2

THE CROWD STORMS INTO THE NEWSPAPER OFFICE
WE WANT FOSDICK!!
SO DO I!! BUT-SOB!-MY PAPER CAN'T HAVE IT ANY MORE!!

3

PLEASE, MR. BULLMOOSE- TELL US WHAT HAPPENED!! WE'RE GOING CRAZY!!
JUST GIVE US A LITTLE PEEK!!
JUST A HINT?
GO BUY YOUR OWN CARTOONIST!!
11-22
Al Capp

Washington, D.C., *Times-Herald* by the *Post* of the same city. These two newspapers represented completely opposing viewpoints. The readers of the *Times-Herald*, however, easily made the transition to the *Post*: the latter had had the sense to continue the comic strips of the *Times-Herald*, which apparently constituted the most interesting feature of the newspaper for its readers. Similarly, when the New York *Daily News* absorbed the *Mirror*, it added the latter's comics to its own series.

Another type of problem concerns reader behavior vis-à-vis the comic strips: Does the reader make a choice among them? A survey conducted yearly in Minneapolis from 1949 to 1956 revealed certain typical attitudes. The conclusions are definite: the person who begins a comic strip reads it fully, in 95 percent of the cases. The individual who reads one strip tends to read the others (50–55 percent of the cases). There are only two attitudes: those who read all the comic strips, and those who read none of them. There are very few intermediate positions; the distribution curve of readers is of a most rare type: a "V", with the "pro" group on one side, the "con" group on the other, rather than the usual bell-shaped curves in which the intermediate positions predominate. The most frequent position among fans is to prefer certain series, but to read them all. It appears, on the other hand, that the reduction in the size of the strips has somewhat disgusted readers. Morning readers continue to read everything; in contrast, a slight tendency to selectivity is noticeable among the audience (especially feminine) of the evening papers. It cannot be said that this fact is due to television.

Other investigators have concentrated on the nature of the enjoyment the comic strips afford their readers. In 1949 Leo Bogart conducted an investigation among low-paid workers in a district of Manhattan. Some were recent immigrants; these considered the comic strips childish because they saw their American-born children reading them; they themselves had not known them in their youth. Thus Bogart noted that the least-educated subjects showed the least amount of interest in the comics. In this clearly determined social group the reading of the comics is a habit, and even a rite performed by 85 percent of those interviewed. The privation or interruption of the habit is keenly felt. It has been said that Mayor Fiorello La Guardia of New York read the comics over the radio during a newspaper strike, before the war, in order to satisfy the feverish curiosity of the people, as well as of the children, who had been deprived of them. Since then this tactic has been imitated on similar occasions.

The Frenchman has difficulty in imagining the perenniality of comic-strip heroes, because he has known several waves of them, each one of which annihilated its predecessors. "Spirou" and "Tintin" are short-lived in comparison with "The Katzenjammer Kids," which has been in existence for seventy years, or "Bringing Up Father" (fifty-five years). Moreover, for the Frenchman there is a complete break when he changes over from the illustrated magazine to the newspaper; the characters of his youth disappear from his sight. The American spends his entire life in the company of the same heroes, and can establish his own landmarks in relation to theirs. They are connected with his earliest memories; they are his oldest friends; often, through wars, crises, changes of residence and changes of job, and divorces, they are the most stable elements of his existence, to the point, according to Bogart, that adults experience a hostile reaction to new strips, which introduce a change in the immutable circle of familiar faces.

Apart from this ritual aspect, what pleasure in the comic strip was experienced by the very average people he observed? This pleasure also seemed to him a very "average" one. The comics introduce variety and fantasy into these monotonous lives. It is not true that they arouse antisocial impulses or distract readers from the realities of life: their reading is, in the group being investigated, too superficial an experience. On the other hand, and for the same reason, their cathartic role must not be exaggerated. They supply a useful

---

1, 2, 3. Al Capp, "Li'l Abner." Copyright News Syndicate. Al Capp likes to depict readers of the comics as fanatics. In the episode from which these pictures are taken, Bullmoose the millionaire has, out of pure sadism, bought the rights to a highly successful series ("Fearless Fosdick," a comic strip within a comic strip, and a parody on Dick Tracy). He has imprisoned its author and is keeping his work, which Bullmoose burns each day before the enraged and pleading crowds, without deigning to tell them what is happening to their hero.

Another question on reader behavior was answered by a survey of rural readers of the *Centre Daily Times*. It might have been supposed that the continuity strips are less likely to be read occasionally than the daily gag strips. The survey revealed that such was true: comic-strip fans read them regularly, whether or not they are continuing. In fact, series like "Blondie" and "Dennis," which are limited to the daily gag, have a lower percentage of occasional readers than the continuity strips. This result tallies with that of the Minneapolis survey: The reader who likes the comics reads everything; the reader who does not like them reads nothing.

1. Schulz (Peanuts, the child, and the comic books), "What a beautiful gory layout!" Copyright U.F.S.

2. Al Capp, "Li'l Abner." Daisy Mae is jealous of Li'l Abner's passion for his favorite comic-strip hero. Copyright News Syndicate.

but limited outlet; they are an amusement, a silent show in a conventional language, offered to millions of isolated individuals in their reading, not to an assembled and electrified crowd. The pleasure experienced by the educated readers described by D. M. White seems to be much more positive, without being essentially different.

The same inquiry revealed the role of the comics in social intercourse. Being a neutral subject familiar to everyone, they provide a topic of conversation, a friendly opening gambit between people who are not well acquainted with each other, "a ready-made satirical imagery, immediately applicable to real people and problems." The implication seems to be to certain social conventions: to be compared to a comic-strip character is always friendly, never offensive. One discusses the doings of the characters as if they really existed, but it must be made clear that the speaker does not really believe in them, if he does not want to be mocked. Consequently, those who, having missed an episode of their favorite series, try to find out from their friends what happened to the hero must do so with caution. The technique is rarely commented on. Bogart cites only one such case: that of a policeman who admired the draftsmanship of "Prince Valiant." He notes that a serious conversation about the comic strips is an indication that they are considered as an art form. One could not expect to observe such a fact in the milieu under consideration. Bogart's observations on the role of the comics in social intercourse are revealing. He tells of the attitude of a building superintendent who, while he liked only certain series, read them all in order to be able to talk about them.

Just as the comics contribute to the unity of the individual's life, some authors see in them a major element of American unity, while others actually regard them as the only common element binding together the great majority of Americans. One could also investigate the following hypothesis: since they are read by the entire family, they represent a factor of community and agreement between the various age groups. The comic book, by reintroducing a distinction between child and adult reading, is a disruptive factor. Is this one of the reasons why it is so violently resented?

There is no European equivalent of this already quite detailed portrait. Also, there exists no complementary portrait of the enemy of the comic strips, since Robinson and White did not find him where they had expected to hear an enemy growling. In an analysis that is subtle but perhaps too a priori, Leslie Fiedler sees in the attacks on the comic strip the expression of a lower-middle-class group that claims to be cultured and a supporter of culture but that is satisfied with a substitute. "It is not the literate, fully educated man who is leading the attack, but the semi-educated man who feels threatened." For Fiedler, this man reads Cronin and the *Reader's Digest*. Perhaps. It is certain that the most vigorous attacks in France have come from a type of intellect whose platitudinous character is evident from ten yards away. The writings of members of this group always reveal a total ignorance of what they are attacking; the reader is not always sure that they are any more knowledgeable in what they defend. Possibly this is the last stage in an evolutionary process (after all, the comic strip is not a world apart). In the last century these narrowly rationalistic minds attacked philosophy, religion, science, and history. The evolution of ideas has banished them from these disciplines. Driven back from one post to another, they found themselves reduced to the comic strip: there was nothing else left.

In Europe practically nothing is yet known about the comic-strip audience. In contrast to the situation prevailing in the United States, there may possibly be several distinct audiences, reflecting the extreme heterogeneity (in quality, content, and place of origin) of production. (Europe imports comic strips from all over the world.) The Italian magazine *Linus,* which publishes "Peanuts," "Li'l Abner," "B.C.," "Pogo," and other intellectual strips, is read principally by readers aged 16–28, most of them students. This age category constitutes approximately 70 percent of the total readership. The supporters of SOCERLID (Société d'Etudes et de Recherches des Littératures Dessinées [Society for the Study and Research of Pictorial Literatures]) in France, are different: 65 percent of them are over 29, and of this group 15 percent are over 40. The distribution of job categories is much more varied, and the professions are particularly well represented. Investigations of newspaper reading conducted between 1948 and 1954 are useless in this area because they were badly conceived. The investigators divided the comic strip into two categories; in one category it was lumped in with humorous drawings, in the other, with the picture novels. The definition of the categories was vague: "Professor Nimbus" constituted the first category, and seems not to have been considered a comic strip. This muddled investigation revealed the existence of "for" and "against" opinions, as in the United States, with a minority undecided, and showed that the comics have a stronger appeal than any other newspaper feature.

Alex Raymond, "Flash Gordon."
Copyright King Features Syndicate, Inc.

9

the world of the comic strip

In the eyes of those who believe they can analyze the comic strip by glancing over two or three magazines, the world of the comic strip appears simplistic. On the contrary, however, it represents an incredible network of lucid observations, traditions, some of which are thousands of years old, influences, and relationships between the characters. To disentangle this network requires patient, methodical work assisted by a comprehension that is born only from many years' acquaintance. American sociologists have done precisely this, and have thus been able to draw up a preliminary, and in some respects quite thorough, comprehensive survey of the world of the comics. (Needless to say, Europe, where the comic strip is regarded as being nonexistent, has no useful equivalent.)

F. E. Barcus has made a statistical study of the evolution of the types of comic strips between 1900 and 1959 in three leading Boston newspapers—a total of 778 titles. He notes that the series centered upon the family, children, and daily life have never represented less than 60 percent of the titles (93 percent in 1915; 91 percent in 1925, after a slack period); on the other hand, fantasy (including science-fiction) has fluctuated between only 1 percent and 5 percent. Adults have always constituted 75 percent to 80 percent of the comic-strip population; adolescents are rare (5 percent). Long variations affected the strength of the serial strips, which rose steadily from 1920 to 1949, and then dropped. Animals dropped from 32 percent in 1910 to 12 percent in 1959. Their frequency curve is the opposite of that for children, which has three peaks: 1905 (35 percent), 1925 (42 percent), and 1940 (28 percent). Some subjects are affected by short variations. The war strips very clearly reflect the intensity of American participation: 4 percent in 1915–1920, 18 percent in 1940–1944. Series devoted to business and international topics flourished after the wars, but then rapidly declined. All these phenomena reflect a combination of current events and their impact on the collective imagination, and the policies of the syndicates, which exploit the rhythms of interest and indifference of the public—an unknown, and probably variable, rhythm.

In another survey, Barcus made a very detailed analysis of the Sunday strips for March, 1943, 1948, 1953, and 1958, of four newspapers that carry most of the great American series, as if he were analyzing an actual population group. The world of the comics is a contemporary world inhabited by adult Americans, who pass a great portion of their lives in funny situations and cope with family problems. When they do not fit into this category, they live in a world of adventure, the problems of which are related to crime, love, and war. Humor reigns supreme, with 64 percent of the total, as against 19.2 percent for adventure (a proportion inflated by the survey of 1943 and the war then in progress). It is an urban world (Americans seem to enjoy contemplating their powerful cities in the comics, and McCay and McManus were the poets of this urban world): 73.8 percent of the comic strips whose locale is the United States take place in a city. In contrast, foreign countries are presented as rural in 80.9 percent of all cases. Four out of five series take place in the United States, 90 percent of them in our own time, fewer than 1 percent in the future, 9 percent in the past. Only 3 percent of the series are peopled solely by children; 40 percent, however, contain only adults.

The characteristics of the population are very revealing: 72 percent of its members are men, hence this is a masculine world. They are usually middle-aged, whereas the women are very young or obviously elderly. Needless to say, 80 percent of them are Americans. One Negro was found. Ethnic minorities and foreigners supply 17 percent of the heroes and 36 percent of the villains. From the social point of view,

WELL--HERE IS BROADWAY-THE GREAT WHITE WAY-THE RIALTO OF AMERICA-WHAT DO YOU THINK OF IT?
IT'S ALL RIGHT-I SUPPOSE-IF ONE LIKES ELECTRIC LIGHT BULBS-
NEWS REEL
THE CONVICT OR TIME ON HANDS

1

When the small, quiet city dozes in the tranquillity of a winter evening...

2

1. George McManus, "Bringing Up Father." Copyright King Features Syndicate, Inc.
2. Maurice Tillieux, "Gil Jourdan." Copyright Ed. Dupuis.

TARZAN GRIMACED AS HE SWAM THROUGH THE NOISOME ODORS RISING FROM THE SLIMY WATER AND FROM THE LOW, MARSHY BANK BEYOND. GREAT, UNBLINKING EYES HUNGRILY WATCHED THE MAN SWIMMING DIRECTLY TOWARD THEM.

Burne Hogarth, "Tarzan." Copyright U.F.S.

Two special worlds dealing with the same subject: the jungle and its monsters.

Alex Raymond, "Flash Gordon." Copyright King Features Syndicate, Inc.

LED BY PRINCE RONAL, FLASH, DALE, AURA AND BARIN STRIKE OUT IN THE GENERAL DIRECTION OF THE GREAT TREE HIGHWAY.

A VENOMOUS TREE LIZARD, IN SEARCH OF PREY, DROPS FROM ITS LOFTY PERCH ONTO RONAL'S BACK.

6 percent of the characters cannot be classified. Of the remainder, 67 percent belong to the middle class, 12 percent to the lower classes, and 15 percent to the rich. As regards occupations, fantasy reigns supreme: 23 percent have have no definable occupation; 17 percent engage in unusual activities, and only 36 percent have ordinary jobs (two-thirds of these are men). Women may be doctors or teachers, but are not in positions of authority over men. Forty percent of Americans have a profession, contrasted with 27 percent of the ethnic minorities.

The goals pursued by this population are primarily pleasure, power, love, friendship, and justice. Another investigator, Spiegelman, notes that egotistical goals are disapproved of but are frequent. Married people seek love, financial security, and power; single people are much more diversified and more likely to have altruistic goals. In 81 percent of all cases the goals sought after are attained; evil men are successful in 63 percent of the cases (84 percent for good people). Among the methods of arriving at one's goal, action and intelligence dominate (27 percent), followed by trickery (15 percent), charm (particularly feminine) in 13 percent of the cases, force in 10 percent; in only 5 percent of the cases are established institutions involved. But the most successful methods are not the most frequently utilized ones: institutions are effective in 92 percent of the cases, intelligence in 84 percent, force in 73 percent.

The contrast between married and single people is depicted in very curious terms. The men lose their ambitions when they marry, whereas the feminine will to power increases; the woman abandons the search for pleasure; the male does not. The single man is tall and handsome; when he marries he becomes small, fat, and bald. When she marries the woman becomes taller than the man, but she puts on weight and becomes ugly.

Another survey, conducted by Gerhart Saenger, was devoted to male-female relationships in the strips of nine New York newspapers in 1950. The combined results of these two surveys show that the single person is always equal to any situation, but when he marries it is his wife who copes with problems. The single person, even in the humor strips, always persists in his undertakings, whereas more than a third of married men lose all continuity of ideas. The married man becomes irrational and more easily influenced than his wife, and fails more often. In the humor strips the married man and the single man offer their love without much success. In the adventure strip, on the other hand, it is the woman who offers her love to the hero, who maintains a prudent reserve. "Love is dangerous, for it leads to marriage, a situation in which the man loses his strength. He can preserve it only by fleeing women, who are an obstacle to the true goal of his life, the search for adventure" (conclusion of G. Saenger). According to the same analysis, marriage goes contrary to the man's new goal, which is to rest! His wife prevents him from doing so. Everyone is familiar with the old strip in which the young wife Blondie drags Dagwood, who claims he is sick, out of bed and, pushing him out into the snow, orders him to go and earn his living.

Studying the King Features Syndicate's comics in January, 1950, Mr. Spiegelman raised the question of attitudes toward foreign ethnic groups. He noted that foreigners and Negroes are restricted to the adventure strips and are all distant, either in time or in space. He found no American Negro: The Negroes are Africans in distant jungles, and furnish both likable characters and villains. There is no contemporary Indian: the Indian appears in historical strips, where he is cast in a "good-guy" role. Irish-Americans have been completely adopted: 15 out of 19 have a major role, 14 a "good-guy" but comic role. The same is true of the Italians and the Slavs. The attitude toward the British is ambiguous: as ancestors they are courageous and likable; as contemporaries, five out of seven are comic and disagreeable. Frenchmen appear

---

If the principal characters of the comic strips often fall within a limited range of stereotyped characters, the blame must be placed on the comics editors of the syndicates. They classify the strips in several clearly defined categories, their characters in several basic groups, and are careful to see that the selection offered by their syndicate contains a complete series of these categories. The artist nevertheless succeeds in developing the character he is told to portray, and even the spirit of the series; this is so, for example, with Roy Crane, who transformed "Wash Tubbs" (originally set in the film world) into an exotic adventure strip more in accordance with his preferences. The author has greater liberty, however, in the minor characters, which he creates as he wishes. These characters, more authentic, alive, and picturesque, sometimes have such a vivid life of their own that they succeed in dethroning the hero of the series. Popeye was in the beginning a supernumary, as was Snuffy Smith (who later replaced Barney Google). Captain Haddock of "Tintin" at first appeared in an occasional minor role; the strength gradually acquired by his personality finally resulted in his becoming a permanent character. Hipshot, the gunslinger, is the real hero of "Rick O'Shay."

1. Alex Raymond, "Flash Gordon." Copyright King Features Syndicate, Inc.

2. Frank Godwin, "Conni[e]" Copyright Ledger Syndica[te]

Several minutes later, the Titanian ship and its prisoner enter the inner city

3. William Ritt and Clarence Gray, "Brick Bradford." Copyright King Features Syndicate, Inc.

FOR A BRIEF SECOND THE THREE SURVIVORS SEE THE SHIMMERING OUTLINE OF THE MYSTERY PLANET BEFORE IT VANISHES FOREVER INTO ITS OWN DIMENSION

4. Sydney Jordan, "Jeff Hawke." Copyright London Express Features.

5. Alain Saint-Ogan, "Zig et Puce au XXIe Siècle" (Blighter and Flea in the 21st Century). Copyright A. Saint-Ogan.

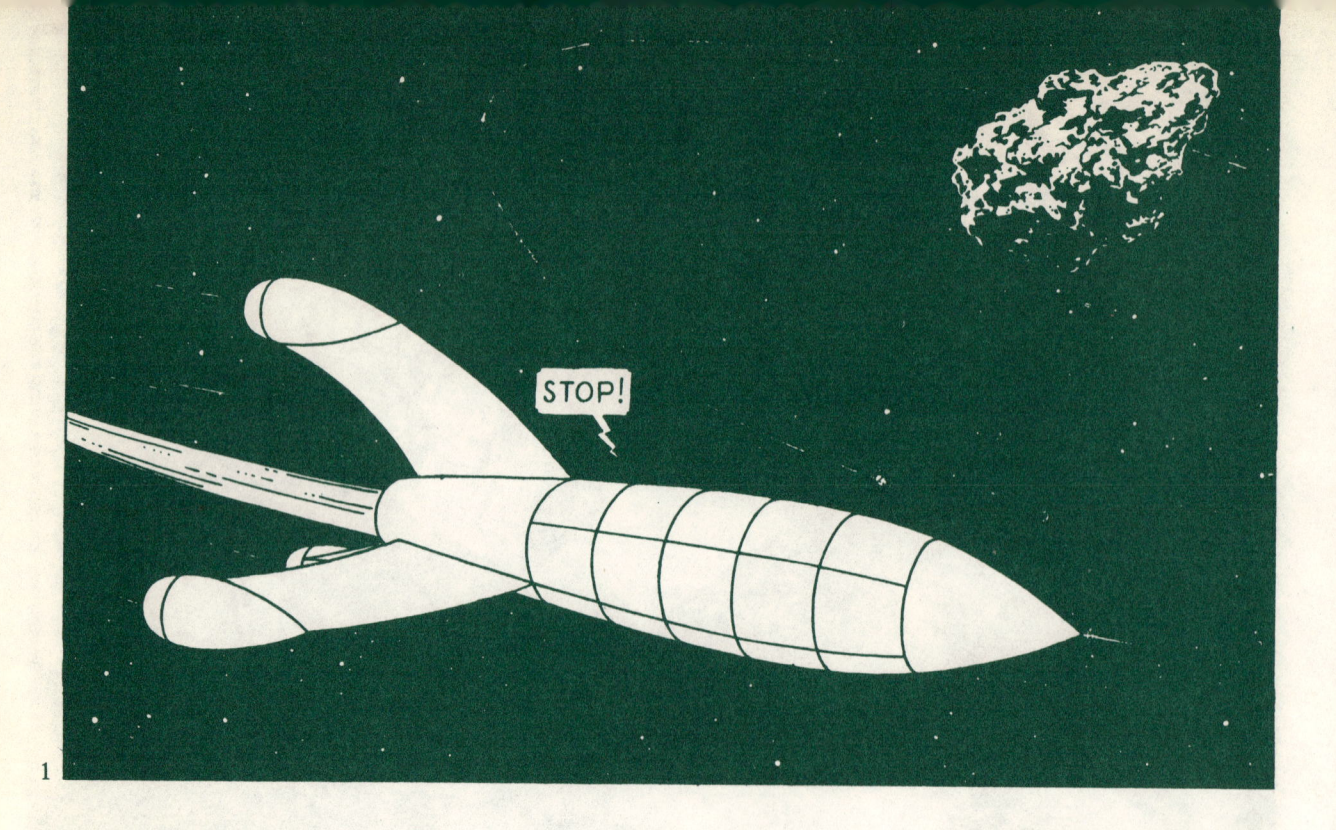

1 STOP!

2 QUELQUES HEURES PLUS TARD, UNE VILLE FANTASTIQUE APPARAIT DEVANT LES YEUX STUPÉFAITS DES AÉRONAUTES.

4 " POUR BRISER L'ASSAUT DES PARTISANS, TORG REGROUPERA LES TROUPES QUI LUI SONT RESTÉES FIDÈLES. MAIS SI NOUS PARVENONS À NOUS EMPARER DE LA STATION DE RADIO-TÉLÉGRAPHIE, LA VILLE SERA ISOLÉE ".

only in humor strips. The Germans appear in only one series; three out of five are sympathetic and funny. The sampling used in this analysis must be considered with reservations, for its principle ignores certain internal laws of the comic strip, as we shall see. It is very evident, however, that the American minorities are ignored, that only their ancestors are admitted to the comic strip. Generally speaking, foreigners are liked, but at a distance. F. E. Barcus concludes by drawing attention to the controlled nature of this image of the world given by the comics. "Such distortions may well reflect underlying needs and desires of the population more exactly than we wish to acknowledge.

All these surveys can be reproached with a common failing: they place all the series on the same level. Actually, since we are seeking the relationships between the comics, the public, and reality, the relative success of the various strips should be taken into account. When one series is read ten times more often than another, we may believe that it reflects the public's taste ten times more accurately and has ten times more influence on the public's imagination. Each strip should be assigned a coefficient in proportion to the total printing of the newspapers in which it is published. Important differences would certainly appear in the new percentages obtained. This would eliminate a factor that distorts the results: certain types of strips have undoubtedly remained exceptional solely for the accidental reason that the genius of the artist has discouraged imitation. Let us not forget that the waves of proliferation of a given comic-strip type are inflated by the syndicates' policy of commissioning imitations of a strip they saw was successful. Raymond, Foster, and Hogarth have made it very difficult to make use of the Middle Ages, mysterious Africa, or the science-fantasy epic. The international printing of these success strips must compensate, at least partially, for their unusual nature.

No study can be made of the world's armies without taking into consideration their total effective force; this is what has been done for the comic strip. The extensive surveys carried out on the comic strip as a whole must be completed by serious analysis, both quantitative and qualitative. L. W. Shannon has attempted such a study of Harold Gray's "Little Orphan Annie" over the two-year period of 1946–1947. He concluded that the unchanging little girl with the vacant eyes is the spokesman for the conservative ideals of the middle class. She stresses faith, hope, confidence in Providence, charity ("but not too much charity"), the value of help spontaneously offered by neighbors and friends, not ordered by government fiat. She is against swindlers, politicians, governmental slowness, and foreigners in search of American military secrets. A second survey of the Sunday strips from April, 1942, to July, 1950, shows that Annie spent 59 out of 110 weeks combating foreign (Russian) agents, and 15 weeks battling a gang of young hooligans who

---

1. Hergé, "Tintin—On A Marché sur la Lune" (Tintin—We Walked on the Moon). Copyright Casterman.

2. Scolari, "Saturno Contro la Terra" (Saturn Versus Earth).
Caption, No. 2: Several hours later, a fantastic city appears before the astronauts' astonished eyes.

3. J. F. Dille and R. Calkins, "Buck Rogers." Copyright National Newspaper Syndicate.

4. Poïvet, "Les Pionniers de l'Espérance" (The Pioneers of the Hope). Copyright Vaillant.
Caption No. 4: "To break the partisans' assault, Torg will reassemble the troops who have remained faithful to him. But if we can succeed in seizing the radio-telegraph station, the city will be isolated."

A survey of cartoonists conducted several years ago by H. F. Wiggin revealed that 65 percent of them came from small cities or from rural areas. Two-thirds of them belonged to the middle class; one-quarter of them had grown up in poverty. 54.84 percent were Protestants (which reflects the national proportion); 10 percent were Jewish (they constitute 3.24 percent of the American population). Their incomes varied from $7,500 to $150,000 per annum; 42 percent earned more than $25,000. 70 percent of them were between 40–49 years of age; 58 percent were high-school graduates. All had studied art (this was very rare before 1930). They formed a very stable, family-oriented group: 92 percent were married; for only 8 percent was it their second marriage. 68 percent had two or more children; 21 percent had four or more children. These characteristics inevitably have an influence on the comic strip. Moreover, many of them utilized their memories in their strips: in "Just Kids" Ad Carter used his childhood playmates (one of whom died in France in 1918). Chic Young gave the Bumsteads a son when he himself had one; his own child died, but in "Blondie" he made the son grow up. Many cartoonists portray in the hero the man they themselves would have liked to be. (Harold Foster, among others, expressly admitted this.)

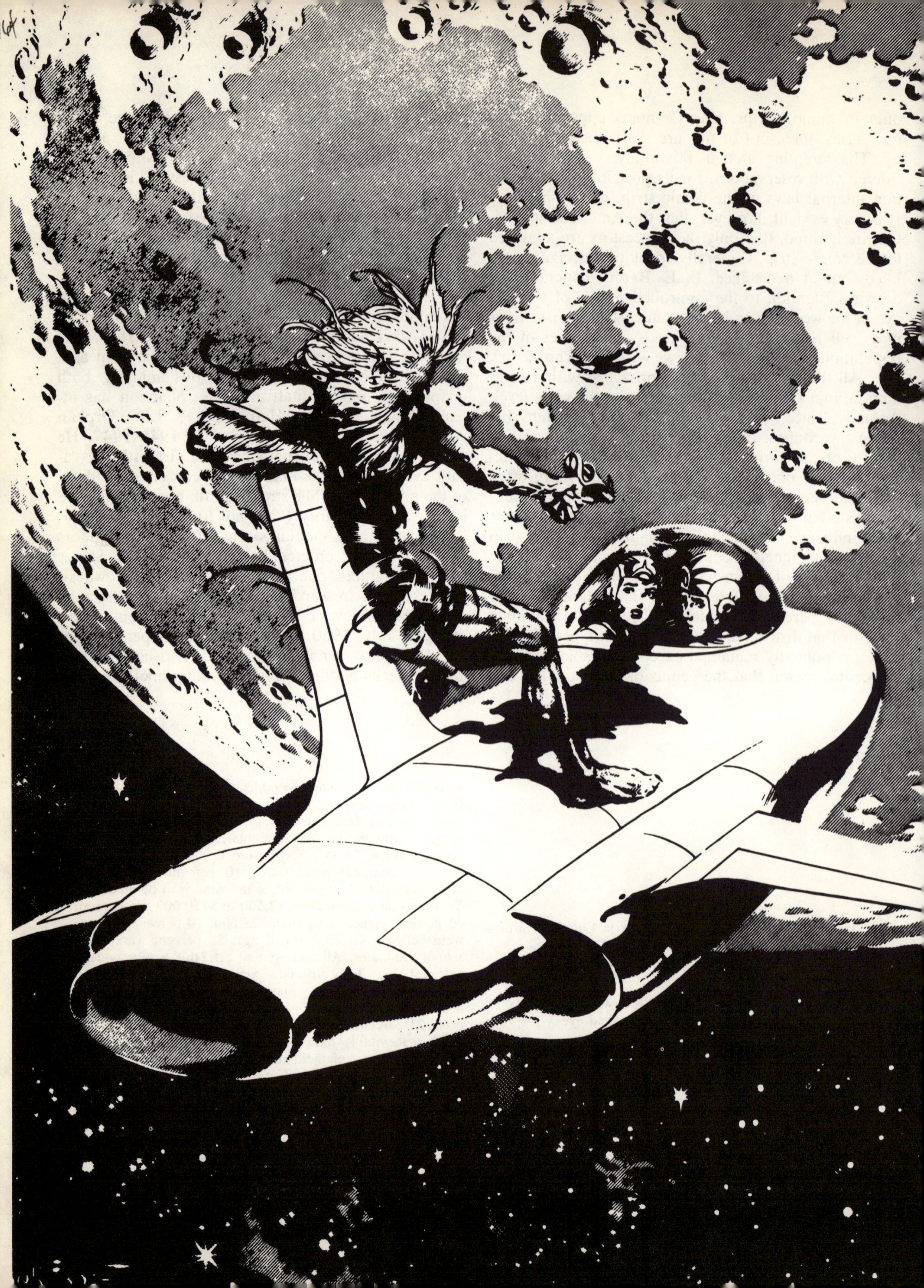

had organized a racket. That is, she protected Capitalism against Communism, and the small, honest businessman against social outcasts. The remainder of her time was spent helping the poor and the unfortunate. Gray, a fierce opponent of Roosevelt, the New Deal, and federal interference, constructs genuine parables. He tells how Annie, thanks to a buried treasure, builds an autonomous community of orphans; but in trying to seize the treasure the Internal Revenue agents cause a landslide, and the treasure is lost to everyone. We see Annie living comfortably with vagabonds and millionnaires—preferably with farmers, poor but honest people, but never with workingmen. She frequents poor people whose misery is due to purely personal, not social, factors.

As for her protector, the millionaire Warbucks, he is presented as the great capitalist who fights to assume his social function, which is to be charitable to the poor—the ideal of the European medieval period, which permitted wealth on this condition. His method—work, think, act better and more often than other people, do things in his own way, and leave the authorities alone—is exactly that of the Rockefellers' and Carnegies. ("Gasoline Alley," which is owned by the same syndicate, sometimes shares this attitude by its optimism, its emphasis on the civic virtues, and an occasional tirade against the concept of social class.) At present Annie and Dick Tracy (which also belongs to the Chicago *Tribune*) are waging an endless campaign against the deliquescence of justice and the paralysis of the police by the theories of conscience-stricken jurists and neurotic sociologists.

In another, purely quantitative, analysis devoted to "Li'l Abner," A. Brodbeck and D. White demonstrated the mechanism of that strip's family relationships in reference to certain studies of contemporary American society. The American boy is supposed to be "bigger" than his parents: it was noted that the Yokum parents, who were originally of almost normal size, began to shrink after several months, and finally became miniscule in comparison with their son. The father is a puppet; it is the mother, Mammy Yokum, who transmits the traditional knowledge to her son. As for the other women, Daisy Mae, Li'l Abner's wife, is sweet, submissive, innocuous, and quickly resigned; city women are scheming, superficial, and wanton. All the women (except Mammy Yokum) try to destroy the independence of the male, particularly on "Sadie Hawkins Day," when the single men are hunted down across the fields, in an epic chase, by a horde of disheveled females showing all their claws. Another characteristic trait: food is the expression of the mother's love for her son, and it is quickly evident that in moments of crisis Li'l Abner fortifies himself by wolfing down enormous plates of food.

Suggestions for investigation could be multiplied. For instance, some consider "Beetle Bailey" an antimilitaristic series. Actually, when we analyze it we see that basically its criticism is directed at officers who are too old or too young, and at the enlisted man, who, though likable, is irresponsible. Sarge, the noncom, a bellowing but solid and paternal man, and the always calm Captain Scabbard, who has more confidence in Sarge than in his boyish executive officer, keep the unit functioning properly—a perfectly traditional viewpoint. It would seem, then, that Mort Walker has no really hostile intent; far from being antimilitaristic, he consciously or unconsciously depicts the traditional criticism of the army made by the largest segment of the career army men—the regimental officers and higher noncoms. The field to be explored is immense, and has hardly been touched. Several perhaps hasty and subjective surveys of a given period, type of characters, or series, have been begun. In 1927 Lehman noted the anarchism underlying the strips of that period:

"Their characters often defy, with total immunity, human and natural laws . . . they have no sense of propriety . . . accept no restraint . . . they have little consideration for priority rights and their preservation. They handle valuable objects with complete disdain and destroy great quantities of wealth in various forms."

Leslie Fiedler notes that the mythology so particular to the comic books is only a transposition (perhaps instinctive?) of the fairy tales, in which the urban jungle replaces the forest. It is true that this suggestion accounts for the extraordinarily stereotyped nature of these stories, whether in their scripts or in the physical appearance and attitudes (of which there are only four or five, quasiritual) of the characters, or the superhuman nature with which they are endowed by design.

Another criticism concerns Spiegelman's survey of the attitude taken in the comic strips toward foreigners. The basis for the study (a single publication) is too narrow, the topic for study (the attitude toward the Germans) ridiculous. We gather that these five Germans on an island are the Katzenjammers. Not only is their number too small to permit the drawing of conclusions; in addition, Spiegelman ignores an essential characteristic of the comic-strip universe,

Frank Frazetta, "Buck Rogers." Buck Rogers has an unexpected encounter near the Moon.

166

Opposite:

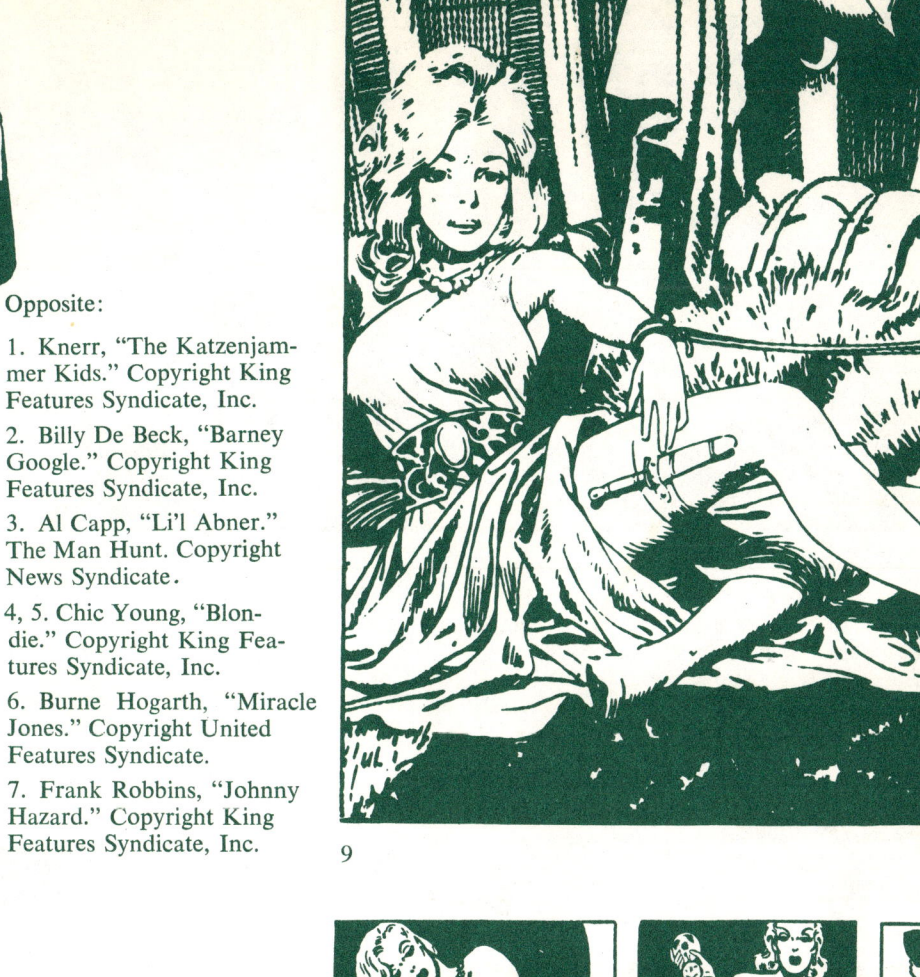

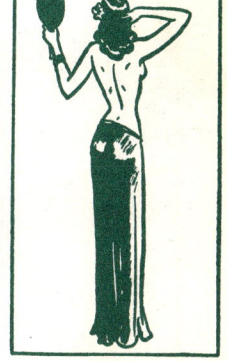

1. Knerr, "The Katzenjammer Kids." Copyright King Features Syndicate, Inc.
2. Billy De Beck, "Barney Google." Copyright King Features Syndicate, Inc.
3. Al Capp, "Li'l Abner." The Man Hunt. Copyright News Syndicate.
4, 5. Chic Young, "Blondie." Copyright King Features Syndicate, Inc.
6. Burne Hogarth, "Miracle Jones." Copyright United Features Syndicate.
7. Frank Robbins, "Johnny Hazard." Copyright King Features Syndicate, Inc.

WOMAN

8. Milton Caniff, "Terry and the Pirates." Copyright Chicago Tribune–New York News Syndicate.
9. Harold Foster, "Prince Valiant." Copyright King Features Syndicate, Inc.
10. Milton Caniff, "Male Call." Copyright Milton Caniff.
11. Alex Raymond, "Rip Kirby." Copyright King Features Syndicate, Inc.
12. Stan Drake, "The Heart of Juliet Jones." Copyright King Features Syndicate, Inc.

"In the middle of the day? That's not like you, Juliet! . . ."
"And when he left, Ace said he was going *to town*. You were both coming from the *opposite* direction when I met you!"

Time in the comic strip: the baby (see page forty-six) becomes a little boy (1), then a youngster (2). Today he is the father of a family (3).

1, 2. Frank King, "Gasoline Alley." Copyright, Chicago Tribune–New York News Syndicate.

3. Bill Percy, "Gasoline Alley." Copyright Chicago Tribune–New York News Syndicate.

which invalidates surveys as soon as we compare them with reality: every continuous comic strip creates and then perpetuates its own universe, sometimes unchanged, with its own laws and its own conventions. This is particularly true of the older series, because they have endured and because they were born at a time when the need to copy reality did not exist. Are we really to believe that the Katzenjammer scene that we reproduce here reflects the reality of social relationships? A Negro man thrashing a white child, in the presence of an adult white who is doubled up with laughter? Next to it, the picture of the lazy mountaineer who lets his wife work had a certain relationship to the realities of life among poor whites, but it is no longer current; it has become folklore.

When Dirks created the Katzies, they may have reflected the picturesque characteristics of German-Americans. They were still considered Germans in 1917, since their title had to be changed. In the forties this was no longer true. Their behavior is so uncharacteristic that the French prewar public never realized that its beloved Pam and Poum belonged to the hereditary enemy seed. The same is true for a great number of comic strips, and possibly for all of them in varying degrees. They create genuine myths that the public accepts without question and that embody in more or less recognizable form aspects of reality dating from the time of their creation. A simple example of this is seen in clothing. Pol Vandromme has noted that the public no longer sees Tintin's garb—golf knickers typical of the thirties. His readers will find fault with Hergé over the accuracy of an airplane, but accept this outmoded style! Similarly, Jiggs still dresses in turn-of-the-century styles. In older strips, by a phenomenon that one might have believed was limited to iconographical influences among ancient civilizations, a detail that is no longer recognizable continues to be perpetuated. In "The Katzenjammer Kids," Hans, the little blond boy, wears a black vest with a white scalloped collar. Who realizes today that this is a black velvet vest with a lace collar, a remnant of that ridiculous fashion launched around 1890 by a moving novel, *Little Lord Fauntleroy,* which had worldwide success and was the despair of little boys "dressed like girls"? Preceding even the Katzies, Christophe had led the way by giving Fireman Camember a uniform that had disappeared long before.

On a less superficial level, the analysis of human relations in the comics reveals traits that appear to belong to the nineteenth century. It is well known in the history of mental habits that a long interval separates a reality from its entrance into the collective imagination—so long, that the situation has in the meantime changed. Moreover, it must not be forgotten that many artists have introduced into the comics their own childhood memories, which, until around 1930 and even later, went back to the 1880's. The discrepancy between reality and imagination appears several times: the peak period of the aviation strips, for instance, was reached after the truly heroic period of the air age. The reporter-detective is one of the hero types of the thirties. He reflects a real situation: one of the techniques of sensationalism was to entrust investigations to reporters . . . between 1870 and 1900!

Thus the relationship of the comic strips to reality is a complex one. On the whole, the comic strip is indeed a witness to its age, and everything is to be found in it, but the degrees of transposition are very unequal. We have attempted to survey, in our illustrations, the past sixty years as seen in the comic strip. It could be developed in greater detail; it could also be nonexistent if we had recourse to other series. No future historian will be able to suspect the existence of Nazism behind the peaceful scenes in "Vater und Sohn," which systematically ignored that phenomenon. "Blondie," the only strip conceived for a worldwide audience, is interested solely in human relationships: husband-wife, parents-children. This so-called "typical" American family has no car. In contrast, "Bringing Up Father" is a chronicle of American life; a chance investigation always discovers in it actual objects, the latest fashion, the newest gadget. Only one

---

The way having been paved by the continuing story, the introduction of time in the comic strip was by Frank King's "Gasoline Alley." The hero, at first a bachelor, married and had three children (two of whom were adopted); all of them are now married and have children of their own. This is the most striking (but not the only) example. Perry Winkle recently married; his elder sister is a mother and widow. Chic Young has made the son and daughter of the Bumsteads grow up. Prince Valiant has four children; his eldest son is now the same age as Valiant was at the beginning of his adventures.

This introduces the factor of the hero's aging. The customary solution is to have the children grow up normally and to let the parents remain unchanged or age more slowly than is usually the case. Ultimately, however, the question of the hero's death will have to be faced—every artist undoubtedly counts on being able to leave the problem to his successor!

Time is a major element in the originality of the comic strip as a narrative art: by imposing a rhythm on its publication, it cadences its narrative. Only the comic strip can enable reader and character to live the same time; only the comic strip can continue a story for decades. Series published in complete episodes in book form (comic books) are deprived of the rhythm of the genuine comic strip, and tend to be illustrated pseudobooks.

1. Winsor McCay, "Dream of the Rarebit Fiend," *Aviation* (1909). Copyright McCay Company.

2. Pinchon, "Bécassine": Call-up of Women, First World War. Copyright Gauthier-Languereau.

3, 4, 5. George McManus, "Bringing Up Father." The twenties: bobbed hair, short skirts, the radio. Copyright King Features Syndicate, Inc.

6. Percy Crosby, "Skippy": The financial crisis, 1930. Copyright McClure N.S.

7. Martinek and L. A. Beroth, "Don Winslow of the Navy": Evacuation of American civilians during the Spanish Civil War.

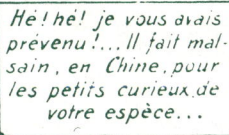

8. Hergé, "Le Lotus Bleu" (The Blue Lotus). Japanese aggression against China. Copyright Casterman.

Balloons for No. 8:

1. Ministry of War, Tokyo. Stop. Chinese bandits have blown up railroad line between . . .

2. . . . Shanghai and Nanking. Stop. No major damage. Stop.

3. Well, we'll make it major. . . .

4. This is Radio Tokyo. . . . The Chinese bandits stop at nothing in their daring! We have just learned that they have attacked . . .

5. . . . the Shanghai-Nanking railroad line. After blowing up the track, the bandits . . .

6. . . . stopped the train and attacked the passengers . . .

7. . . . a great number of whom have been killed while trying to defend themselves.

8. Twelve Japanese subjects were among the victims. After the attack . . .

9. . . . the bandits, about one hundred in number, fled with their booty.

10. *Tokyo News!* Special edition! Chinese bandits attack train! Latest news . . .

11. . . . and Japan must remember that she is the guardian of order and civilization in the Far East. . . . Hail to our heroic soldiers who are leaving to defend this noble cause! . . .

16. [At the League of Nations] . . . and, once again, Japan has fulfilled her mission as the guardian of order and civilization in the Far East! . . . If, to our great regret, we have had to send troops into China, it was to defend China herself! . . .

17. Look, I warned you! . . . China's not a healthy place for busybodies like you. . . .

9. Milton Caniff, "Terry and the Pirates." The war in the Pacific. Copyright Chicago Tribune–New York News Syndicate.

THE YANKEE WOMAN IS NEXT!

1

PUTT, PUTT, PUTT
DAWN. THE REFUGEES ARE QUIET, WATCHING THEIR HOMELAND FADE INTO THE DISTANCE... A WOMAN SOBS... A MAN BRUSHES AWAY A TEAR.

2

BRUSQUEMENT LA MER S'EST SOULEVÉE, S'OUVRE AVEC DE PUISSANTS REMOUS ÉCUMEUX. JAILLISSANT DES PROFONDEURS, EN ÉMERSION ACCÉLÉRÉE, UN GRAND SOUS-MARIN DE CROISIÈRE, SANS LE MOINDRE SIGNE DISTINCTIF DE NATIONALITÉ, VIENT DE SURGIR AUX YEUX DE DAYTON, SIDÉRÉ...
?!!?
N-27
UNITED STATES
a.m. 40 A

3

I DON'T GET IT! —THE ARMY IS SUPPOSED T' OWN THE HELICOPTERS...
AN' THE NAVY IS SUPPOSED T' BUILD BRIDGES AN' STUFF
MILTON CANIFF

4

ROY CRANE 7-11

5

THE U.S. RETURNS TO NORMALCY
Students Wildly Indignant about Nearly Everything
THE U.S. MARINES ARE BRUTES
OUR PARENTS ARE WAR-MONGERS!!
AL CAPP
5-1

6

LSD IS A POWERFUL HALLUCINOGEN! IT MAY SOMEDAY PROVE TO BE ONE OF THE MOST USEFUL DRUGS! BUT IT'S GOING TO REQUIRE MUCH ADDITIONAL RESEARCH BY DEDICATED PROFESSIONALS ...NOT AMATEURS WHO ARE TAKING IT FOR "KICKS"!
BRADLEY EDGINGTON 12-19

7

event is difficult to find in the comics: the Great Depression, which upset the American's world too deeply for him to wish to see it in the comics. We find only echoes of it, as in our example (Percy Crosby's "Skippy"), in which the child repeats what he has heard.

The comic strip is a product of the Atlantic civilization. The Katzenjammer Kids and Buster Brown are part of the trend that, beginning with Rousseau's Emile, has made the child a literary subject. It is a mistake to ignore them when studying this subject, for they belong to it as much as those other comedians, Tom Sawyer (1876) or Kipling's *Stalky and Co.* (1899). "Little Annie Rooney" belongs completely within the tradition of persecuted childhood; she is a sister of Victor Hugo's Cosette and of David Copperfield. Sickles is no Saint-Exupéry, but there is a general trend that marks the entrance of aviation into the collective imagination, and both belong to it. In the case of Harold Foster, there is a direct link with the Victorian novels of knighthood. Here again the academic world ignores this fact, and yet exhaustive works have been devoted to successors of Chrétien de Troyes that are not as good as "Prince Valiant." Another error is to study, for example, America as seen by European opinion, and to ignore the comic strip (and the popular novel). Several series deserve thorough analysis, and reveal that this literary genre, which embarrasses so many superior minds, is a repository of many influences, some of them ancient.

The solitude of the adventure-strip heroes has occasioned much comment and even protest. There was an epidemic of marriages in the comics after 1940; but gradually, through deaths and disappearances, they were obliged to return to solitude and permanent girl friends. (It has been forgotten that the latter are ancient, starting with Roland's fiancée, who appeared only to die.) The conventions of the adventure comic strip are directly related to those of the epic, which require, very logically and without any need for appeal to psychoanalysis, the hero's total freedom. Moreover, this solitude is also that of the heroine—Connie had no ties, for example—and of the child (which fact reduces to naught all the sexual implications some commentators wished to find in the hero's solitude): Blighter and Flea, Tintin, and Bibi Fricotin have no known relative likely to impede their liberty. Hans and Fritz Katzenjammer have only their mother (the Captain is not even a relative). Even as a boy Terry was alone, not to mention professional orphans like the two Annies. Here the comic strip reflects an ancient prejudice that is not confined to literature but is revealed in real life by the eternal reproach—"he's not the same man"—addressed to so many leaders (Nelson, Morgan, the Robin Hood of the southern cavalry, and others) after their marriages. In the comics the wife is a tyrant, her husband a puppet. Too close a comparison with contemporary society would be unwise, for the picture is the same in the humorous literature of the Middle Ages.

Let us pause for a moment at "Flash Gordon,"

Picture No. 3, caption:
The sea suddenly becomes rough, and heaves in powerful foaming surges. A large cruising submarine rapidly emerging from the depths, and bearing not the slightest indication of nationality, has just appeared before the eyes of the astonished Dayton. . . .

The News Seen By:

1. Milton Caniff, "Steve Canyon." The Middle East troubles. Copyright Publishers-Hall Syndicate.

2. Roy Crane, "Buz Sawyer." Refugees fleeing Castro's Cuba. Copyright King Features Syndicate, Inc.

3. Vic Hubinon, J. M. Charlier, "Buck Danny." Space exploration. Copyright Editions Dupuis.

4. Milton Caniff, "Steve Canyon." The Vietnam war. Copyright Publishers-Hall Syndicate.

5. Roy Crane, "Buz Sawyer." The Vietnam war. Copyright King Features Syndicate, Inc.

6. Al Capp, "Li'l Abner." Student protests. Copyright News Syndicate.

7. Bradley and Edgington, "Rex Morgan, M.D." The problem of LSD. Copyright Publishers-Hall Syndicate.

It has often been said that the language of the comics is incorrect and distorted. In 1943 G. Hill made a survey of 16 series chosen from among the favorite strips of children. A count made over 24 days supplied 9,302 words out of a total of 28,808. It appeared that while the vocabulary was simple, slang, misspelled words, onomatopoeias, and foreign words accounted for no more than 5% of the total. Only 10% of the words were names. Given names were very numerous, in view of the predominance of person-to-person relationships in the comic strip. Series which utilize a technical slang (aviation series, for example), phonetically reproduce a local accent, or create a distorted and disjointed language ("Pogo") are unusual in the American comic strip, which however has strongly influenced American vocabulary, creating numerous expressions which have quickly become popular (hot dog, jeep, wimpy, and many others which were popular for a time).

1. THEY SAY THE TROUBLE WITH THIS COUNTRY IS TOO MUCH CLASS CONSCIOUSNESS — THAT IT'S BEING OVER DEVELOPED. YOU'RE IN ONE OF THE THREE BIG CLASSES, CAPITAL, LABOR AND THE PUBLIC. NOW LET'S SEE JUST WHERE I STAND. I PUT IN EIGHT HOURS A DAY WORKING HARD — HEAD AND HAND — AS HARD AS ANYBODY. YOU CAN'T DENY I'M A WORKING MAN. SO I'M **LABOR**. I SAVED A LITTLE COIN LAST YEAR AND BOUGHT A COUPLE OF BONDS. YOU SEE I'M **CAPITAL** TOO! AND FURTHERMORE, I GUESS I'M THE BIRD THAT PAYS SKY PRICES FOR NECKTIES, GASOLINE, PIE AND OTHER NECESSITIES. I SURE AM THE **PUBLIC** IF ANYBODY IS! I'LL SAY THEY'RE GOING TO HAVE A JOB UNSCRAMBLING ME!

2. WELL, WE'VE BEEN PRETTY LUCKY THIS YEAR — GOT OUR GRAIN HARVESTED IN SPITE OF THE FLOODS — HAD THE MONEY TO HIRE PLENTY OF HELP AT THE RIGHT TIME — A LOT OF FARMERS LOST ABOUT EVERYTHING THIS YEAR —

EVER SINCE WARBUCKS HELPED US PAY OFF THAT MORTGAGE AND LOANED US CAPITAL TO OPERATE THE PLACE WE'VE BEEN MAKING MONEY — INSTEAD OF ALWAYS BEING JUST ONE JUMP BEHIND LIKE WE WERE BEFORE WE'VE BEEN JUST ONE AHEAD ALL THE TIME —

OF COURSE WE DIDN'T WASTE ANY MONEY JUST BECAUSE WE HAD IT — WE'VE BEEN CAREFUL AND LIVED ABOUT THE SAME AS WE ALWAYS DID — NOTHING FANCY BUT COMFORTABLE — BUT EVEN SO WE OWE ABOUT EVERYTHING TO MR. WARBUCKS·

AND IF YOU GET RIGHT DOWN TO THE FACTS I GUESS WE REALLY OWE MORE TO LITTLE ANNIE HERE FOR IF IT HADN'T BEEN FOR HER WE WOULD NEVER HAVE MET MR. WARBUCKS IN THE FIRST PLACE —

AW, YOU DON'T OWE ME ANYTHING. IF YOU HADN'T TAKEN ME IN AN BEEN NICE TO ME I WOULDN'T HAVE BEEN HERE FOR "DADDY" TO FIND, WOULD I?

3. WHAT IS THIS **CHRISTMAS** YOU TALK ABOUT — YOU SAY IT'S A CELEBRATION OF **PEACE** AND **GOODWILL**?

YES, AND PEOPLE GIVE **GIFTS** — THE **STORES** ARE **JAMMED** — PEOPLE OUTDO EACH OTHER WITH FINE, COSTLY GIFTS — THEY FIGHT EACH OTHER IN THE **MARKET** FOR THE PRIVILEGE — THEN THEY HAVE **PARTIES** —

THEY GET **DRUNK**, CHASE EACH OTHER'S **WIVES** AND THEN DRIVE **SPEEDY MACHINES** INTO TRAFFIC JAMS AND **KILL** EACH OTHER IN **ACCIDENTS**.

WHY DON'T THEY PASS A **LAW** AGAINST IT?

The Opinions of the Chicago *Tribune:*

1. Frank King, "Gasoline Alley." A speech against the concept of class warfare.

2. Harold Gray, "Little Orphan Annie." The hardworking but unlucky small farmer praising the bighearted capitalist who has helped him.

3. Walt Kelly, "Pogo." Pogo explains Christmas to the old man on the unicorn. Copyright Publishers-Hall Syndicate.

4. Walt Kelly, "Pogo." Copyright Publishers-Hall Syndicate.

5. Al Capp, "Li'l Abner" (Fearless Fosdick). Ignoring the violence in the streets, Detective Fosdick prefers to pick on a balloon seller who has no license. Fosdick kills forty-two people in an (unsuccessful) attempt to capture him. Copyright News Syndicate, Inc.

THE MONSTER-KILLERS

1. Burne Hogarth, "Tarzan." Copyright U.F.S.

2. Alex Raymond, "Flash Gordon." Copyright King Features Syndicate, Inc.

which seems to float in unreality, but which on the contrary possesses an astonishing wealth of themes and traditions. Its theme is simple: three Earthlings (the hero, the young woman, and the scientist) land on the planet Mongo, where numerous races and kingdoms are suffering under the rule of the Emperor Ming, a thorough tyrant. Hunted down from jungle to jungle and from kingdom to kingdom by his agents and armies, they try to counterattack by fomenting revolts, which are always crushed (the final triumph of liberty was hastily concocted by Alex Raymond at the outbreak of the war). "Flash Gordon" is primarily related to, and at the beginning was greatly inspired by, the science-fantasy novels of Edgar Rice Burroughs, who had placed an earthly adventurer in a similar situation on Mars; like Mongo, Mars presented a combination of medieval society and technical progress. Other episodes, however, are more reminiscent of the poetry of Abraham Merritt (particularly in "The Moon Pool"). Above and beyond these ties with contemporary science-fiction, Flash Gordon is the direct descendant of a certain type of Anglo-Saxon hero, for example, Peter Wilkins, hero of a novel of 1750, and, more remote in time but a very definite influence, Robin Hood, in his struggle against authority. Upon penetrating more deeply behind the obvious sources, we discover the spirit of the work, and perceive that this is a completely typical epic. Before 1938, when Raymond rationalized Mongo, we find the same type of unbalanced society characteristic of the novels of the Round Table: there is no economic life, and fortified towns and castles rise in the midst of deserts. The successive episodes rarely unfold in contiguous countries; there is always a voyage (by air), shipwreck, and discovery of an unknown country with extraordinary features. This is the ancient type of narrative that the ancient Irish called *imrama* (navigation): the hero Maeldun discovers the underwater island, that of the giant ants, or huge birds, just as Flash discovers the land of winged men, the country under the sea, that of the caverns, and so on. Raymond has peopled his work with an astonishing bestiary: he demonstrates that he was very consciously thinking of Hercules, Perseus, and other vanquishers of monsters. To return to less conscious influences, however: Raymond has made of Flash an epic hero so deserving of this name that the definition given of Tristan in a preface by Gaston Paris fits him exactly:

"The hero, a demi-god rather than a man . . . a killer of deer and wild boars, and skilled in dismembering game, an incomporable fighter and jumper, a daring navigator . . . invincible in battle, a killer of monsters, protector of his followers, merciless to his enemies [this does not apply to Flash], living an almost superhuman life, a constant object of admiration, devotion and envy."

Every word of this could be illustrated by pictures from "Flash Gordon." However, this strip cannot be included in the same class with authentic epics. Its affinities link it instead to the baroque novels of knighthood of the Renaissance, Amadis de Gaule, the angry Roland, Persiles. In both cases there are departures in search of adventure, queen-magicians in love with the hero, the jealousy of his female companion, episodes that could succeed each other indefinitely, bizare names. "Flash Gordon," like these earlier models, is completely divorced from religion. It could not, however, adopt their frank sensuality.

We must realize that the comic strip is not an isolated phenomena completely divorced from all tradition—on the contrary. Insofar as it is a so-called "popular" art, it is receptive to many more traditions and influences than the "official" arts, which are more or less sclerosed or trapped within themselves. We must also realize that the practice of identifying certain forms of imagination, certain techniques, and certain ages is historically false. For example, the epic is not only a written form confined to a part of antiquity and the Middle Ages; it is also a form of imagination that can be expressed by means other than writing. Here again the comic strip belongs to a movement. For fifty years we have been living a great age of the epic, but it has been manifested particularly in the cinema and in certain comic strips. Their conventions, and those of the Western, are also its conventions. There also exists a written current, recognizable in science-fiction, that is particularly striking in the works of Eddison and Tolkien. It is obvious that the boundaries of the discussion must be widened and that the comic strip is not the only genre whose existence is misjudged. There exists an entire trend that does not fall within the framework of traditional studies and that has not even been recognized, because it should belong to the domains of art history and the history of literature—both sluggish disciplines undeserving of the name of "history" and which have not yet realized that everything that exists merits study, particularly when its audience is counted in the thousands of millions every year. Sociologists have studied the phenomenon, but they have scarcely progressed beyond tabulations of percentages. We hope we have demonstrated that the world of the comic strip is not so simple as it is believed to be and that it is closely linked with reality, both present and past. Statistics have destroyed the myth that the comics are filled with violence. It is certain, on the other hand, that they preach individualism: for this reason they have had the honor of being persecuted by all the totalitarian regimes.

HOGARTH.

Burne Hogarth, "Tarzan." Copyright U.F.S.

10

narrative technique

Having become a method of expression, thanks to a special artistry that is embodied in each cartoonist in the form of a style, the comic strip has now become a vehicle of communication like the movies and television. Like these methods of communication, however, it is caught between the picture and the text, and its fundamental problem is the respective apportionment of these two constituent elements. In the case under consideration, the picture becomes of primary importance. Originally the comic strip was hardly more than a series of illustrations for a text regarded as the basic element, since written narrative constitutes the fundamental narrative method of civilized man. This text unfolded without consideration for the illustration, and only when the text was utilized for description of, and comment on, the action of the cartoon in order to complement and make the latter more intelligible did an authentic comic strip come into existence.

For a long while the only manifestation of the written expression was a text placed beneath the picture. This is the case in such "ancestors" as Christophe's "Sapeur Camember" or "La Famille Fenouillard", and was generally the case in the European (French, Belgian, and Italian) comic strip until before the thirties. This procedure was even refined in Italy by the use of doggerel verses ("Bonaventura," "Quadratino," and others), and the Italians went so far as to omit the "balloons" of the American strips in order to replace them with texts in verse (Dirks's "The Captain and the Kids," and George McManus's "Bringing Up Father"). Later the text was incorporated into the picture, occupying spaces used or even deliberately left empty for this purpose; this practice very often resulted from the rejection of the "balloon," which disturbed (sometimes seriously) the esthetics of the picture. Three of the greatest cartoonists—Harold Foster, Alex Raymond, and Burne Hogarth—clung to this method, which preserves the integrity of the picture.

Beginning in 1900, however, the first "balloons" (or "phylacteries," to use the technical term) appeared; they consisted of a white area emphasized by a dark line that delimited a vaguely circular space intended for the text. The line issues from the mouths of the characters in a threadlike appendix, which gives the impression that they are dragging a balloon by its hanging appendage. The first balloons ("Yellow Kid" and even "Buster Brown") were shapeless and badly drawn: they introduced an unesthetic element that shattered the general harmony of the picture and even (on occasions when they were badly placed) completely destroyed the esthetics of the cartoon. The text once again became the great threat to the comic strip: it tended to invade the latter and to give priority to insipid chatter and needless gossip. This trend became particularly evident in Europe, especially in the adventures of Buck Danny (Charlier and Hubinon) or even in the works of Jacobs—although in the latter, the balloon, which had quickly become rectangular, fitted perfectly into the strip by geometric fusion. This tendency can sometimes be found in Walt Kelly's "Pogo," but here the balloon is part of the general esthetics or at least the mood, especially in the form of Gothic letters or varied typographical characters.

To this use of the balloon can be related the infinitely varied expression of sounds, onomatopoeia, unexpressed thoughts, memories, dreams, and so on. The most usual manifestations are in the form of a picture of a lighted electric bulb, symbolizing the sudden appearance of a "luminous" idea after a period of great perplexity, or of a circular saw cutting into a log (Knerr) to indicate the sonorous snores of a

1. John Cullen Murphy, "Ben Bolt." Copyright King Features Syndicate, Inc.

2. Martin Branner, "Winnie Winkle." Copyright Chicago Tribune–New York News Syndicate.

3. Milton Caniff, "Male Call." Copyright Milton Caniff.

4. Mell Lazarus, "Miss Peach." Copyright Publishers-Hall Syndicate.

5. Hergé, "Tintin." Copyright Casterman.

6. Walt Kelly, "Pogo." Copyright Publishers-Hall Syndicate.

7. Walt Kelly, "Pogo." Copyright Publishers-Hall Syndicate.

8. Roba, "La Ribambelle." Copyright Ed. Dupuis.

Balloon No. 5:
"This must be a big one! Just listen to that racket!"

9. Morris, "Lucky Luke." Copyright Ed. Dupuis.

10. Franquin-Roba, "Spirou et les Hommes Bulles" (Spirou and the Bubble-Men). Copyright Ed. Dupuis.

11. Uderzo-Goscinny, "Astérix et Cléopâtre." Copyright Dargaud.

12. Knerr, "The Katzenjammer Kids." Copyright King Features Syndicate, Inc.

13. Walt Kelly, "Pogo." Copyright Publishers-Hall Syndicate.

14. Franquin, "Spirou et les Plans du Robot" (Spirou and the Robot's Plans). Copyright Ed. Dupuis.

15. Franquin, "Jidehem." "Gaston."

Balloon No. 11:
"How do you say 'speak'?"

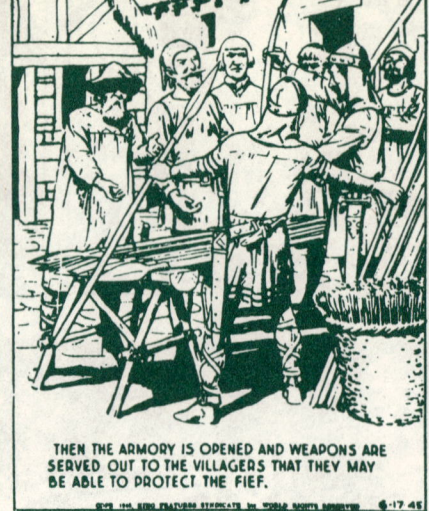

1. Harold Foster, "The Medieval Castle." Copyright King Features Syndicate, Inc.

2. Alex Raymond, "Flash Gordon." Copyright King Features Syndicate, Inc.

3. Burne Hogarth, "Tarzan." Copyright U.F.S.

4. Schulz, "Peanuts." Copyright U.F.S.

sleeper. This symbolism is also expressed in the accumulation of a variety of graffiti: to denote swearwords, the expression of which is forbidden by the moral code; it may even depict entire scenes illustrating a dream or a memory, as is often the case in Knerr's "The Katzenjammer Kids." This usage was particularly prominent, on the one hand in the works of Segar, one of whose characters, Professor Picric, invented a "solidifier of dreams" that causes the phantoms in the balloons to become tangible, living characters, and on the other by Pat Sullivan, whose lovable "Felix the Cat" utilized, with remarkable presence of mind, the contents of the balloons created by his imagination.

As for the picture itself (the cartoon, to use the technical term), it constitutes the basic element (we might call it the "vocabulary") of the comic strip. The frame of this picture was originally square or rectangular, its relative dimensions varying with the requirements of the layout. In 1905 it became panoramic in the works of Winsor McCay, extending outward in narrow horizontal (or vertical) rectangles, and thus giving an impression of amplitude, depth, and reality. McCay was not satisfied with this innovation, however, and went so far as to utilize the variable frame, enlarging or reducing his "field" in accordance with the dramatic and theatrical requirements of a page. Going still further, he used the same setting for two different actions, thus rediscovering after a fashion the ancient method of the simultaneous setting in the medieval theatre.

The frame, however, remained rectangular. Its tendency, in the twenties, was to indulge in an occasional whimsy by way of other geometrical forms: circles, ovals, and ellipses (the circles usually contained close-ups), but these attempts (see *Histoires en Images*) provided only a superficial variety, and quickly became a rigid, uninteresting system. In France between 1937 and 1948, Pellos struck out in a new direction by adopting a chaotic layout (see "Futuropolis") in which the various cartoons interpenetrate along incredible contours and combine following broken lines, zigzags, and half-circles, thus strengthening the dramatic tension of the page, which finally explodes in a visual and psychological shock of great intensity. It should be noted, moreover, that this layout is in perfect harmony with the author's nervous, unrestrained style. Ten years later, in "Atomas," Pellos adopted the "stellar" arrangement, in which the cartoons radiate from a central picture that commands the rest of the page. We can now readily understand how the general composition of the page plays an active role in the general esthetics and the dramatization of the story.

It may happen that the frame finally disappears and the pictures follow in succession, separated only by white spaces with indefinite contours, as in the strips of Herriman's "Krazy Kat." Herriman proved to be as imaginative and inventive in layout as he was in his narratives and settings; he indulged in a riot of elaborations as unexpected as they were varied, in which the cartoons are shuffled like a hand of playing cards, isolated in the center of a page without a frame, in polygonal circles similar to photographic diaphragms, the whole effect heightened by a symphony of colors that causes the pictures to dance. In our own day the younger Dirks has attempted to repeat (but with less vigor and whimsy) these same techniques in "The Captain and the Kids."

It was inevitable that the comic strip, a pictorial method of expression, would one day realize its kinship with the cinema and borrow some of its techniques, adapting them for its own particular use. For example, for a long time cartoonists had been satisfied to draw scenes in frontal view. Harold Foster and a few of his contemporaries introduced the innovation of using downward-angle and upward-angle shots, which brought about the elaboration of a dense, authentic narrative style. These attempts were rarely copied; this was especially true in Europe, where the artist became trapped in a retrogressive type of layout. It is true that the requirements of page composition and variations in size imposed by publishers remind us, especially in our time and even in the United States, of the severe restrictions on page layouts, but it is certain that very few artists realize the necessity of expressing themselves graphically by the creation of a dynamic movement in the composition of a page or a strip.

With these considerations we are led to a study of narrative techniques as such. The aim of this technique is to relate a story that unfolds in a series of events, the temporal development of which is achieved by successive leaps from one picture to the next, without any interruption in the continuity of the narration. The latter is concerned with the relationships that exist from cartoon to cartoon, from strip to strip, and even from page to page, and, of course, between each of these different constituent elements.

We may define several forms of narration by reference to time, the fundamental criterion of every story, that is, by reference to the relative position of events in their chronological order. First there is simple narration, in which a single plot is developed in a series of cartoons arranged in logical order of their temporal development. This type, in which the scenes unfold in their normal succession, is the one most frequently encountered. Then there is parallel

184

1. Dale Messick, "Brenda Starr." Copyright Chicago Tribune.

2. George Wunder, "Terry and the Pirates." Copyright Chicago Tribune.

3. Joseph Gillain, "Valhardi Contre le Soleil Noir" (Valhardi Against the Black Sun). Copyright Ed. Dupuis.

4. Jacques Martin, "Le Franc—Le Mystère Borg" (Le Franc—The Borg Mystery). Copyright Casterman.

5. Stan Drake, "The Heart of Juliet Jones." Copyright King Features Syndicate, Inc.

6. Eddy Paape, "Marc Dacier." Copyright Ed. Dupuis.

Balloons #3:
On the evening of the 18th . . .
"What a job!"
"Two minutes to eleven—almost time."

Balloon #4:
Jeanjean suddenly stops short.
"Look! Isn't that the Jaguar we saw yesterday?!"

Balloons #5:
"Are you so stupid as to believe you can force me to love you by threatening to marry Eve?"
"You don't believe it?"
"Just wait a minute!"
"What should I do? What can I do?"

Balloon #6:
Suddenly . . . "Doc! Lucas! Quick!"

7, 8. Burne Hogarth, "Drago." Copyright Post Hall Syndicate.

9. Ed. P. Jacobs, "Le Mystère de la Grande Pyramide" (The Mystery of the Great Pyramid). Copyright Ed. du Lombard.

10. Burne Hogarth, "Drago." Copyright Post Hall Syndicate.

11. Morris-Goscinny, "Lucky Luke Contre Joss Jamon" (Lucky Luke Against Joss Jamon). Copyright Ed. Dupuis.

12. Roy Crane, "Buz Sawyer." Copyright King Features Syndicate, Inc.

13. Cabu, "Le Grand Duduche." Copyright Ed. Dargaud.

14. Johnny Hart, "B.C." Copyright Publishers-Hall Syndicate.

15. Walt Kelly, "Pogo." Copyright Publishers-Hall Syndicate.

16. Roy Crane, "Wash Tubbs." Copyright N.E.A.

17. Roy Crane, "Buz Sawyer." Copyright King Features Syndicate, Inc.

Balloon #8:
"Look! It screws out of the base!"
Balloon #11:
"Run, old boy—we've got to beat it! They followed my trail!"
Balloons #13:
"Mr. Léon Kitrone, I'd like to present our hero, Duduche!"
"My . . . My selections aren't quite perfect. . . . Please be understanding!"

Winsor McCay, "Little Nemo." Copyright McCay Company. With permission of Mr. Woody Gelman.

narration, in which two or even more plots are simultaneously developed by juxtaposition of various scenes. This method attests, at least in its detail, to an indifference to time, and unites spatially distant actions the simultaneity of which was not obviously necessary in order to justify the demonstration. This technique, often utilized by Chester Gould in "Dick Tracy," resembles that used by the novelist John Dos Passos in literature. Its advantage is that it gives an impression of authentic, teeming life, while occasionally disturbing the general development of the story, the principal theme of which may be lost by the reader.

Lastly, there is "accelerated" narration, definitely the most interesting and most fertile type, which decomposes the action into a series of successive frames temporally very close to each other, frames that depict the situation from various angles. Christophe's narration of the insults endured by Fenouillard on the bridge of the steamer is a forerunner of this style; a contemporary example is John Prentice's delineation of the suspenseful scene in which an enormous mastiff is lying in wait for the hero, Rip Kirby. This technique, which is well suited to the expression of rapid action by a succession of cartoons, enables the artist to achieve effects no text could express.

Since 80 percent of European and American artists appear to be (or wish to be) ignorant of these methods of expression (especially of accelerated narration), and neglect the techniques of layout and arrangement that are the primary features of the comic strip and are germane to it, we shall limit our study to those cartoonists who have made fruitful innovations and have advanced narrative art in the comic strip. Burne Hogarth, Milton Caniff, and Frank Robbins, among others, sought to express animation, movement, and the appearance of temporal or spatial continuity within a cartoon, and this problem of kinetics was to monopolize the major part of the artists' efforts.

One of the most striking examples of accelerated narrative technique is found in a Tarzan page drawn by Burne Hogarth, which demonstrates the author's preoccupations and leads to a type of composition that sacrifices plot to esthetics. Let us consider a specific case.

First scene: a panoramic view of Tarzan in profile, running.

Second scene: same plane, background shortened, character seen from behind. The lines of force of the effort increase, and we feel an augmentation of internal tension.

Third scene: closer general view, the dramatic content of which indicates the hesitation of the surrounded Tarzan, who is searching for an escape.

Fourth scene: vertical view, in which Tarzan, surrounded, is about to make a supreme effort (p. 178).

In a single cartoon, Hogarth could have created an ambience by summarizing the scene in a long text, but by decomposing the action and opening up with a panoramic view (first scene), he created suspense and made the reader realize the bond between the antagonists (scenes 2 and 3) in the inevitable sequel that makes them opponents. The sudden appearance, in the foreground, of the Negroes who surround Tarzan is a shock device, and achieves a high dramatic and kinetic tension.

As regards the general layout of the pictures, until 1945 Hogarth utilized the four-strip system created by H. Foster. That year saw the birth of Hogarth's own beloved brainchild, "Drago." This strip, with its silhouette-like characters on a white ground, elimination or interruption of the frame, silhouettes standing away from circles sometimes decorated in Japanese fashion, and variety of types of frames, was an abortive attempt to break away from "Tarzan's" traditional-type frames. Upon resuming "Tarzan" in 1947, Hogarth adopted a new formula better suited to the dynamics of his style: three horizontal and three vertical strips. Over this grille, composed of nine equal rectangles, he ranged at ease, combining them in twos and threes, vertically, horizontally, or in four-block squares, thus obtaining a flexible, serene layout that accentuated his violently energetic style, and permitting variations in size that would be the envy of the movie, imprisoned in the immutable frame of the screen. In his last forty-six pages Hogarth once again modified his layout by limiting himself to three vertical strips over two horizontals. His draftsmanship then achieved maximum expressiveness by the extensive use of panoramic views and very dramatic scenes.

We should also mention that the lettering of the text was treated as carefully as the image with which it had to harmonize—whence the disastrous effect of translation. The same held true for the title crowning the strip.

Without continuing the development of the layout, as Burne Hogarth had done, Milton Caniff was one of the first to adopt the cinematographic style by careful attention to framing and lighting, and by his realization that rhythm and layout are closely linked. Caniff stresses that the layout acts through its appearance as a single unit; each cartoon is seen only from the viewpoint of dramatic significance, and acquires its full value and meaning only in relation to the surrounding cartoons. In "Rip Kirby" John Prentice adopted this technique, in which blacks and

1. Milton Caniff, "Terry and the Pirates." Copyright Chicago Tribune–New York News Syndicate.

2. Milton Caniff, "Steve Canyon." The first Sunday supplement, published on January 19, 1947. Copyright Publishers-Hall Syndicate.

STEVE CANYON
by MILTON CANIFF
WHY, IT'S STEVIE CANYON! ME SISTER IN SHANNON WRITES THAT YE PAID HER A PERSONAL CALL!
THAT I DID! SHE LOOKS FINE!
GLAD TO SEE YOU BACK, MR. CANYON! MY BOY GOT THE SOUVENIR YOU SENT FROM EGYPT!
GOOD!
CHECKING IN, SARGE!
CAPTAIN CANYON! I REALLY SWEAT YOU OUT THIS LAST TRIP! HEY! I HAVE A FINANCIAL STATEMENT FOR YOU... YOU'LL NEVER REGRET HAVING BACKED ME ON THIS DEAL!...
WANT A FLOWER FOR YOUR BUTTONHOLE, MR. CANYON?
NOT TODAY, POSIE — BUT YOU AND YOUR MOM ARE ABOUT DUE TO SEE A MOVIE ON ME...
GOING UP?
THIS CAR, MR. CANYON! —AND FOR YOU WE DON'T WAIT TILL IT'S FULL! RIGHT, IRMA?
R-R-RAJAH!
OH... HERE IS MR. CANYON, NOW...
HORIZONS Unlimited
IT'S A MR. DAYZEE, SECRETARY TO COPPER CALHOON, THE BIG SHE-WOLF OF THE STOCK MARKET...
HMM—THEY CALL HER "THE COPPERHEAD" I WONDER IF SHE HOWLS OR HISSES?
MR. CANYON?... MISS COPPER CALHOON WISHES TO ENGAGE YOUR PROFESSIONAL SERVICES! PLEASE COME TO MISS CALHOON'S APARTMENT AT ONCE...
...BUT WHAT IF I DON'T WANT TO PLACE MY SERVICES AT THE COMMAND OF MISS COPPER CALHOON?
MIS-TER CANYON! PEOPLE DO NOT REFUSE WHEN SUMMONED BY COPPER CALHOON!
AND ALL THIS TIME I THOUGHT I WAS A PEOPLE! GOOD MORROW, MR. DOOZIE!
WHY, MR. DIZZY, WHAT YOU SAID!..AND ME SO YOUNG AND IMPRESSIONABLE! ...THE CLICK YOU HEAR WILL MEAN YOU'RE SOLOING!
WELL, IT WOULD HAVE BEEN NICE TO HAVE MONEY TO PAY THIS OFFICE RENT BUT I GUESS IT'S BAD FORM TO GET INTO REGULAR HABITS LIKE THAT...
COPPER! YOU HEARD ON THE EXTENSION WHAT STEVE CANYON SAID!.. I HAVE NEVER BEEN SO---
I WANT THAT MAN!! ...GET HIM!
1-19

190

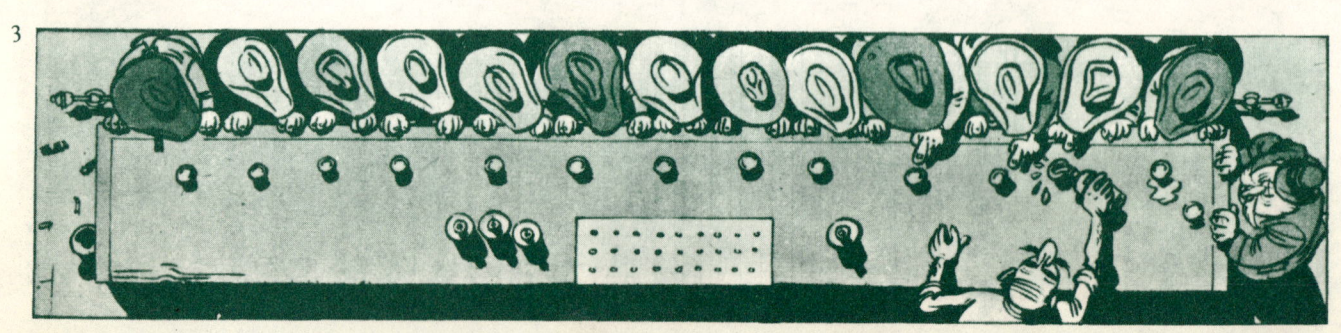

1

2

3

whites contrast violently (as in Caniff's work), with results whose excellence has been demonstrated daily for years. Alex Raymond was able to demonstrate the progressive development of the picture from stasis to dynamism; in "Flash Gordon" unusual angles, infinite depth, almost unlimited material techniques (the only limitations being the artist's possibilities), and innumerable trick pictures follow in endless succession. These techniques (especially the last of the three) have on occasion been astutely utilized in Europe by Hergé and Morris.

It must be admitted that very few cartoonists know how to interpret correctly the techniques adopted from the cinema; they are satisfied to assemble a variety of cartoons without any unifying plan to bind this medley into a whole. Close-ups, angle shots, general views, and others are all combined in defiance of good sense, without any consideration for the possible psychological significance of the frames being utilized for strictly descriptive purposes.

However, Gir (in "Fort Navajo"), Gigi (in "Scarlet Dream"), Hugo Pratt, and Crepax, seem to have understood the fundamental theories and possibilities of these techniques, and are making intelligent use of them in skillful compositions and attempts to achieve the best esthetic effect.

Regarding color, we note that it has been used particularly as a realistic element intended to accentuate the qualities (or defects) conferred on the comic strip by other techniques. Color, however, creates new esthetic problems, for it introduces tonal relationships and colored harmonies that must combine with, and even replace, the black-and-white relationships. These preoccupations may considerably modify the general effect of a page; and in the work of a conscientious artist, color composition raises new problems in addition to the usual ones. It often happens that a color page, "emptied" of its substance by publishing requirements, loses a great part of its value, especially when the expression of shadow-light relationships has been completely dependent on color: we then obtain flat or chaotic pictures.

Mention should be made of the originality of Leonard Starr, who with the help of color created his own narrative system. He achieved this by abandoning realistic utilization of color and playing with tones as if with black and white. In addition, he introduced narrative continuity by the creation of a controlled colored atmosphere that is repeated in various forms in each individual cartoon of the strip. By carrying light over from one cartoon to the next, he introduces a feeling of strangeness and alienation to which the reader cannot remain indifferent. George Wunder has realized that it is possible for color not to conform to reality but that it can help to create a psychological mood, and especially to reinforce the psychological and dramatic effects of the picture or the narrative by frequently daring applications.

All the foregoing considerations pertained to the "realistic" comic strip, and (with few exceptions) did not take the humor strip into consideration. Needless to say, the latter could have adopted the methods, problems, and improvements of the realistic strip, but it has its own requirements. It particularly tends to live within its frames and to form a self-contained unit. In the humor strip, as a general rule, the strip or page requires continuity only within its own limits and, in general, hardly needs to concern itself with a continuous sequence from one strip to the next. Moreover, the humor strip once again raises—and urgently—the question of the relationship between text and image, for in this case the text, which is intended to reveal a play on words or punch line, is very often of primary concern, and the picture usually serves only to reinforce or support it, the most favorable condition being achieved when the pictorial gag and the written gag combine and reinforce each other. Here again, the comic strip as such must be totally committed to the picture; the pages of Knerr's "The Katzenjammer Kids," consisting entirely of pictorial gags and atmosphere, or the strips of Johnny Hart's "B.C.," prove that the text can very well remain in the background. The work of George McManus ("Bringing Up Father") furnishes abundant proof that the humor strip can successfully make legitimate esthetic claims that in this case are expressed in remarkable demonstrations of a baroque art developed to the highest degree.

It may happen that the humor strip is also continued from one strip to another or from one page to

1. Harold Foster, "Tarzan." Copyright U.F.S.

2. Burne Hogarth, "Tarzan." Copyright U.F.S.

3. Morris, "Lucky Luke." Copyright Ed. Dupuis.

1, 2. Burne Hogarth, "Tarzan." Copyright U.F.S.

3. Harold Foster, "Prince Valiant." Copyright King Features Syndicate, Inc.

"GOT TO GIVE IT TO YOU IN THE CLEAR... THE KEY PHRASE IN THE THING IS "SALT-RISING BREAD""

BON VOYAGE!

ALEX RAYMOND

Opposite:

1. Milton Caniff, "Steve Canyon." Copyright Publishers-Hall Syndicate, Inc.

2. Alex Raymond, "Secret Agent X-9." Copyright King Features Syndicate, Inc.

3. Alex Raymond, "Flash Gordon." King Features Syndicate, Inc.

4. Alex Raymond, "Jungle Jim." Copyright King Features Syndicate, Inc.

John Prentice, "Rip Kirby." King Features Syndicate, Inc.

DON'T CUT ANY MORE! I WILL WRITE THE FORMULA FOR YOU...
© King Features Syndicate, Inc., 1964. World rights reserved.
JOHN PRENTICE 3-3
QUICKLY, THEN, DOCTOR. AND ACCURATELY.
THERE'S LEE, ALL RIGHT ... KNOW HIM FROM HIS PICTURES... BUT WHO'S THE MAN WITH THE KNIFE?
A WEAKENED LIFELINE SUDDENLY GIVES WAY.
© King Features Syndicate, Inc., 1964. World rights reserved.
A PLUNGE TOWARD ROCKY DEATH...
© King Features Syndicate, Inc., 1964.
THE ROPE...IT'S BROKEN!
MUST... GET... HER UP!
© King Features Syndicate, Inc., 1964. World rights reserved.
JOHN PRENTICE 3-6

Pellos, "Futuropolis." (See opposite for translation)

Hugo Pratt, "Sargento Kirk."

another, becoming a genuine narrative that goes beyond the scope of the single joke based on a fundamental theme, whose daily variations constitute its humorous expressions. This is often the case in Schulz's "Peanuts."

Our conclusion, then, is an affirmation of the indisputable narrative value of the comic strip, in the service of which complex techniques should be utilized so that it may become what in truth it is: a total and authentic art form.

"Futuropolis":

Summary of preceding chapters: Having saved his friend Maia from the Abyss, Rao, ordered off on a distant mission by the masters of Futuropolis, is attacked by a huge bear, and almost perishes. He then finds himself alone: By order of the masters, Maia has abandoned him.

XVI. Rao felt his heart filling with anger and rebellion. He had risked his life a hundred times, disobeyed the highest orders, and given up his people, in order to save this girl, and she had done nothing to appease the anger of the masters and try to come to his aid?

This time all was over! These laws were inhuman; this obedience was too often rewarded with ingratitude! He wanted nothing more to do with this race in whom cold reason had left no place for the feelings of the heart. From now on he would live alone in the wilds, far away from everyone!

Yet he stayed where he was, thinking. . . . As he looked around, he suddenly saw his weapon—that scepter-like weapon charged with continually replenished lightning power, which he thought he had lost in the battle. He seized it joyfully, and suddenly felt stronger, invincible!

With new energy, he began walking.

But after several hours, for the first time he felt fatigue overtaking him. Under his torn clothing, he was cold. In addition, he was hungry. He looked in his belt for his supply of concentrated food.

Terrified, he realized that he had lost it! An irreparable disaster! What would become of him? . . . But he refused to be defeated. On the contrary, this new event aroused his courage. Since he had renounced his own people, from now on he would live like primitive man, who ate the flesh of animals!

He had now arrived in a less desolate region, carpeted with stubby grass instead of snow. . . . Upon reaching the crest of a low rise, he saw on the other slope a small flock of animals pasturing. Remembering what he had learned, he decided that they were deer.

Excited by hunger and the sight of this game, which awakened in him buried instincts inherited from his distant ancestors, he leaped, carried away by a wild energy, forgetting his wounds, his fatigue, his worries, and revivified by strange new forces. . . .

The flock fled, with great leaping bounds, and he went after them. Despite his weariness, his body was so supple and strong that he felt he could quickly do battle with these agile animals. And he delayed making use of his weapon in order to prolong this exciting struggle.

Finally, he decided the moment had come. . . . Under other circumstances he would have admired these gentle, timid animals and respected their lives. But he had become a primitive creature of wild instincts. Choosing his victim among the flock, he aimed his infallible weapon in its direction.

Before he could complete this movement, a violent shock paralyzed his arm. A dazzling flame enveloped and momentarily blinded him. When he regained his sight, and consciousness returned to his confused brain, he saw that he was now holding only a remnant of inert metal.

He instinctively raised his eyes.

Then he saw in the sky a long, missile-shaped object, which was moving rapidly south. Suddenly he understood. The creative genius of the masters of Futuropolis must have quickly invented a flying machine, which until now had been unnecessary. . . . This was what had given him the shock!

It had undoubtedly been sent to watch him, punish him if need be, and force him to admit defeat! . . .

No! He accepted the overwhelming struggle! He would not submit to this merciless law! He would prove to himself that it was possible to live elsewhere than in this world where everything, even the human heart, was made of steel!

Balloons:
"Room, Buddy!"
"Hang it! Styx has tricked me!
"Aha! You thought you could get away from me! If Zarda were here, she'd appreciate the situation. Ha, Ha!"
"Good habits are never lost. . . . What do you intend to do with me?"
"Use you. The fumes you are about to breathe will kill you only after forty-eight hours . . . unless you swallow the antidote. . . . So I'm sure I'll have your close cooperation."

Robert Gigi-Claude Moliterni, "Scarlet Dream."

Balloons:
Meanwhile, in another hotel in Venice . . .
"Miss Roselli! I need a car immediately! May I borrow yours, honey?"
"What's the big hurry! And what's this word 'honey'?"
"Okay! But be careful you don't have any accidents!
Stella and Johnson are still on their vacation . . .
"We'll stop in Napoli. . . . Then in Sicily . . . We'll rent a motorboat. . . ."

Crepax, "Neutron." Copyright Crepax/Figure.

202

1

Vite, capitaine, vite, sautons!... Notre wagon s'est détaché et va redescendre la pente...
Sautez, vite!...

2

HA HA HA HA HA HA HA HA HA HA HA HA HA HA HA HA HA
Eh bien! ça promet d'être gai!
TRRRING TRRRING
Allo, j'écoute...
Allô-ô-ô-ô, j'écou-ou-te!
Non, madame, ce n'est pas la boucherie Sanzot ...Non, madame, vous avez formé un faux numéro...
TRRRING! TRRRING! TRRRING!
Vas-tu la boucler, oui ou non, espèce de vieille perruche bavarde!...
Allô-ô-ô-ô, j'écou-ou-te!

3

60

Balloons (opposite):
1. "Quick, Captain, let's jump out! Our car has got loose and is going to roll back down the slope!"
"Jump, quick!"

2. "Well, this is going to be fun!"
"Hello!"
"H-E-L-L-L-O!"
"No, lady, this isn't Sanzot's Butcher Shop . . ."
"No, lady, you've got the wrong number . . ."
"Are you going to shut up or not, you noisy old parrot!"
"H-E-L-L-L-O!"

Balloon No. 4:
"Watch where you're driving, Boss!"
Hergé, "The Adventures of Tintin."
1. "Le Temple du Soleil" (The Temple of the Sun).
2. "Les Bijoux de la Castafiore" (The Jewels of the Castafiore).
3. "L'Etoile Mystérieuse" (The Mysterious Star). Copyright Casterman.
4. Maurice Tillieux, "Gil Jourdan." Copyright Dupuis. A magnificent example of narrative technique.

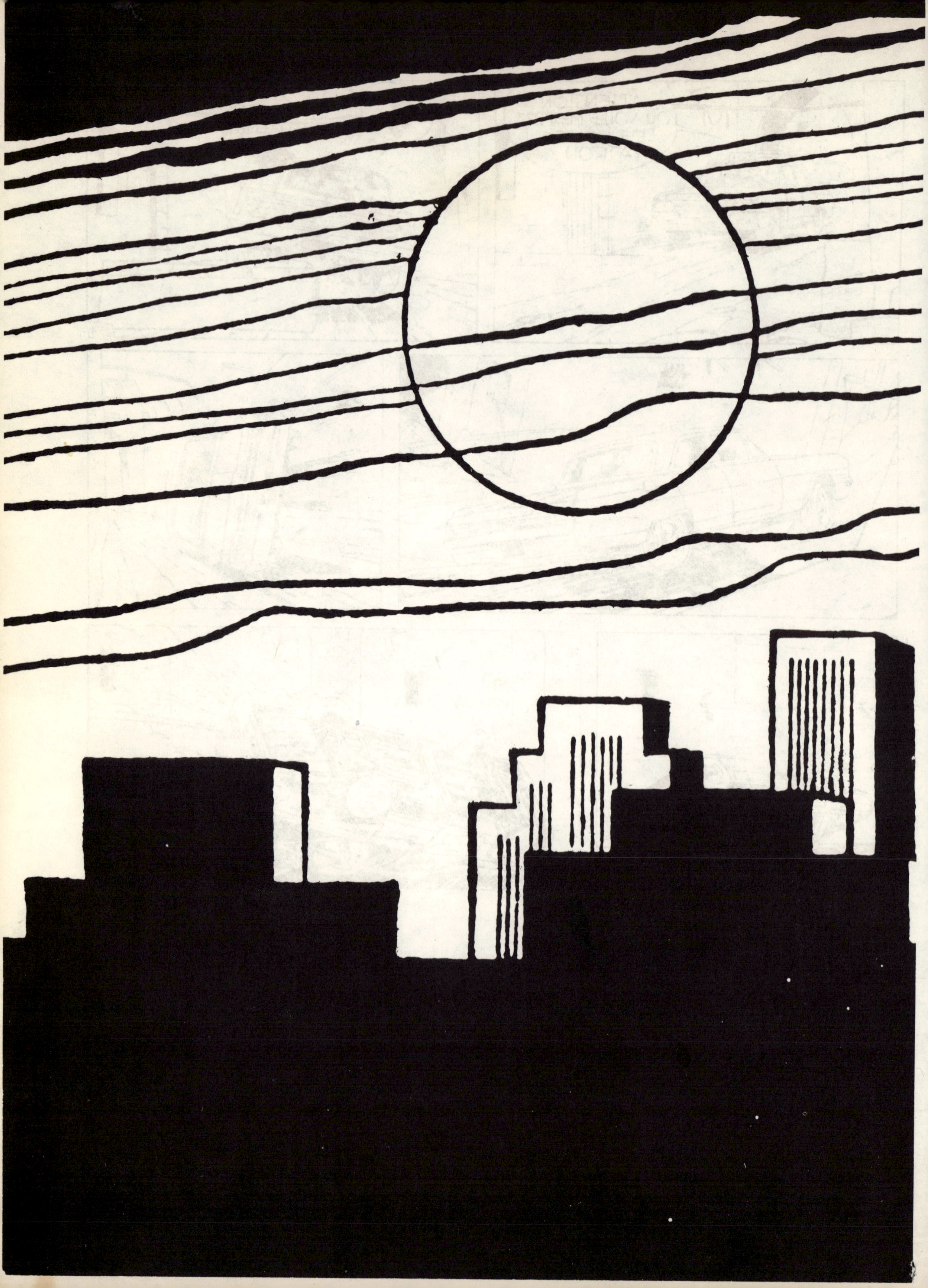

11

esthetics and signification

At its inception, in the days of the first casual drawings by Dirks and Opper, the style of the comic strip was borrowed from magazine illustrations and newspaper caricatures. Winsor McCay was its first artist, the first to acquaint the comic strip with the achievements of the other graphic arts. He was influenced by the illustration of the English fairy-tale books, but his technique was inspired particularly by Art Nouveau. His surfaces—flat expanses laid out in a complicated puzzle—are often outlined with the heavy black stained-glass-window line frequently seen in *Belle Epoque* posters, particularly those of Mucha and Eugène Grasset (this type of line is still being used, for example, by Al Capp in "Li'l Abner"), and his colors—purples, oranges, greens, dark blues—also belong to Art Nouveau.

While McCay invented an astonishing imagery, it was not typical of the comic strip, and created no "school." James Swinnerton was the first to simplify draftsmanship, eliminate pen scribbling, and depict his characters with a clean outline supported by the carefully delineated black areas of their clothing ("Little Jimmy"). His example, as well as that of the French and English posters with their cut-out silhouettes, and the influence of masculine dress with its black garments, did not eliminate mediocre scribblers, but it did contribute to the creation of the first comic-strip style, which was characterized by the vigor of black silhouettes geometrically arranged on a white background, sometimes forming almost abstract areas. Cliff Sterrett ("Polly and Her Pals,") and George McManus ("Bringing Up Father") are perfect examples of this style. The former claimed to have been influenced by cubism; McManus, whose style was very decorative, was also influenced by fashion design (his first career), but he was above all a perfect stylist, simultaneously creating characters, costumes, and setting.

Another trend developed during the twenties: hatched drawing, much favored by Harold Gray and Herriman. This style found its master after 1930 in Frank Godwin ("Connie" and "Eagle Scout" in collaboration with Paul Powell).

During the same period, the poster style and advertising drawing were evolving in the direction of realism. All during the twenties its influence was felt in the comic strip, at first imperceptibly, then with increasing strength. Finally, in 1929, a well-known poster artist, Harold Foster, introduced realism into the comic strip.

This appearance of classical realism—or rather idealism—in the comic strip, beginning with Foster's adaptation of "Tarzan," followed by Alex Raymond in "Flash Gordon" and Burne Hogarth's version of "Tarzan," launched a relatively short but exciting phenomenon that had widespread repercussions: in a few years (1930–1940) the comic strip absorbed the entire tradition of classical painting and draftsmanship. The choice of the character of Tarzan by United Features Syndicate was most decisive. His naked body permitted of no caricatural approximation: an artist with a knowledge of anatomical drawing would have to be hired, and, since "Tarzan's" supernumaries were animals, he would also have to be an excellent *animalier*. The episodes, which took place in the African jungles, required that he be

Chester Gould, "Dick Tracy." Copyright Chicago Tribune– New York News Syndicate.

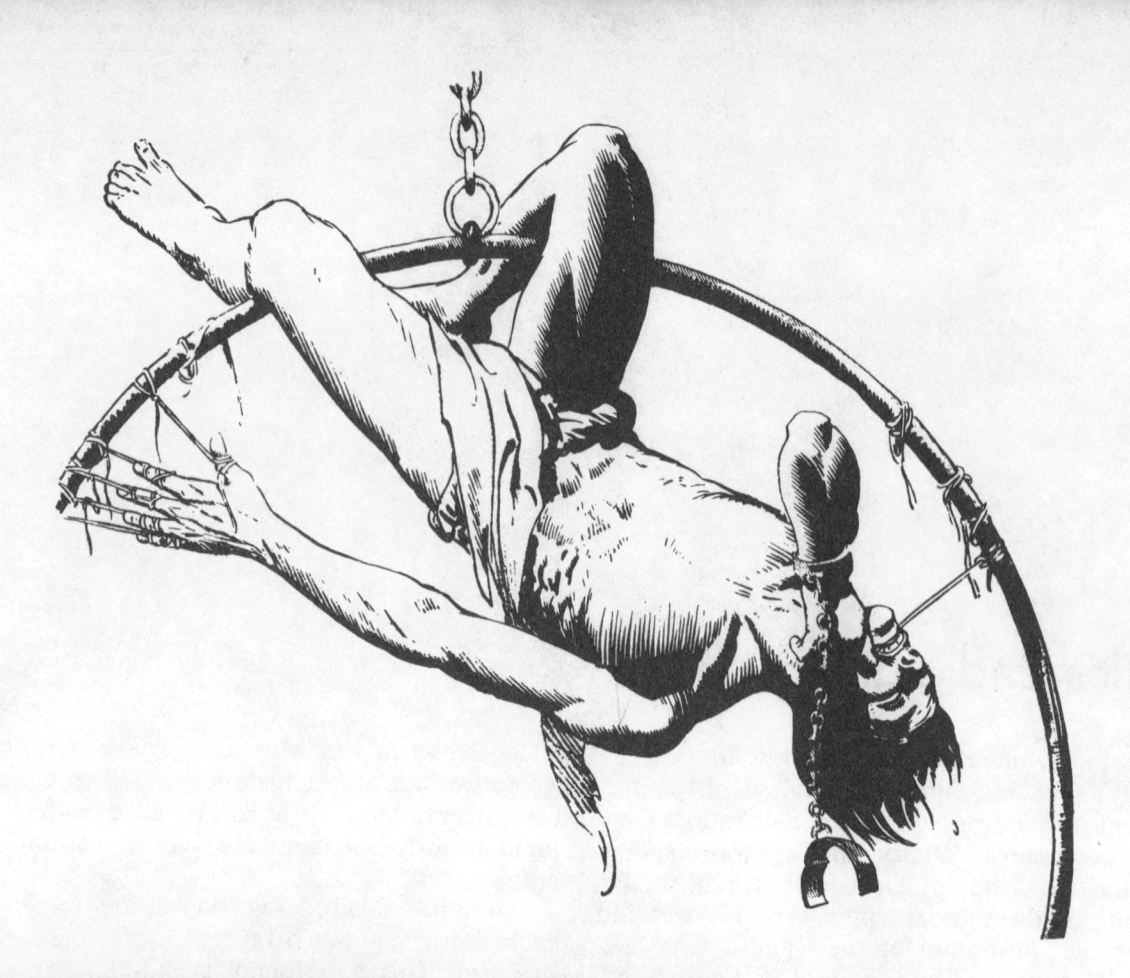

1

2

UNABLE TO STAND THE SEARING HEAT, MING'S SOLDIERS RETREAT IN DISORDER----

3

4

5

The Classical Heritage:
1. Harold Foster, "Prince Valiant." Anatomy.
Copyright King Features Syndicate, Inc.

2. Alex Raymond, "Flash Gordon." Composition.
Copyright King Features Syndicate, Inc.

3. Alex Raymond, "Jungle Jim." The Portrait.
Copyright King Features Syndicate, Inc.

4. Frank Godwin, "Rusty Riley." The Portrait.
Copyright Editor Press.

5. Burne Hogarth, "Tarzan." Composition.
Copyright U.F.S.

1

2

AS FAR AS THE EYE CAN SEE IN ALL DIRECTIONS ARE THESE STOCK YARDS, 25000 PENS, 75000 PEOPLE EMPLOYED IN EVERY MINUTE, NIGHT AND DAY, SUNDAYS INCLUDED, OF THE 365 DAYS, FIFTY CATTLE, SHEEP AND HOGS ARE DRESSED FOR DINNER HERE! IT IS HARD TO BELIEVE, BUT IS ONLY TOO TRUE! MUST YOU GO?—

YES! IT IS GETTING LATE! WE WILL TAKE YOU DOWN TOWN AND LEAVE YOU, MUCH AS WE HATE TO DO SO. WE MUST BE IN MILWAUKEE NEXT SUNDAY!

equally skilled in evoking the luxurious vegetation in the midst of which "Tarzan" unfolds. Thus an artist with classical training was needed.

(Let us recall that "Tarzan" also helped to introduce the cinematographic narrative and the scriptwriter to the comic strip. Until then the cartoonist had been the creator of the entire work. Many people protested against this specialization, particularly Foster himself, who abandoned "Tarzan" to be the sole author of "Prince Valiant.")

The next step was drawing from live models (currently practiced by Alex Raymond), following the most classic methods of drawing: skeleton and large basic masses, then the muscles, and finally the hair and clothing. With realism came another requirement: the hero must always be recognizable from all angles, since this new type of drawing was accompanied by a new narrative style that varied the angles of vision and occasioned much improvement of the characters. The comic-strip author is facing a genuinely new situation in the history of art: he is obliged to produce portraits by the hundreds, and a live model, as well as systematic collections of photographs, is indispensable to his work. The series of faces of the Emperor Ming (in "Flash Gordon") is certainly the most remarkable collection of portraits in the comic strip. In Foster's work the faces are slightly less varied, and their psychological expression is less developed. Godwin, with his skillful pen crosshatching techniques, is a master of old people's heads.

Animal drawing was the special domain of Foster and Hogarth in "Tarzan" and "Prince Valiant"; they enriched its history with an unexpected postscript in which we discover superb fragments (the gigantic octopus at the bottom of the well into which Prince Valiant is about to be thrown, innumerable horses, Hogarth's angry lions, a gleaming black panther by Foster), but their contemporary successors have not been able to maintain their standards. The animal, even the horse, is disappearing from the comic strip, or is becoming a mythical creature known only from photographs. Only Roy Crane, who has his own stable, and Stan Lynde ("Rick O'Shay"), a Montana cattle raiser, still know what a live horse is.

Perspective in the comic strip was not a discovery of the thirties: it had become too much a part of ordinary vision not to have been known before then. It was found in the street scenes of "Yellow Kid," of course, but it was in Winsor McCay's work ("Little Nemo") that it was first used for more than the routine of ordinary illustration. McCay was a master of architectural perspective. He employs it constantly, in the successions of his baroque palaces, in his shots taken from the feet of skyscrapers, and in his urban landscapes, in order to suggest urban infinity and immensity. When he cannot include a sufficiently large area in his panoramas, he does not hesitate to abandon classical perspective for a spherical perspective that is one of the innumerable surprises of the comic strip. Since McCay, no one has fully exploited the possi-

1. Harold Foster, "Prince Valiant." Animal Drawing. Copyright King Features Syndicate, Inc.

2. Winsor McCay, "Little Nemo." In the hands of Winsor McCay, perspective was the first tradition of classicism to be adopted by the comic strip. He even attempted curvilinear perspective; this view of the Chicago stockyards is not the only example to be found in his work. With permission of Mr. Woody Gelman. Copyright McCay Company.

The comic strip closely resembles the illumination in its method of execution. The illumination was executed in workshops by specialists; unpublished studies have even demonstrated that specialization was far advanced, at least in the fourteenth and fifteenth centuries. There was a supervisor who assigned the work of illustration, decided on the layout, and sometimes made sketches. His team consisted of a calligrapher, who did the lettering, an illuminator for the scrollwork borders, colored letters, and miscellaneous ornamentation, and one or more painters who did the actual illustrations. Poorly erased instructions of the supervisor can be seen in the margins of certain manuscripts: "Job, Ch. IV: An old man who speaks to Job and shows him a dead lion," "Seventeenth Book: Here, how the Emperor of Germany and King Louis of France besieged Damascus," "Rémy, leave this space empty; I shall do the face which belongs here" (note from the calligrapher to the illuminator). It was recently discovered that there was also a color assistant: under the colors can still be seen conventional signs, visible by transparency, which are always the same for a given color. The painter drew in the miniatures, noted their color by means of a code, and turned them over to another worker for coloring.

210

1

2

The Landscape:

1. William Ritt and Clarence Gray, "Brick Bradford." Copyright King Features Syndicate, Inc.

2. Roy Crane, "Buz Sawyer." Copyright King Features Syndicate, Inc.

3. Etchevery-Quello (Martin Sièvre), "Les Aventures de Ragnar." Copyright Vaillant.

Picture 3: Every wave is now an insurmountable mountain. Olaf's boat is caught in a trough. He can no longer see the others. The sail is lowered. The Vikings, who are part of their ships, face the storm.

4. Harold Foster, "Prince Valiant." Copyright King Features Syndicate, Inc.

CHAQUE VAGUE EST MAINTENANT UNE MONTAGNE INFRANCHISSABLE. LE BATEAU D'OLAF S'EST TROUVÉ PRIS DANS UN REMOUS. IL A PERDU LES AUTRES DE VUE. LA VOILE EST BAISSÉE. LES VIKINGS, QUI NE FONT QU'UN AVEC LEUR BATEAU, AFFRONTENT LA TEMPÊTE.

Hogarth, "Tarzan." Copyright U.F.S.

bilities of perspective, which is merely utilized in a competent manner.

The pictorial landscape, which also followed in the wake of "Tarzan," is an achievement of the thirties, less evident in "Tarzan" and 'Flash Gordon" (where it is somewhat unrealistic) than in "Prince Valiant." Foster was originally a painter; a worshiper of nature in her wild state, he has lived in the Canadian Northwest, a fact that is evident in his work. Every possible type of landscape can be found in "Prince Valiant": lakes, forests, swamplands, and fjords, under sunlight or rain, all of them immense, all sprawling under vast expanses of sky. "Prince Valiant" is one of the few adventure strips that have seasons of the year. Several other cartoonists occasionally allot a role to landscape —Robbins (his landscapes are dark and massive), Clarence Gray (who was particularly fond of moonlight reflections on the sea), Milton Caniff (an impressionist in black and white)—but only Fred Harman ("Red Ryder") and Roy Crane ("Wash Tubbs," later "Buz Sawyer") can rival Foster, in very different styles. Harman was also a painter of Western scenes, the spacious landscapes of which play a major role in Red Ryder's rides. Crane introduced atmospheric perspective into the comic strip; he is a master of misty perspectives of distance. The two gray tones in double-tone paper permit him to overlap mountainous areas, or islands in the sea, behind a vigorous foreground, with effects frequently evocative of certain Chinese landscape paintings.

Also in the thirties (prolonged beyond this period by Hogarth in "Tarzan"), composition entered the comic strip. Since the early days the cartoonists had naturally followed certain elementary rules for arranging figures in the picture. McManus very often situated them at random. Improved methods borrowed directly from the Renaissance and Baroque artists were used by Raymond and Hogarth, who was an admirer of Michelangelo. For several years, beginning in 1935, he created numerous compositions in the form of spirals, pyramids, and St. Andrew's crosses, in which all the movements are balanced. His pictures were articulated on diagonals or on the fourth or one third of the sides, and, for two or three years, on the Golden Number (Burne Hogarth claims that this was purely instinctive and that he did not make use of a geometrical grille). Hogarth attempted to endow not only his pictures but also his pages with a unified composition in which movements correspond, are reversed, or balance each other in every direction. Foster's composition, less obviously geometrical, is more calm and more Davidian, yet astonishingly skillful in the placement of the characters.

It is possible to distinguish a baroque period (or at least a baroque current) in the comic strip, represented by Hogarth and Raymond (who abandoned it rather abruptly to concentrate on drawing dignified, impassible silhouettes). McManus made an important contribution to this trend with his frenzied setting for "Bringing Up Father," an exaggeration that is characteristic of his work during the thirties.

Other classical rules can be detected in the comic strip. The practice of enlarging the foliage to the scale of the picture, well known to Poussin and his contemporaries, was generally applied by comic-strip artists (for example, in the work of Roy Crane), as was the practice of sacrificing the less important parts. (The reduction of an entire landscape to a wavy line is an extreme application of this principle.)

Whereas the classical style was conceived for color, for the Sunday strips, around 1938–1940 the group Caniff-Andriola-Robbins perfected a different, very black-and-white style that was to become the wonder of the daily strips, and from then on this dualism of style became very prominent in the comic strip. The black-and-white style, in which the cartoonist skillfully distributes India ink with a brush, is more pictorial than graphic. This style, with its violent contrasts of light and shadow, recalls the lighting effects of the film; its fluidity makes it more suitable for a cinematographic type of narration, whereas in the works of Raymond or Foster there was a risk, due to the perfection of the draftsmanship, of concentrating interest exclusively on the picture, considered as an end in itself. Here again, however, this was actually a deliberately brutal application of the chiaroscuro of

---

"Wishing to give a new quality to the drawing of the Sunday strips, I wanted to link each picture with the others in a single total design. Despite the divisions between the pictures, I was seeking a total animation of the page, such as Michelangelo had achieved in the Sistine ceiling, divided into distinct panels but united in a single grandiose schema.

"Being aware of such structural styles as the golden number and dynamic or bilateral symmetry, I was most impressed by Mannerism and the Baroque: Caravaggio's 'Entombment,' Rubens' 'Lion Hunt,' Géricault's 'The Raft of the Medusa' and many others. I have never ceased to marvel at Michelangelo."

—Burne Hogarth, from an unpublished letter

MR. JIGGS I BELIEVE
HOW DO YOU DO MR. JIGGS-
DIDN'T I MEET YOU BEFORE?
McMANUS
6-4

1

2

3   In a moment the fight breaks out!

4   "He's disappeared.... Yet I wasn't ten yards behind him."

The Style of the Twenties:

1. George McManus, "Bringing Up Father." Copyright King Features Syndicate, Inc.

2. Edgar Martin, "Boots." Copyright N.E.A.

3. Frank Godwin (and Paul Powell), "Eagle Scout Roy Powers." Godwin was noted for his mastery of the technique of cross-hatching. Copyright Ledger Syndicate.

4. Frank Godwin, "Connie." Copyright Editor Press.

216

Milton Caniff, "Terry and the Pirates."
Copyright Chicago Tribune–New York News Syndicate, Inc.

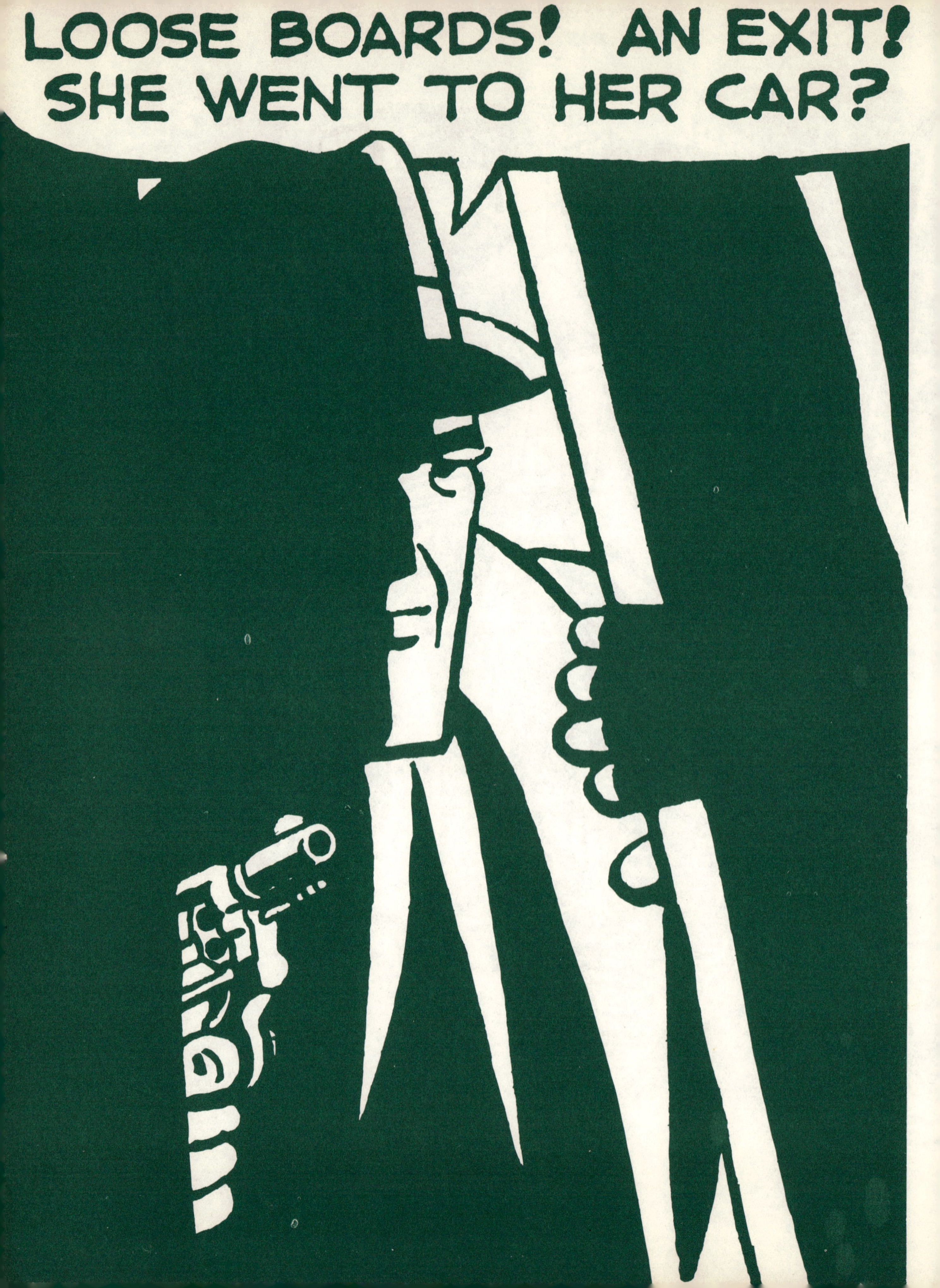
LOOSE BOARDS! AN EXIT! SHE WENT TO HER CAR?

the painters. From the technical point of view the contrast between Raymond and Caniff is analogous to the one that separates Piero della Francesca from Caravaggio. In the "black style," cinematographic framing replaces pictorial composition, which has also disappeared from the color strips. By continuous experimentation, Roy Crane perfected his own style; he too made vigorous use of blacks, but preferred to use the silhouette, on a background of gray or white. The cross-hatched style *à la* Godwin disappeared from the United States with the death of this artist after the war. On the other hand, it is universal among the Latin artists and in England; Salinas and Del Castillo are virtuosos of this technique. The texture of Del Castillo's backgrounds occasionally betrays the influence of Villon. In addition, since the forties the illustration of the "sophisticated" magazines has had an influence on the realistic strip.

Reaction to this realism has taken the form of a trend toward the creation of a new caricatural style, in which an extensive knowledge of distortion, decisive line, and placement of figures in the pictures is hardly concealed; "Li'l Abner," "Peanuts," "B.C.," and "Wizard of Id" are its principal representatives. An important use of white backgrounds obliterates space in a manner reminiscent of certain characteristics of contemporary painting (see the studies of Francastel).

Numerous other influences—particularly of Walt Disney—have affected the comic strip. Disney propagated a round, firm, elastic style marked by equilibrium of movement, which played a considerable role in the French children's strip. ("Pogo," by Walt Kelly—who trained in Disney's studio—is derived in large part from this style.) The influences of Degas and his line, and of Toulouse-Lautrec's posters, are still strong. The enormous objects, in shadow in the foreground, so often utilized in "sophisticated" strips to create the mood, are a direct descendant of the double bass whose keys can be seen in the foreground of Toulouse-Lautrec's "Jane Avril" poster. Color is often utilized in a manner reminiscent of Lautrec's use of it in a Moulin Rouge poster ("La Goulue"), in which the brownish silhouette of Valentin le Désossé is a close-up against a very luminous middle ground and a background of silhouettes.

The cartoonists also welcomed novelties that had been tried and then practically abandoned in painting: for example, the decomposition of movements. It is common, in the humor strips, to depict a character several times in the same picture in his successive poses; Wilhelm Busch and many other humorists had been doing so for years. In our day Lucy skipping rope ("Peanuts") is the true descendant of Duchamp's *"Nu Descendant un Escalier"* (Nude Descending a Staircase).

We believe we have demonstrated, by means of the illustrations in this book, that based on these influences and successive styles the comic strip has created original works of which it can no longer be said that they are not art. Its most original contribution has unquestionably been in the area of black-and-white esthetics, from 1920 to our own day. The examples given here could be multiplied a hundredfold; in this regard we may invoke Leone Battista Alberti's plaint, expressed in his *De Pittura:* "I would that educated painters realized that it is possible to exercise great industry and considerable art in the use of black and white exclusively, and that one must possess rare intelligence and perfect skill in order to properly utilize these two colors." We prefer to let these illustrations speak for themselves.

We must now try to place the comic strip within

The introduction of graphic realism into the comic strip raised the problem of the balloon. This symbolic element does not fit well into a realistic background and space. This was the same problem that faced painting when it began to turn toward realism in the fifteenth century, with regard to saints' halos, a symbolic element that, like the balloon, hung free in the air. Foster and Hogarth refused to place balloons in their drawings. Raymond used them in the beginning, then gave them up. Both before and since that time, certain series ("Felix" and "Pogo," for example) have directly attacked the problem, and treat the balloon as a real object that can be grasped, collided with, and deflated. Other artists are satisfied to pay careful attention to their placement and to harmonize their outline with the drawing of the picture or the frame. Some artists color them lightly. Trials were made of "negative" (that is, black with white letters) balloons (see Coulton Waugh, *The Comics*). Although it was not apparent at first sight, and although as late as 1925 not all the artists themselves were convinced of it, the dynamism of the line around the balloon is nevertheless a decisive factor in the drawing's success, which may be destroyed by a weakness in the line.

Chester Gould, "Dick Tracy." Chester Gould's style is expressionist, like that of Gray, but with a different technique: hardness of line, brutality of effects. Copyright Chicago Tribune–New York News Syndicate, Inc.

220

3

4

1. Alex Raymond, "Rip Kirby." Copyright King Features Syndicate, Inc.
2. John Prentice, "Rip Kirby." Copyright King Features Syndicate, Inc.
3. Fred Harman, "Red Ryder." Copyright N.E.A.
4. Leonard Starr, "Mary Perkins, on Stage." Copyright Chicago Tribune–New York News Syndicate.

1, 2, 3. Milton Caniff, "Terry and the Pirates." Copyright Chicago Tribune–New York News Syndicate.

4. Milton Caniff, "Steve Canyon." Copyright Publishers-Hall Syndicate.

5. Roy Crane, "Buz Sawyer." Copyright King Features Syndicate, Inc.

6. Frank Robbins, "Johnny Hazard." Copyright King Features Syndicate, Inc.

1. Frank Robbins, "Johnny Hazard." King Features Syndicate, Inc.

Balloons, No. 2:
"Spring! . . . It's a ghost! . . .
Don't come near me! . . . No! Don't hurt me! . . ."
"Oh, it's you, Pete! Answer me! Where's Jake?"

2. Joseph Gillain, "Jerry Spring." Copyright Dupuis.   3. Hergé, "Tintin." Copyright Casterman

4. Franquin, "Spirou." Copyright Dupuis.

Caption, No. 5:

Midnight! In the small Schtroumpf village, all is calm and quiet. . . .

5. Peyo, "Les Schtroumpfs." Copyright Dupuis.

Arturo del Castillo, "Randall."
Robert Gigi and Claude Moliterni, "Scarlet Dream."

its widest perspective, as has already been attempted for the study of its content. We have just seen that it can already be included in a network of relationships that link it with contemporary art. In some of its accomplishments it has absorbed the classical heritage; in all of them it depicts being and objects, simulates space, reveals a subject. Starting from this point, we can formulate certain working hypotheses. We may present the comic strip as a traditional (because a popular) art, the equivalent of those Quattrocento Florentine workshops that turned out works in accordance with Trecento rules for an intellectually retarded clientele. Or we may entertain the opposite hypothesis: the comic strip has hundreds of millions of readers, is gaining in importance, and has created its own style, based on those styles that have influenced it. It could therefore be considered, together with the cinema and photography, as the only contemporary living art. According to this hypothesis, painting, which has been cut off from the public for the past forty or fifty years, has withdrawn from the life of the world and its major events.

From this follows the consequence (and further problem) that in its most developed forms the comic strip propagates conventions and an esthetics that derive in large part from classical figuration, whether directly or through the intermediary of illustration and caricature. Under these fundamental aspects, it is the ring in the water of the Italian Renaissance that continues to spread over the surface of the pond. We must therefore determine the role that may be played by the comic strip in reaching (as it has been doing for approximately thirty years) civilizations that possessed a different figurative culture (note the great success of the American strips in prewar Japan, for example) or none at all (as in Africa), or, as in the Occident for the past sixty years, social classes that had not progressed beyond a naïve or caricatural imagery hardly capable of introducing them to the subtleties of composition by pyramid or Divine Proportion, as used by certain cartoonists.

Other working hypotheses could be suggested. The film and the comic strip may achieve unification of vision on a world scale, and this on a Western foundation. The way was paved, though on a very small scale, by commercial artwork disseminated by early peddlers, which influenced Japanese engraving and the pictography of the American Indians in the last century, just as it had influenced the Persian or Hindu miniature in the seventeenth century. On the other hand, the comic strip may succeed, four and a half centuries later, in adapting to the needs of the general public the simplified principles of an art that broke with the public at the time of the Renaissance, with its investigation of perspective and anatomy and the enigmatic subjects of Botticelli or the reliefs of the Temple of the Malatestas. Let us remember that in the opinion of certain specialists, popular art is a vulgarization of the achievements of the art of the elite.

It seems possible to distinguish, as a preliminary and very crude working hypothesis, a kind of alternation between the narrative-type arts and those arts that depict only the momentary or the immutable. The former tell a story with the assistance of a series of pictures. An example is furnished by the narrative arts of Egypt and the Orient, which depict the pharaohs' campaigns, abundantly illustrated and described on the temple walls.

After the art of Greece, which portrayed the moment, the end of the battle in which Achilles kills Penthesileus but not the events of the fight, which unfolds in its friezes the simultaneous aspects rather than the successive phases of a complex scene, Roman (and perhaps even Hellenistic) art partly reversed this trend with its triumphal columns of the emperors, which relate their military campaigns in a continuous spiral. The medieval period is, together with our own, the golden age of narrative art. In Old French, and even in sixteenth-century French, the word *histoire* (story, history) meant "picture." The seventh-century Ashburnham Pentateuch is decorated with genuine plates in which the pictures are separated by narrow white lines or architectural constructions. The characters (in the story of Jacob and Esau) move from one picture to another. Narrative series flourished particularly in the Romanesque period and down to the sixteenth century. The lives of Christ and the saints required series of pictures the sequence of which was imperative and which was strictly adhered to because it was based on history, theology, and morality. Legends of knighthood and commemorations of victories are depicted in the same manner; the Bayeux Tapestry is not a unique specimen. With the Renaissance there was a rupture; narrative art survived obscurely in popular imagery. While it is true that tapestry ensembles and series of paintings were devoted to lives of Alexander or Don Quixote, the pictures were not sequential. The end of the nineteenth century witnessed the rebirth of figurative narrative art, now more important than ever, with its two parallel and related manifestations, the film and the comic strip, both born together in the nineties.

Needless to say, this alternation is simply a working hypothesis, but it should point up the interest of a unifying viewpoint that will make possible the comparison and integration of phenomena too often regarded as anomalies that art history finds embarrassing and that it would prefer to ignore.

1. Roy Lichtenstein, "Viki" (1964). Leo Castelli Gallery

2. "Eddie Diptych" (1963).   3. "I know . . . Brad" (1963).    4. "OK Hot Shot" (1963).

Galerie Ileana Sonnabend, Paris

12

narrative figuration

Narrative figuration is not a continuation of the comic strip. The presence of certain paintings in the exhibition organized by the Musée des Arts Décoratifs, and this chapter itself, coming at the end of a book devoted for the most part to the history, esthetics, and sociology of the comic strip, could lead to confusion and the attribution to the authors of this book of intentions they do not possess. To determine the reasons for this undertaking, and the limits of my collaboration with the members of SOCERLID, we must recall that the problem of narrative figuration has been dealt with in earlier books that make a new historical exposé and analytical study of narrative categories unnecessary. The international exhibition of "Narrative Figuration in Contemporary Art" that I organized and presented at the Galerie Creuze, under the auspices of that gallery and the Galerie Europe, in conjunction with the fourth biennial of Paris in October, 1965, led to the publication of a brief essay, to which the reader may refer if he desires a general knowledge of a phenomenon that touches upon a great variety of artistic activities and that, although firmly bound up with the idea of figuration, is presented in frequently complex categories that make reference to marginal ideas, such as those of the impression or the series (Reutersward, Arnal) on the border line of representation.

Until now exhibitions of and writings on narrative figuration have simply attempted to establish the sociological substantiation of what was neither a new pictorial trend nor a school established on a philosophical or political basis, but simply a method of expression, implying both a reference to temporal dimension in the elaboration of the canvas, and an evolution of the process by which the spectator interprets this same canvas. Thus the global perception of the work, as implied by the creative action in lyrical abstraction or "action painting," was succeeded by a progressive perception according to an evolution in time. This led to the establishment, in our previous exhibits, of sections devoted to what we propose to call, for the time being, "evolutive figuration," by internal itineraries (Bruning, Naccache) or metamorphosis of an object or of a character (Boshier, Arroyo).

In this new chapter that we are beginning in the study of pictorial narration, our interest will be concentrated on the picture itself, in its structure and its structural conventions, rather than on its membership in one or the other of the narrative categories we have already studied. However, a very brief survey of these categories, in order to enable the reader to follow us, will not be amiss.

In addition to internal itineraries and metamorphoses, a primary category is constituted by "anecdotal narration," in continuous form or in successive scenes of which the development may appear perfectly explicit (Foldès) or, on the contrary, may debouch on a poetic system that presents profound ambiguities of interpretation (Périlli). A second category includes "narration by juxtaposition, in a single composition, of planes situated in space-time pairs that differ from each other. . . ." This is the category most prevalent in recent contemporary painting.

Lastly, a major place should be allocated to "narration by compartmented subjects" (the polyptych is a variant of this), which achieves remarkable development in "narration by episodes." In this case, the artist has recourse, from canvas to canvas, to an exact story, to events that occurred at a definite time, or to definite characters whose actions make possible differ-

---

In no painter is the presence of the comic strip so tangible: Yet Lichtenstein executes a genuine re-creation of the theme, a synthesizing and purifying operation by which he achieves a new language. He strips the picture of all narrative content.

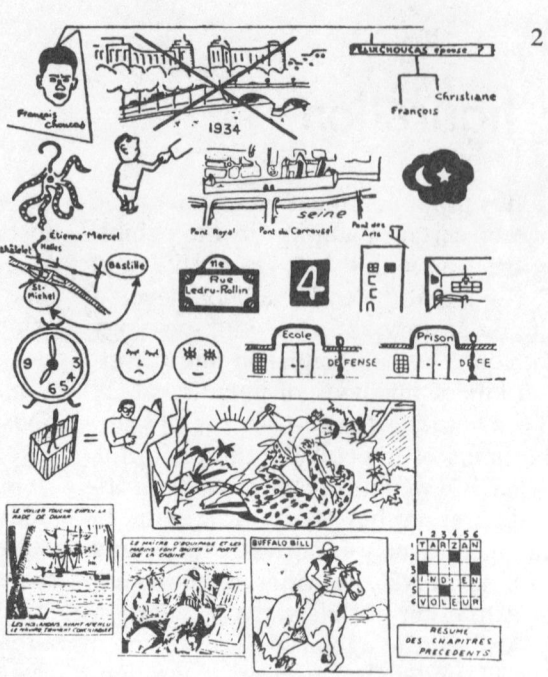

LE GRAND MAGAZINE D'AVENTURES

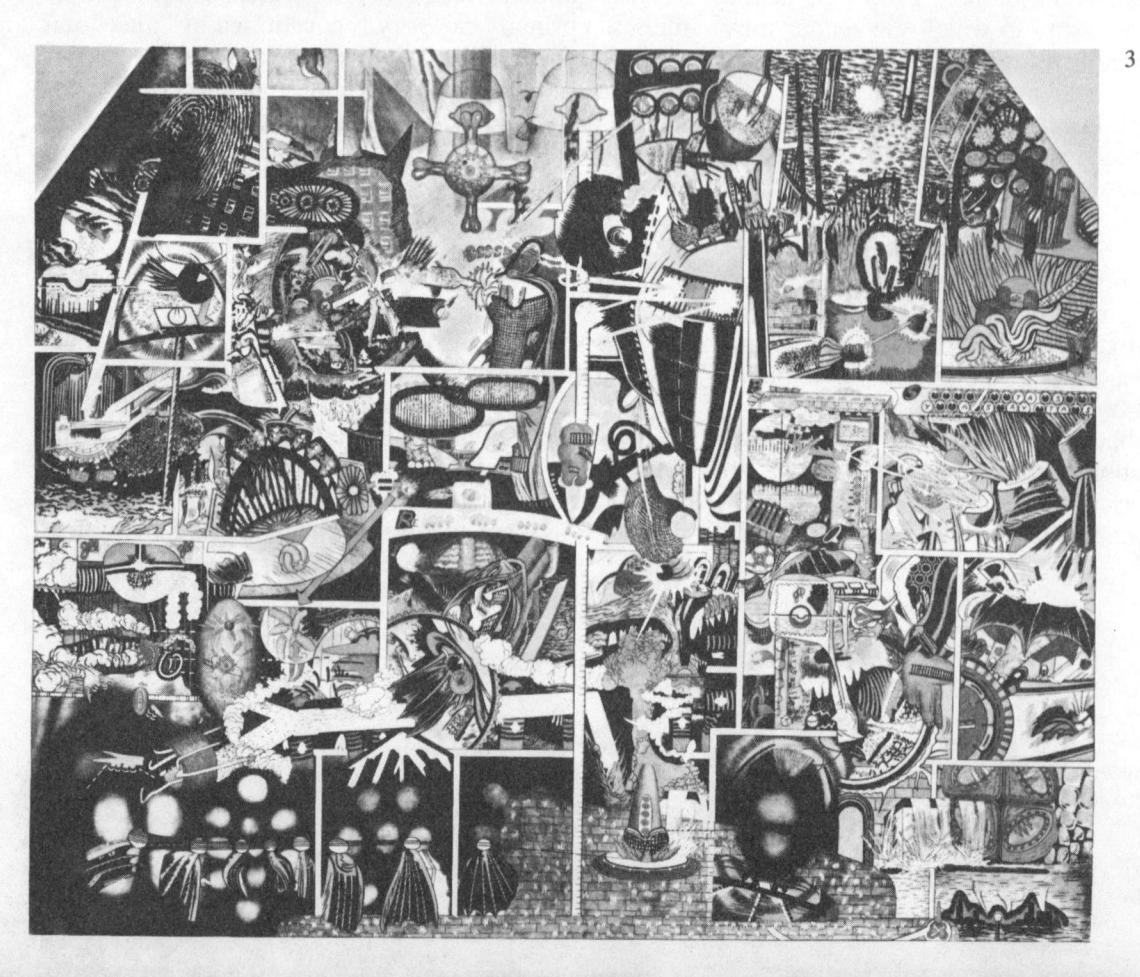

ent compositions. Thus Berni has built his entire work of the past few years around two heros, Juanito Laguna and Ramona, and Rancillac has devoted a recent exhibition to the events of 1966. So too, Arroyo, Aillaud, and Recalcati have on two occasions painted works composed of several paintings devoted to a single theme: "A Passion in the Desert," and "Live and Let Die, or the Tragic Death of Marcel Duchamp."

We must now return to a consideration of the content of the term "narration," which in the course of this book may have been assigned different meanings. In the etymologically narrative context of the comic strip, the function of which is always to tell a story, it was natural to understand this term in a restrictive sense and to limit it to the continuity of pictures linked by a single action over a very short period of time. It would be necessary to determine the acceptable margin of elapsed time between two pictures acceptable if they are to form a narrative continuity. Pictorially, on the contrary, in most cases the aim is not to "tell a story" or even to "give information" (which the public obtains through other rapid and powerful methods from the press, television, and movies). The astonishing thing is precisely that, considering the presence in our society of such traumatizing elements, and in spite of pictorial trends generally hostile to the anecdote that have been active since the end of the nineteenth century, we are witnessing today a regeneration of the "narrative" picture. Thus everything depends on the definition of the word, which, while it is given a restrictive meaning by specialists in the comic strip, should on the contrary be, in the pictorial field, the object of a "semantic expansion."

A narrative work is any artistic work that relates by its style and composition to a figurative representation in time, without necessarily being in all cases a "narrative." This definition is both sufficiently narrow to eliminate the traditional figurative representation involving a scene or an object isolated from all content and continuity, and sufficiently broad to permit the study, as a group, of artists who have deliberately chosen to depict duration and those whose work even temporarily includes this problem, without thereby constituting for them a deliberate commitment to the narrative genre. It is not necessarily the intention of such artists to supply either explicit or strictly discursive information, but to achieve an adaptation of reality by submitting it to their own decoding key and by performing the filtering operation necessary for the establishment of a divergence, a hiatus, and a transposition between this reality and the work of art. The choice of constructive elements and styles of expression inherent in the very nature of the pictorial act never permits an assimilation to the methods and aims of either the comic strip or the cinema.

PAINTING AND THE COMIC STRIP

Until recently, the history of the comic strip as a distinct phenomenon related to the sociological evolution of our century bore only an incidental relationship to painting. Then, in the course of the fifties, there appeared the first reactions to lyrical abstraction's style of immediate communication, and the inventory of the products of our industrial civilization began to be evoked by and integrated into the work of art. In the very conception of the picture, only a painter like

---

1. Oyvind Fahlström, "Krazy Kat" (1962), private collection, New York.
2. Maurice Lemaître (Galerie Stadler, Paris). "Le Grand Magazine d'Aventures," in *Canailles* (1964). A supertemporal monograph which includes pages published in the first issue of the magazine *Ur*. The introduction into this drawing of scenes borrowed from illustrated magazines is justified by the author as an allusion to the youthful reading habits of François Choucas, his hero, as "an escape and at the same time an invitation to surpass himself." These inclusions form a parenthesis in a narrative, autobiographical sequence based on the drawing. Lemaître finished this page at the moment when Isidore Isou was creating *Les Journaux des Dieux* (The Journals of the Gods), a hypergraphical novel.
3. "Setting" (1962), Moderna Museet, Stockholm.

The use of the "balloon" in painting is directly adapted from the comic strip. In addition to Lichtenstein and Fahlström, who were openly inspired by it, Alechinsky introduced this method into his "talking drawings." Foldès and Hiraga fill their "balloons" with unintelligible scribbles, while Rancillac leaves his completely blank. With the help of balloons Michenet establishes a visual relationship between certain characters and their thoughts. In "Le Puits Artésien" (The Artesian Well) Cheval-Bertrand uses them to link two pictures.

Périlli organizes scenes the legibility of which is not evident, and in which filiform figures with the elegant airs of insects stand out against vividly colored backgrounds. They are often combined with written comments, as in "Eléments pour la Reconstitution d'un Acte d'Amour" (Elements for the Reconstitution of an Act of Love), with the collaboration of Jean Clarence Lambert. This pictorial poetry transports us into a world that is simultaneously alien to, and heavy with allusions regarding, our own world—a kind of possible double that reconciles science-fiction and the legend.

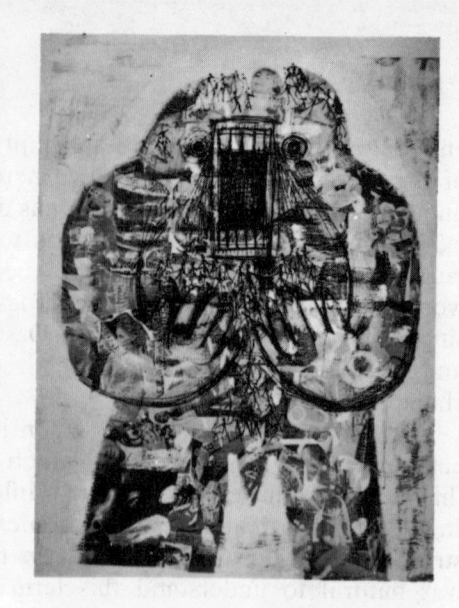

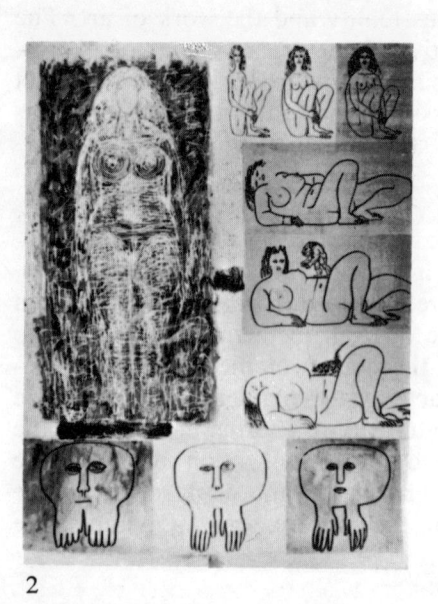

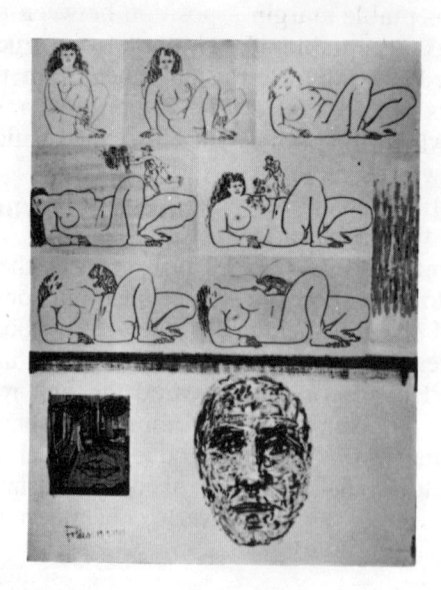

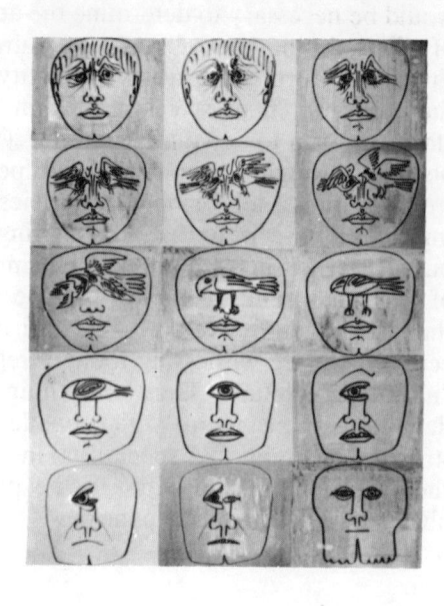

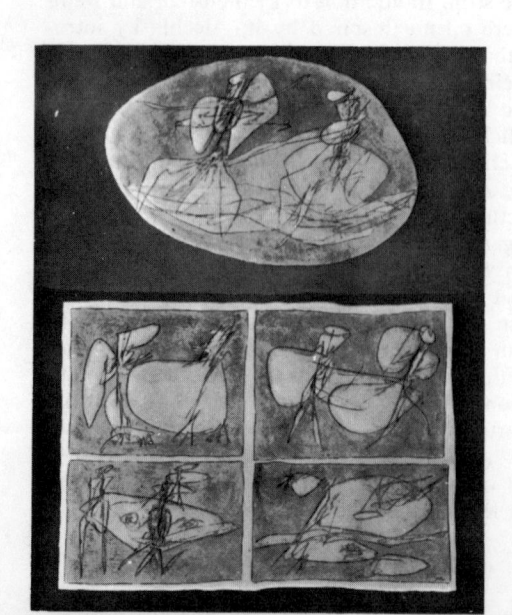

1. Peter Foldès, "Synthèse Narrative ou le Livre d'Heures de Leviathan" (Narrative Synthesis, or the Book of Hours of Leviathan) (1965), Galerie Europe, Paris. Foldès, obsessed by the narrative spirit, in 1948 composed a compartmented painting with nine pictures in evolution: "Lampe Électrique et Papillon de Nuit" (Electric Light and Moth). In his motorized paintings, films, and pictorial compositions, he seeks to achieve a kind of narrative gesture of man battling with his demons. His characters, who have no permanent identity, undergo metamorphoses in accordance with the caprices of a fluid, crafty imagination in order to animate small, perverse tales, the acid morality of which leaves us with a feeling of malaise.

2. Achille Périlli, "Transmutation des Amants" (Transmutation of Lovers) (1964). Photo Oscar Savio, Galleria Marlborough, Rome.

Hélion seems to us directly related, when he breaks with geometrical abstraction, to a type of draftsmanship that was fashionable among the humorists of the thirties. The idea of integrating into a canvas or drawing elements borrowed directly from the characters of the comic strips has arisen only quite recently. There is the famous example of Schwitters, "For Kate," which dates from 1947; and in Maurice Lemaître's "Grand Magazine d'Adventures" (a selection from his *Canailles*) we discover sequences that reproduce episodes from "Tarzan," "Buffalo Bill," and other illustrated stories for children.

In the works of many other painters such direct borrowings are also rare or of brief duration. Rauschenberg has on several occasions made such borrowings; Fahlström, an entire portion of whose work is an attempt at various solutions, has given us (1962) a free interpretation of "Krazy Kat."

More frequent borrowings have been made by certain painters (for example, Télémaque and Rancillac), from characters of Disney, Hergé, or other artists; Superman and Tarzan appear in the works of Jean-Louis Brau. In the works of these artists the reference to entities that occupy an obvious place in the heritage of everyone's childhood arises, sometimes from a reminiscence involving analogies of images and situations, sometimes from a desire to utilize a directly intelligible vocabulary that simplifies communication to an extreme degree. In recent years we have witnessed the proliferation of these borrowings, which also draw upon the adult comic strip. One of the strangest attempts has been that of the Brazilian Darcy Penteado, who has invented nothing less than comics in Latin, in which Chicago gangsters revile each other in the language of Cicero. To return to Disney's characters, let us recall that Lichtenstein himself was tempted by the integration of Mickey Mouse and Bugs Bunny into a context of abstract expressionism. This took place around 1957; being dissatisfied with the results, he destroyed most of his works.

Lichtenstein, in fact, is after a fashion the symbol of the union of the painting and the comic strip. The fact that he is certainly the most antinarrative painter imaginable is not the least paradoxical aspect of his situation. We know that Lichtenstein does not work in a temporal continuity, but isolates an exact sequence, which he reproduces, enlarges, and solidifies in a kind of extratemporal permanence. The characters he has chosen and elevated to the dignity of gigantic icons incessantly declaim the same sentence, to which no answer will be given. Lichtenstein reintroduces the factor of classical fixity into a moving context, just as after the Renaissance the easel painting isolated certain episodes of the narrative sequences of altarpieces, frescoes, and compositions by Duccio and Carpaccio.

Criticism has answered the accusation that Lichtenstein is a scrupulous and servile imitator of the comic strip. It is well known that he completely recomposes the elements borrowed from various episodes of the script, which he enlarges, and covers with solid areas of color and with stencils, in order to obtain contrasting effects between zones treated in a method that evokes, but does not imitate, the stratagem of the impression (the orderly deposits of pigment with which Lichtenstein dots the faces of his heroines bear no resemblance whatsoever to an enlarged typographical screen). As for his texts, they are often borrowed from episodes completely unrelated to the one he has chosen.

This is not the place to explore the ambiguity of Lichtenstein's work; by building on the principle of antisensitivity it discovers a new sensitivity; by banishing the "popular" picture from our environment and restoring meaning to commercial art, it offers us something subtly "different"; its social and moral message is theoretically nil, but it nevertheless demands of us a merciless, unremitting state of awareness. There is no satire, no irony directed at a world of which it is a "portrait"; it does reveal a somewhat amused humility in the face of denunciatory preoccupations sometimes

It has been said that the canvases of Foldès were simply sketches for his films. There is some truth in this remark, if we realize the close relationship which links this painter's plastic works with his short films (*Short Vision, Animated Genesis, Un Appétit de Oiseau* [An Appetite like a Bird's], *Un Garçon Plein d'Avenir"* [A Promising Boy]) and his television shows. Foldès's procedure, which creates modes of expressions simultaneously in three areas, by a reflex of reciprocal movement very indicative of a search for compensation, constitutes a living response to the narration-film dilemma (like Lapoujade, who has also made some excellent films); his universe is reduced to several obsessive themes, to a core of simple reactions. But it is wrong to see in his paintings only preliminary sketches for his films, for they are the development of the same mythological texture in accordance with other laws. To remark that pictorial narration is not continuous like the film is to note and become aware that there is a difference. The magic strength of the image, immortalized in the painting, is incomparably more powerful than the fleeting, irreversible sequence of the film: it exists with the radiance of the icon, in an immediately perceptible permanence.

1

2

3

4

5

6

ascribed to it, and, toward the cartoonists themselves, the politeness due an army of benevolent collaborators.

This "honor" paid by Lichtenstein to the comic-strip authors in "elevating" certain details of their work to the level of art by a unilateral decision is undoubtedly based on an ancient superiority complex on the part of painters vis-à-vis cartoonists, which, far from being lessened by the advent of Pop Art, has been subtly exacerbated. In all honesty it must be said that Lichtenstein has never permitted himself the slightest disdain toward those who furnish his sources; he considers these sources, he has remarked to Alan Salomon, as "an art form, after a fashion." It is true that he immediately adds, "I believe, however, that the people who work on it [the comic strip] do not consider it such." However, it is the commentators, rather than the artists, who draw the sharpest distinction. This undoubtedly results from the fact that his selections are chosen (by Lichtenstein's own admission) from the modern comic book, the quality of which is inferior to that of the classic strips, and this simultaneously satisfies his desire not to be embarrassed by too individualized a character and to find in a certain banality of draftsmanship an echo of the banality of the dialogue from which it derives its most precise effects. For Lichtenstein the comics are still first and foremost "sites of excitement of the imagination . . . and . . . of immense possibilities from the visual point of view."

Lichtenstein's resolutely structuralist course confirms that, just as he does not see in Pop Art a pure and simple return to the realistic picture, so too he does not utilize the sequence of the comic strip in its narrative logic. The content of the story from which it is detached, the hero's personality, the incidences of the social context on the subject and the factor of sociological instruction the strip may represent are of only secondary interest to him. It is in the pure forms of the faces and in the conventions of the composition; it is in the relationship between the effect of tridimensionality obtained by certain graphic artifices and the deliberate use he makes of them; it is in the increasingly detailed study of the optical screen on two planes, that is, in a conceptualization of appearance, that Lichtenstein is pursuing his adventure—one of the most intelligent in Pop Art.

Apart from this example, almost unique in its purity, which seems alien to the problems of narrative figuration, the relationships between the comic strip and painting remain fragmentary. As in the case of Lichtenstein, the narrative artist considers the comics as sociological raw material that can be utilized in the same manner as the advertisement (Télémaque), the picture novel (Rancillac), the technical diagram (Alleyn), the magazine illustration (Foldès, Bertini, Sarkis), the newspaper article (Naccache), the art reproduction (Ferro), or quite simply the ready-made object that serves as a milestone in the development of the interior journey (Télémaque, Monory). This is the fundamental difference between two art forms that are never so remote as when they seem (as in the works of Fahlström) to resemble each other. The comic-strip artist submits to the external reality of the

1. Ian Voss, "Sans Titre" (Untitled) (1964).

2. "A Demi Mots, à Demi Gestes" (Half in Words, Half in Gestures) (1965). Galerie Mathias Fels, Paris. Photos André Morain.

3. Yannis Gaïtis, "Les Fous Volants" (Flying Madmen) (1966). Merlin Gallery, Athens; Galleria Schneider, Rome. Photo André Morain.

4. Key Hiraga, "Fenêtres" (Windows) (1966). Galerie Lambert, Paris.

5. Bernard Rancillac, "Journal Intime d'un Pied" (The Intimate Diary of a Foot) (1965). Galerie Blumenthal-Mommaton, Paris. Photo André Morain.

6. Hervé Télémaque, "My Darling Clementine" (1963). Galerie Mathias Fels, Paris; Galerie L'Attico, Rome.

Starting from a compartmented division in strips, which placed quite undefined characters in ambiguous situations, Voss has increasingly clarified his draftsmanship, made his faces clearer, and given life to an easily identifiable humanity. In clarifying his purpose, however, the painter abandoned the usual narrative structure of strips and compartments in order to adopt a more chaotic layout. That is, the suggested but illegible continuity of his early compositions contrasts with his present discontinuity, which is legible but repudiates narrative conventions. The characters are grouped in precise situations in the form of small playlets, in short, ironical episodes that can be perfectly described and interpreted but that are not linked to each other by any logical continuity. Moreover, the method of work Voss has adopted betrays this deliberate dispersion: he first attacks the strong points of the painting by drawing the principal scenes, then tightens his screen until it completely fills a space that stands out against a uniformly monochrome background: yellow, ocher, rose, or green. The uniform tonality of the canvases permits the characters to play their games freely in a spic-and-span, malicious chromatism that adds still more to the humor of the drawing.

1. Group Cronica (Valencia), "La Quantité se Transforme en Qualité (Quantity Transformed into Quality) (1966).
2. Oyvind Fahlström, "The Cold War," Phase 8. (Sidney Janis Gallery, New York).

story whose development he must make as explicit as possible by a series of graphic methods and conventions. In this sense, the literary desire to multiply the methods of communication satisfies the fundamental purpose of the comics. In most of the pictorial cases we shall mention, on the contrary, the artist's goal is not to achieve explicit language, but to open to the spectator a secret world of subtle connections in which each image, like a reverberated echo, reflects a mental double and reveals to us an increasingly hermetic secret. Even when the purpose is to communicate a certain number of clear ideas, as in the works of Foldès, Rancillac, and Arroyo, the plurality of meanings and the quality of possible annotations prolong the radiation of the image.

Lastly, the desire to achieve speech, to transform the filter of the vision of the real, is present in all painters, even in those who proclaim, out of antiformalist convictions, an integral realism. Where the comic-strip artist applies his art to the expression, by simple signs and univocal layouts, of the behavior and feelings of his hero and the nature of the events that occur in his life, and to the facilitation of the rapid interpretation of the pictures, the painter imprisons himself in a conceptual prison, and communication is achieved only at the price of an initiation. From this results the use of prefaces, critical exegeses, interviews, and the extreme disparity of viewpoints that are still further complicated by elucidations and commentaries. This "truth" of the work, never achieved, at first escapes the creator himself, who demands plurality of interpretations, expects an answer from the Other, and most frequently suggests relative approaches rather than affirmations.

Lastly, by its development in time and the codification of its language, by the succession of episodes, the discovery of which is dependent on sometimes infrequent newspaper and magazine deliveries, the comic strip may play on all the narrative possibilities: flashback, simultaneity of action, plurality of vision of a single series, psychological penetration of the various characters, and so on.

In painting, whatever the novelty of the progressive penetration required by the narrative expression, the "plastic" appropriation of the work remains comprehensive. This is one of the dilemmas that could be rightly posed by the critics of the idea of narration in art: at the end of the itinerary, or of the entrance in depth into the canvas, contemplation escapes from the search for all meaning. Once again the narrative proposition is only a means of interpretation and an indication of the painter's intention to endow his communication with a temporal dimension. The autobiographical or sociological information it provides does not imply any evidence of plastic necessity. Narration is not a label of modernity, an elixir of youth, for painters facing sclerosis, congestion, and stylistic attrition.

Narrative Art and the Cinema

The tremendous power of the animated picture, in the movies or television, is exercised to the fullest extent on the new figurative art. This is a fact that has become commonplace, and supposes a reciprocity. The initiatory and fecundatory function of art in the disposition of the forms of the inner city has in the course of this century, with such movements as cubism, surrealism, and geometrical and lyrical abstractions, been such that the brutal expansion of painting into the universe of the city and the expressions of industrial civilization have led to ambiguity.

It has been said and written that the artist had been following in the wake of the real instead of guiding its perceptional approaches. Appearances to the contrary, and although painters never deny their sources (could they?), the art-reality relationship has not been greatly modified. Certain aspects of the objective world have been privileged, trapped, and singled out, and harsh searchlights have been trained on certain predominant appearances, for examination or fundamental positioning. The example of Lichtenstein and the comic strip is typical, but the artist is not the sterile monopolist that he is sometimes accused of being: he never leaves reality in the same form in which he found it, and in the past few years we have been able to see, even outside the perimeter of art, the influence exercised in turn by Pop Art on

---

The relations between Fahlström and the comic strip stamp a great part of his work. However, Rauschenberg, who introduced Fahlström's exhibition (Daniel Cordier, December, 1962), understands the reason for the tangled expansion that appears in such ink works as "Doctor Livingstone, I Presume." He writes, "The artist has begun with a dense, uncontrolled continuity which has neither beginning nor end, being dependent on a decision or action on his part." He adds that in Fahlström's work, "The figures are free to act and react, to be integrated, to collide or be destroyed, each one always responding locally without the intervention of an esthetic meaning of the quadrilateral composition of the canvas. . . ." Until his most recent works, Fahlström adhered to this freedom, which went contrary to the obligatory order of the comic strips.

1

2

3

the comic strip ("Jodelle") and especially on advertising and magazine layouts, which have attempted to adapt the stylistic traits of the painters. In this case it was still a question of graphic art, of ART: The same static support, the same utilization of draftsmanship. To the interpenetration of techniques and the creative action in painting corresponded the use of plastic procedures in the graphic techniques. The cinema, on the other hand, is a powerful lord that obeys only the laws of its own making, and when it decides to be "influenced" its borrowings are loudly justified, as in the case of Antonioni, and serve to accentuate the unique quality of the decision. The fascination it exercises on many artists is particularly evident among the narrative painters. Here again, however, the problems of the two arts are so different, and the transmutation from one language into the other is accomplished by so many filters, that the dangers of contamination are of secondary importance. It has been remarked that the figures most frequently depicted in the new imagery were those imposed by cinema and television, but this is a truism, for these figures correspond to a certain density and frequency of information that itself corresponds to the requirements of reality and the myths it engenders. To the newsreel's informational purpose, to the incantatory power of the creative film, corresponds the painter's expressive adaptation, which is of a different nature—a genuinely magical operation.

At this point we must reconsider the phenomenon of intellectual fixation represented by the advent of the cinema, a phenomenon whose consequences for the rise of abstraction have been at least as important as those of the discovery of photography for impressionism. The conviction that the problems of the depiction of human action had been solved for all time, and the mechanical precision involved in the new processes of the cinema, at first discouraged any monopolization by art of a narrative development that could be captured in its true rhythm and with methods of transfiguration which themselves sprang from a new art, to be fulfilled in accordance with its own laws. It was forgotten that there was a fundamental insufficiency in the very identification of time in the film with real time, despite the artifices of cutting and montage—the very same insufficiency that had legitimized the first act of figurative representation, the first defiance of death, from time immemorial, by all those who had hoped to immortalize forms by means of the fiction of art. In its development the film cannot be an object of adaptation: it is fluidity and evanescence, like time itself; its interpretation, imposed by the cadence of the images, is irreversible; its performance is almost always collective, that is, subject to universal norms. Thus in some ways the narrative explosion is less a consequence of the cinematographer's projection than a rejection of its limits, and a determination, on the part of the painter, to transcend the temporal-realistic weaknesses inherent in its nature. Like the content of the comic strip, the daily occurence or the story relayed by television or the movie are perceived by the artist as "sociological objects." Under its different forms, narrative figuration thus corresponds to a need for comprehensive adaptation of a continuous or discontinuous reality, grasped in the category of time. Only stabilization on a two-dimensional field of sensitization, such as the canvas, permits the successful completion of this synthesizing operation, this enveloping of the incessant flight of life, this immobilization of the forms that constitute the "story." By

1. Realidad Group, Valencia, "Acero Frio para Ti, Amigo" (Cold Steel for You, Buddy) (1966).

2. Antonio Berni, "Juanito Laguna Part en Ville" (Juanito Laguna Goes to Town) (1961).

3. Bernard Rancillac, "La Fin Tragique d'un Apôtre" (The Tragic End of an Apostle) (1966). Galerie Blumenthal-Mommaton, Paris. Photo André Morain.

In Rancillac's recent works (1966–1967), equality of light and shadow, inspired by certain techniques of printing in color masses, gives us a picture in which color plays the neutral role of an architecture in which the high points are equal to the low points. "Ombre et Lumière sur Cheval" (Shadow and Light on Cheval), "La Fin Tragique d'un Apôtre" (The Tragic End of an Apostle), and "Enfin! Silhouette Affinée jusqu'à la Taille" (At Last! Silhouette Narrowed Down to the Waist) are canvases of silent power in which banal reality is decoded in the ambiguous language of the equation of opposites. In this immobility, the temporal dimension is reintroduced from work to work as if to give a chronicle of our world, from which picturesqueness and dramatic complacency would be rigorously banished.

This painting (in the series devoted to the events of 1966), like that of Berni, constitutes an example of narration by episode.

1

2

3

celebrating the milestones in the recognition of the environment or the historical and sociological continuum, the artist also satisfies the requirements of a moment, one of those periodical returns to the milieu, the surroundings, the society, required for profound circumstantial reasons. In this regard the adaptation of certain habits of framing, and certain optical possibilites to the pictorial composition, make possible a large range of effects: close-ups (Rosenquist, Raysse, Monory, Klasen, Foldès; an Argentine painter, Cuello, even mounted [at the Galerie Levin] an entire exhibition inspired by the televised picture, which makes possible a penetration and violation of the face); panoramic vistas (Recalcati, Monory), brutal close-up of a detail as if by zooming (Bertini, Alleyn, Schlosser), superimpression (Kujawski, Cheval-Bertrand), intersections (Télémaque), the decomposition of movement (Boshier, Malaval, Bignardi, Foldès), and fusion of the character and his surroundings (Arroyo, Rivers).

We could continue this enumeration, and also include in it the influence of the comic strip, which in turn is directly related to the cinema, and so on. But these methods of approach to the picture are only what the painter makes of them, just as they are part of the vocabulary of the film director. Their abuse may become a "tic" or a mannerism.

The Narrative Image

In its various categories, which we summarized at the beginning of this chapter, the narrative image utilizes various formal methods, which include in part the individual styles of the painters and participation in clearly defined artistic families. However, the complexity of the analysis of the narrative phenomenon results from the conjunction of this threefold method of investigation:

1. We have studied the narrative categories in an earlier essay; therefore we shall not consider them here. Far from constituting a permanent system, they merely suggest a preliminary method of approach, which may be completed in more detail.

2. The character of a sociological demonstration that characterized the exhibition of October, 1965, at the Galerie Creuze has revealed the multiplicity of artistic families involved: expressionists, neosurrealists, English and American Pop artists, realists, "lettrists," graphic artists, and practitioners of the mechanical techniques of the new Parisian and Italian imagery were compared and divided into various categories, which permitted an easier interpretation of their canvases. This method, which corresponded to the aims of the exhibition, had the obvious defect of leaving the hasty observer with an impression of stylistic confusion. However, it was impossible to obtain an insight into an idea as ambiguous as that of narration without seeking examples where they were to be found. The necessarily more limited selection in this book and the exhibition at the Musée des Arts Décoratifs permits us to outline:

3. A structural study of the narrative image, linked to more profound reflexes of the painters, a study that goes beyond the narrow circle of techniques and "schools."

I. THE TWO DIMENSIONS

The concept of narration favors that of the written word. The "lettrists," whose works call upon several types of communication (letters and hypergraphy, in addition to the rebus and hieroglyphic solutions), have realized this. Our purpose here is to analyze the image, with which almost all painters (even those who, like Bertini, occasionally utilize signs, numbers, or letters) propose to limit their investigations into language. Once again, this is not an appropriate place for a critical study of "lettrism," or for an examination of

---

1. Eduardo Arroyo, "Robinson Crusoe-en-Île" (Robinson Crusoe on the Island) (1965).

2. Robinson Crusoe: "I began my fortification or wall and, since I was always somewhat afraid of being attacked, I decided to build it very thick and very solid" (1966).

3. "The Princess of Eboli" (1963). Galleria Il Fante di Spade, Rome; Studio Bellini, Milan; De' Foscherari, Bologna. Photos Pierre Golendorf.

"L'Assassinat de Marcel Duchamp" (The Murder of Marcel Duchamp) was a concerted attempt to overthrow the "rhetoric of forms." The scandal it caused was directed perhaps less at the calculated cruelty of the action, the police-like ambiguity of the gesture, than at the manner in which this series of pictures was painted. At a time when the worst neo-Dada exaggerations arouse only worldly echoes, the arrogant shock of conventionalism, like a radical antidote, seemed to Arroyo, Aillaud, and Recalcati the only possible remedy. In the face of unanimous disapproval, Arroyo symbolically withdrew to his island in order to paint sentimental seascapes and construct his fortress. The paintings of the "Robinson" series are perhaps the most insolent and contemptuous of his canvases.

Giani Bertini, "Soudain Erèbe" (Suddenly Erebus) (1966).
Photo Serge Béguier.

the too often deceptive plastic results it offers; we wish only to include it in its place and proper time.

The notion of writing implies that of graphism. Consequently, it is not surprising that a fair number of narrative painters utilize a linear drawing without modeling, in which color intervenes only as an added contribution, frequently at variance with the line and in an extremely simple tonal register. Foldès in almost all his work, and particularly in the three lower panels of his "Livre d'Heures de Leviathan" (Book of Hours of Leviathan), Macréau and Hiraga when they make fantastic figures surge up in counterpoint (Hiraga uses the cloisonné process in his "Fenêtres"), and Gaïtis, who arranges homunculi in successive compartments —all remain on a cursive level, of a hurried and mischievous style that sometimes takes on the accents of a certain naïveté. In the works of Périlli and Novelli, who have exercised a great influence on graphic art, the figures spring, after a fashion, from a stroke of the pen; Novelli's line is nonchalant and full of the unexpected. We may remember the example of a concentric composition that accentuated the effect of planimetry.

In another vein, Ian Voss occupies a special place among the narrative painters.

In this cursive reflex of narration there is an idea of frontality which is that of the blackboard and the page of the schoolboy's notebook. The world is grasped in its primary schematization, the one that most quickly permits the child to transcribe his dreams. The visual artifice of depth is abolished by the artist in order to rediscover this spontaneity of expression, with no intermediary other than the hand accustomed to giving form always to the same type of creature. This sometimes involves haste and repetition, but the graphic artist knows that he is entering the region, at once fecund and perilous, of automatism; he writes his canvas following a very variable arrangement, beginning at one end and ending at another, or on the contrary in successive "packets."

II. INTERPRETATION BY SUCCESSIVE PLANES

We pointed out above that the greatest number of narrative painters were to be found in the category of juxtapositions by space-time planes. It is in this category, too, that narrative "intentions" are the least obvious. Let us consider a famous example, that of Rauschenberg in his period of "combine-drawings." Let us choose one of his pictures, "Kite," in which we see the juxtaposition of an eagle (possibly the symbolic bird of the United States), a U.S. Army helicopter, and a turn-of-the century military parade. If we apply the notion of narration to such a work, it is certainly not to claim that it "tells a story." Simply, we may decide that the conjunction of the three motifs is not a coincidence and that it shares in an intention of signification even if the relationship is established between "images," for these images are charged, for the painter as for the spectator, with an emotive potentiality, a "content" that exceeds their iconographic character, and a power of the second degree. On the other hand, these images are situated in different moments, and perception fastens on and is colored by these moments. Even if the "reader" chooses to see them in the simultaneity of the action that consists of grouping the three of them, the problem of time still exists. These problems are raised in a great number of paintings executed by very diverse painters, notably in Rosenquist's "F-111." To mention them all would be tedious; let us just analyze, in a narrative context, certain modes of penetration chosen by various artists.

The Play of Mirrors or the Reverberation of the Image

Hamilton situates a character in a place the picture of which is rediscovered on the screen of a television set. Some Parisian painters, like Sellier and Michenet, utilize the rear-view mirror and the reflection to determine the position of a mobile (a car) between a before and an after.

It is remarkable to observe that Bertini's recent work, which is based on the utilization of the technique of photographic transfers, and consequently invites an objectivation of the real, actually results in an objectivation of Bertini. It is the painter's own works, particularly those that possessed a certain scandalous content, which are reproduced in a context borrowed from the environment or the event. But in this duplication the laws are often inverted: in a layout *à la* Magritte, a closed space is substituted for an open space, or the false perspective of the painting compensates for that of the documentary ("L'Indifférent Cronos," 1965). This counterpoint causes a withdrawal of the habitual perception of the basic painting, since the latter is reduced by the painter to the state of a photographic object. In this game there is an electricity, a visible transference between the painter and the world, which give depth, density, and complexity to Bertini's canvases. We should note that in certain photographic transfers the operation may take place not only on two but on three planes, since the objectified paintings themselves utilize the technique of the transfer, and depict, for example, Bertini's anatomy on a painted background ("Chien de Garde à Vendre"—Watchdog for Sale). This mirror effect must not, however, conceal the fundamental contribution of the painter's new manner, which is an overthrowing of relationship, an audacious and insolent change of viewpoint.

The realistic image, projected in the outburst of the Bertinian gesture, flows, blends and is integrated therein. In his investigations, beyond his adherences, Bertini is a demiurgic painter. Like a bloodthirsty animal he clutches in his mouth a choice prey: the human beings of our so transitory present, whose faces reverberate from canvas to canvas.

1. Bepi Romagnoni, "Technique de Propagande Politique" Technique of Political Propaganda) (1964), Galleria Il Fante di Spade, Rome; Studio Marconi, Milan.

2. Kujawski, "Les Desespérides" (The Despairides) (1966). Galerie Zunini, Paris.

3. Cheval-Bertrand, "Operette Laïque II" (Nondenominational Operetta II) (1966).

The Explosion of the Frame

In "Où es-tu? Que fais-tu?" (Where Are You? What Are You Doing?) Rancillac provokes the overflow of a subject (the Big Bad Wolf) from one frame into another. Elsewhere he opens windows in the canvas and puts shutters on them, like Foldès, who places real panels on hinges. These techniques are now being practiced by Télémaque and Monory; the latter has carried the idea of explosion to its extreme. With "Les Voyeuses" (The Seers) the painting disintegrates, in the strange atmosphere of a gynaeceum in which young women holding numbers are waiting for an indefinite event. One of them is simultaneously subject and object, and is reproduced twice with the same features in a position antagonistic to herself. Like a veil that is too heavy, the insidious, morbid surface tears open, and the painter can regulate its explosion by different mural positions that may go so far as complete disintegration of the picture. Monory utilizes all the possibilities of this method by blending or alternating the trompe-l'œil, from the slit ("La Vie en Bleu," "Elle," "Bertinoro") to the genuine tear ("La Fin de Madame Gardenia"). In his canvas exhibited at the Venice Bienniale, "Paysages à Géometrie Variable," Martial Raysse also utilized the successive empty spaces of small pictures for the emplacement of a mural composition with various combinations, representing a Nice-Venice itinerary.

The Narrative Object

The role played by the object in contemporary art for the past dozen or more years is well known. In the wake of a reconsideration of the Dada movement, industrial debris and worn utensils have reappeared in America and Europe, in sculptures (where they are used as an amalgam with the help of welding or collages) or in the form of assemblage or mechanical montages. In the system of the New Realism, which was developed at the beginning of the sixties, the object was chosen as such within the categories of quantity and observation, and by its very inertia was viewed in its power of representation of a totality: that of the universe, of which it is an expressive detail. Since then, the young artists have abandoned the paralyzing notion of observation and have returned to a subjective conditioning that is neither a simple snare nor a simple accumulation. Beyond the static parenthesis of the New Realism, we have therefore witnessed a dynamic reevaluation of the object that, however, differs radically from the negative, "nonsense" action of Dada.

In most cases, the relationships established among the various constituent elements of the montage are intended only to produce a visual and mental shock, to effect the passage of an electric current between forms charged with different potentialities. The automobile tire around Rauschenberg's goat is of this nature, as is the chair glued to a canvas, but the spectator is free to extrapolate. Narration begins from the moment when the analysis leaves behind the unformulated and the sensation, and achieves conceptualization.

Let us abandon these ambiguous examples (to which we could add the works of Raynaud [object-image relationship] or Malaval [invasion of the object by a heterogeneous element]) and concentrate on such incontestable cases as those of Niki de Saint-Phalle, Kudo, and Stenvert. During the period preceding the "Nana" phase, Niki de Saint-Phalle was able to utilize the expansion of the object to load her characters with baubles whose power of derision and subversion was added to an often resolutely narrative arrangement, as in the triptych "Les Femmes" (The Women). In this work, all the forces of intervention in the feminine condition were depicted in the form of allegories, by means of objects: bills (Money), *ex voto* in the form of a heart (Feeling), a celluloid doll (The Child), a

The telescoping of forms that seems to occur at great speed under our very eyes, the counterpoint of images on several transparent planes, the accumulation of drawings in an inextricable network of lines, on which the colors themselves overlap—such are the attempts of Romagnoni, Kujawski and Cheval-Bertrand to express the phenomena of simultaneity, superimpression, and optical equivalency brought about by the narrative decision.

Télémaque glues shoes ("Inventaire, un Homme d' Intérieur"), pieces of clothing, also tools and a bag of coal, to the canvas; in his work the object is a signpost or starting point that by the very evidence of its presence releases a charge of subtle analogies. It is, strictly speaking, "integrated" in its place, in a complex network of ideas and sensations.

For Monory, on the contrary, the object is often an element of rupture, a heterogeneous point of fixation. It is the orange the sharpshooter aims, in "Un Autre" (Another), bent double under the tension of aiming, or which in "La Vie en Bleu" (Life in Blue) comes to symbolize life, freshness, and nature, outside the monochrome world of the canvas in which occur the bizarre agonies, the throbbing impotencies, the alibi of sexuality, all the phantasms of appearance. Each time the object contributes an element that is radically foreign in the painted context: the metallic pipe that suggests suffering, the bit of velvet that hangs like a self-reproach from the closed hand (in "Le Vert Assassin"), the open grille ("Le Plaisir"), but which retains its prey, which is too weary to know that it can escape.

2

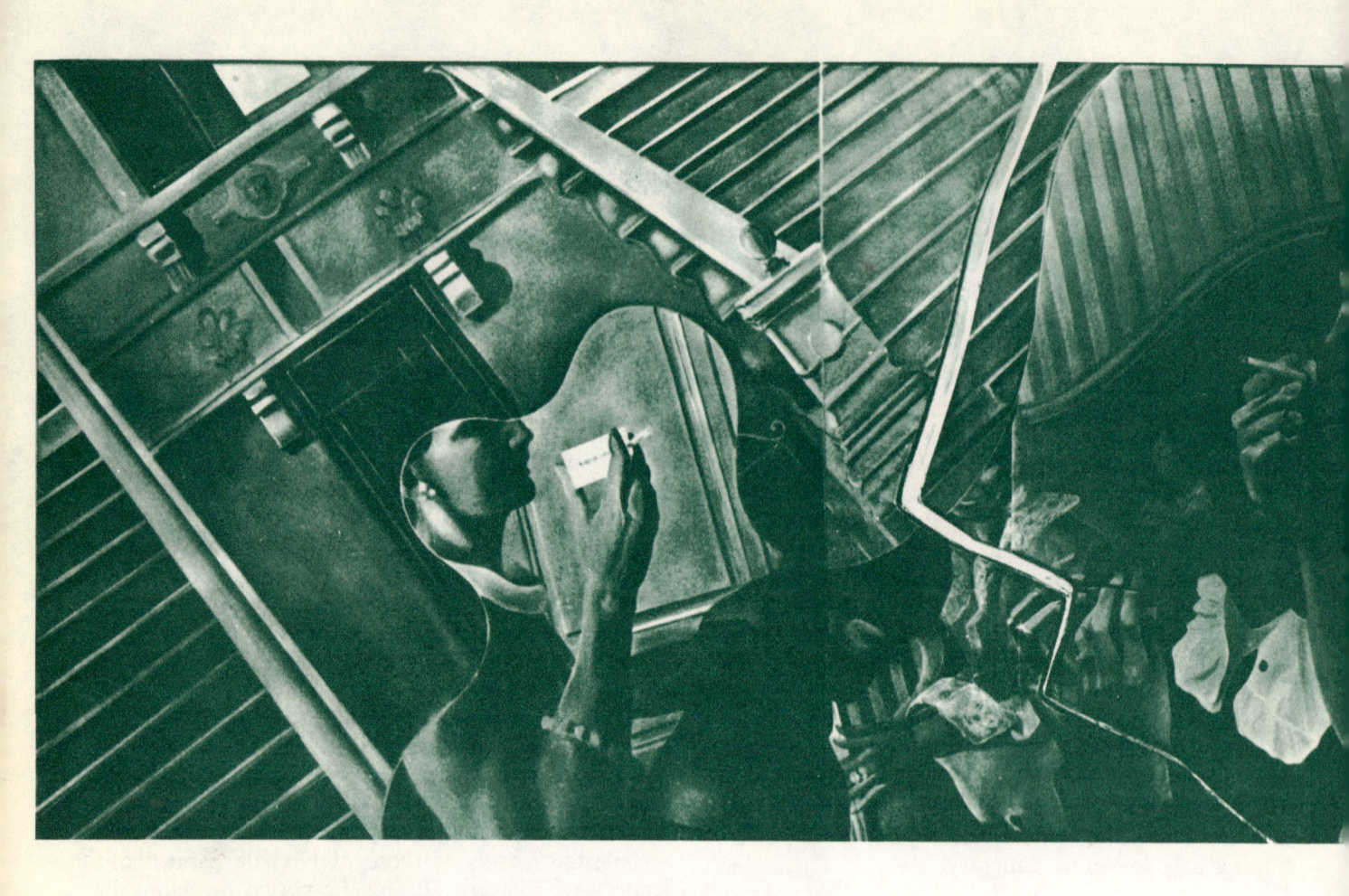

1. Jacques Monory, "Les Voyeuses" (The Seers) (1965).

2. "Le Vert Assassin" (The Green Murderer) (1966); Galerie Blumenthal-Mommaton, Paris; Galleria Schwarz, Studio Marconi, Milan.

3. Hervé Télémaque, *"Inventaire, un Homme d'Intérieur"* (Inventory, A Stay-at-Home) (1966); Galerie Mathias Fels, Paris; Galerie L'Attico, Rome.

247

1

3

James Rosenquist, "F-111" (1965). Robert C. Scull Collection, New York; Leo Castelli Gallery, New York; Galerie Ileana Sonnabend, Paris.

In "F-111," James Rosenquist attempts to express the convergence of a certain number of feelings and ideas that characterize modern man: whatever man's faith in his originality and individuality, he is reduced, by a kind of determinism in the methods of communication, to a common conglomeration and an undifferentiated fate—the common grave, the "steam boiler" of an irresistibly attractive consumer society. In this sense the painting permits a discursive interpretation, articulated on objects and situations that are superimposed upon the fuselage of a modern plane, the bearer of death and at the same time the mainstay of investments, and thus a provider of work and life. In Rosenquist's works the morality of ambiguity is colored by a very special manner of resolving the problems with which it is faced: style and antistyle, dimensions of the canvas compared with those of an ordinary advertising poster, the technique of the film editing and the illusion of materials, a dialectics of the image and relationships of analogy and, as regards the content, humanism and technocracy.

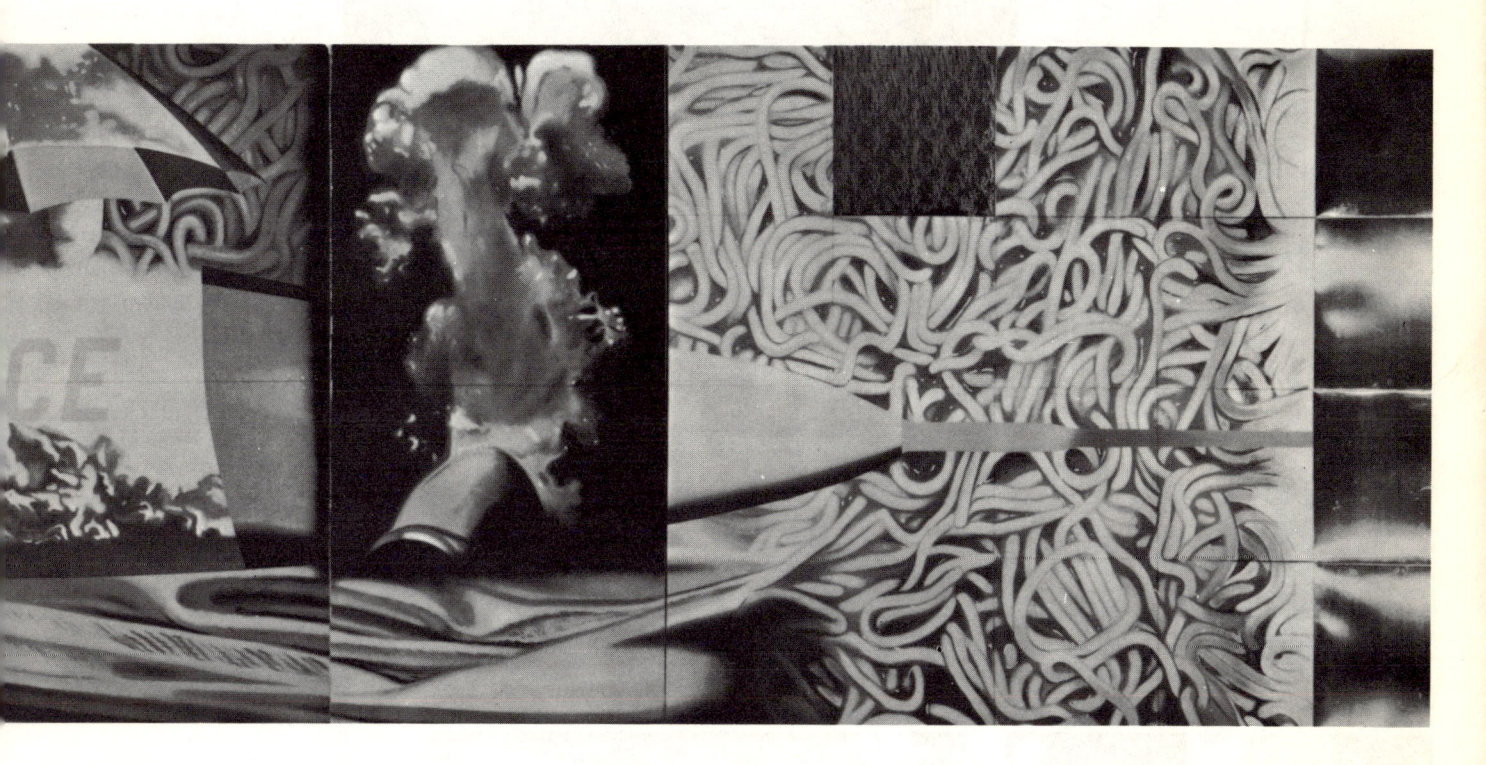

Rosenquist holds up to the public a mirror that is simultaneously the brief description of a moment and a reflection of our mental inertia.

Note the very subtle play of forms and colors that is based on pairs of analogies: tire-cake, parasol-atomic mushroom and a diver's air-rejection tube, folds of a sheet and arabesques of spaghetti, broken light bulb and hair-drier.

1. Robert Rauschenberg, "Kite" (1964). Leo Castelli Gallery, New York.

2. Antonio Recalcati, "D'Après Kafka" (After Kafka) (1964). Photo P. Bijtebier.

3. Valerio Adami, "Le Vasche da Bagno" (The Bathtubs) (1966). Galleria Schwarz, Milan.

4. Peter Klasen, "Le Cobaye ou le Futur Conditionnel" (The Guinea Pig or the Future Conditional) (1966), Galerie Mathias Fels, Paris.

5. Edmund Alleyn, "Science Partie" (1966); Galerie Blumenthal-Mommaton, Paris; Galerie 60, Montreal.

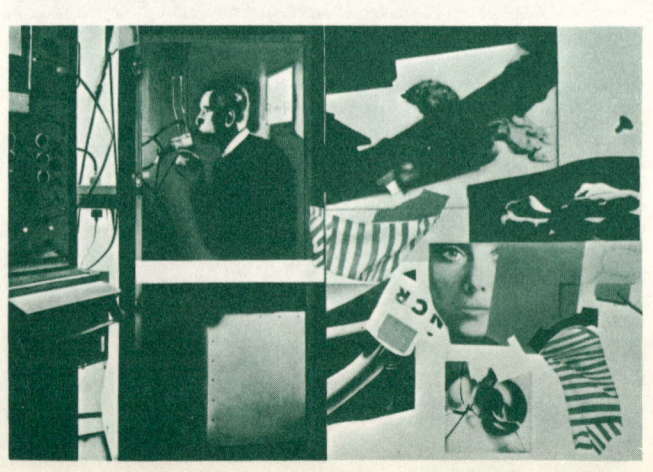

toy plane (War), and so on. Since then, Niki de Saint-Phalle has narrowed her creation down to precise forms—gigantic mother goddesses, wild dancers, ogresses, suffragettes—which tend rather to encircle and define, in his enslavement, the condition of man in industrial societies.

In the works of Kudo, the series of boxes entitled "Votre Portrait" (Your Portrait) is an assembly of the entire apparatus of the conditioned human being, from mechanical tools to the accessories of sexual life. In the midst of these objects with their clean, hard contours, which possess the clear look of newness and the anonymity of the five-and-dime store, the attributes of the human figure appear in a state of advanced decomposition and deliquescence, sometimes in the form of a simple outline. The horror of a world doomed to apocalypse bursts from these aggressive montages, which distill a wholesome malaise. Stenvert fills space with a series of mannequins, wigs, and panels covered with statements of great offensive power, the aim of which is to proclaim an explicit message, a threat, a warning.

With these artists, whose language is communicated essentially through the object, we are obviously twenty thousand leagues removed from simple observation, and are in a completely narrative climate. Here, however, the object is utilized in a very special way. We have several painters in mind; far from leading us back to the purely plastic research of the post-cubist integrations, their concern respects the very nature of the concrete element, but situates it within a counterpoint, within a mental itinerary. Very often, moreover, the very choice of a particular object furnishes us with a key: repetition and obsession imply fetishistic nuances, propitiatory presuppositions, and a complete intimate symbolism rather curious to observe (see Jacques Monory, "Les Voyeuses," "Le Vert Assassin," and Télémaque, "Inventaire, un Homme d'Intérieur").

The Destroyers of the Image

Monory quarters and decomposes the canvas; other artists do not practice this surgical method, but remain within pictorial logic, and multiply the paths. Romagnoni had a special technique for suggesting movement, bustle, the folly of an agitated world: he chopped up the picture into small, very rhythmic fragments, situated in a unique dynamics and optics of speed. Larry Rivers, whose influence on young painters is as least as great as, but less obvious than, that of Lichtenstein, is the originator of the syncopated figures, reductions of characters, partial representations, and detailed anatomical plates of which traces can be found everywhere. Recalcati paints ineffable landscapes, realistic city corners which he perforates with his massive molds—robots with transparent hearts, other selves into which he dissolves. At the end of his life (September, 1966) Cheval-Bertrand had achieved such complexity in his superimpressions that their interpretation seemed hopelessly intricate. The obsessive image, which originated in the somewhat old-fashioned apparatus of the *Petit Larousse*, decomposed before our eyes into successive metamorphoses, into gently mocking evocations. As for Adami, he breaks up reality in order to obtain from it a restructured form (see "Le Vasche da Bagno" [The Bathtubs]).

It is interesting, as Adami suggests to us, to consider in the works of this painter the trajectory that leads from the documentary as inspiration (the photograph and the newspaper clipping) to the final work of art. The image is literally convulsed in order to eliminate certain details, exaggerate others, and reassemble around forms the repetition of which takes on a pulsating character: bunches of fingers with sharp nails, ambiguous mouths that become sexual organs, telescoped bathtubs and chairs, and Picasso-like locks of hair. Adami's universe is one of the most powerfully "reduced" to be found in modern contemporary painting: "reduced" in the sense of a projection of the various components following an analysis in which the role of subjectivity and even of impulsiveness is composed with an astonishing mastery of construction. In Adami's creations the cold eroticism found in other works (those of Télémaque, for example) produces a picture that is implacable in its frenzy, at once illogical and rational, a kind of infinitely complicated puzzle for which the model has been lost.

Kujawski is now achieving superimpression in his works with two layers of transparent plastic: image plays on image; informative data are imprinted on the elongated form of the nudes, and in addition capture the passerby and the landscape in front of which the work is placed.

III. THE REALISTIC IMAGE

Is the ultimate goal of all figuration realism? We hope that everything said above proves the contrary. However, the realist choice is an important factor in contemporary painting. As in the works of Nikos, it may take the form of the pursuit of shadows, photographed through a screen and reproduced on sensitized canvas. This is a game, often with unexpected variations; its surprises, however, conceal a danger of "Boldinism" and certain worldly graces. Bertini appears like a rock among the eddies and artifices of Mec Art, like the character in "Soudain Erèbe" (Suddenly Erebus) clinging to his controls.

Rancillac has certainly been one of the painters most impressed by the animated cartoon and the Disneyan mythology. More openly than Télémaque (who integrated Tintin or Pluto into his canvases, when necessary, like any other "sociological object"), Rancillac at one point made them the central subject of his work, openly utilizing, as do Hiraga and Peter Foldès, the framework of the script and the balloon. In his work, however, the balloon remains white, certainly not silent, but open to all the virtualities of language. In the words of a child looking at them, his canvases have "white ideas." His shift to "the picture of the picture," as Pierre Bourdieu calls it, with an unambiguous reference to events and to the iconography of the picture-novel and the advertising poster, was accomplished in various stages that debouch on the restructuration, in the total meaning of that term, of photographic or documentary facts. This painting poses the problem of moral and political commitment, which, for certain people, is confused with the narrative spirit. It is evident that narrative procedures offer vehicles of expression perfectly adapted to polemical painting of the type now being done by the groups Cronica and Realidad in Valencia, and the Madrileño Genovés.

In the Spanish cultural milieu with its very distinctive sensitivity, historical memories, sarcastic irony, and the chiaroscuro taste for death contribute their austere shadows. The discursive power of a painting by Cronica is obvious, sharp as a sword blade: in it realism is manipulated by all available means—framings, rhythms, enlargements—suggested by the techniques of the film and the comic strip.

Quite different is the adventure of another Spanish painter, Eduardo Arroyo, whose entire work is a narrative frequently autobiographical in nature. Arroyo has successively practiced all the styles of temporalization: "cloisonnés," the polyptych with its series on the Spanish dynasties and Napoleon, the "metamorphoses" with their visible transformations of Bonaparte or Titina Maselli, and lastly "narration by episodes," which he utilized in a personal exhibition, "Twenty Years of Peace" (in which he stigmatized Franco), and in his "Robinson Crusoe" series, as well as in his collective works executed with Aillaud and Recalcati. The total abandonment of all personal style is combined in these joint works with political opinion and the determination to undermine the "rhetoric of forms" and the search for the added fillip of sensation, in which too many painters delight.

But an art whose only language is that of a perfect intelligibility of forms is an act whose seditious nature is ultimately more effective than Dadaistic grimaces. Arroyo might perhaps be capable of losing himself in this game, and he knows it, although the urge to paint is so deeply rooted in him that it surges up just as soon as the restraints are lifted—which is to say, in every canvas.

The possibilities of the narrative picture that we have only too briefly considered in this chapter find in realism their beginning and their end, their birth and their death. In short, narration may kill the plastic presence like an overdose of medicine, and this tendency, which is inherent in the narrative function, finds in the climate of modern painting and in the world in which we are living its most urgent, intoxicating, and also most dangerous justifications.

INDEX

Titles of comic strips are in quotation marks.

For strips that have appeared outside their country of origin, the reader will find their foreign titles (with the name of the country where they were used) and a reference to the original title. For example: "Pim, Pam, Poum" (France), cf. "The Katzenjammer Kids."

Artists known by a pseudonym are listed under both their pseudonym and their real name; under the pseudonym the reader is referred to the latter listing.

"Abentener der Fünf Schreckensteiner," 75.
"Abernathy," Mr., 113.
"Ace Drummond," 69.
Ache (Jean), 95.
"Action Comics," 65.
Adami (Valerio), 250, 251.
"Adventures of the Little Lost Bear," 53, 54.
Aillaud (Gilles), 231, 241, 252.
"Alain la Foudre" (France), cf. "Dick Fulmine."
"Albert and Pogo," cf. "Pogo."
Albertarelli (Rino), 770.
Alechinsky, 231.
"Alix l'Intrépide," 99, 101, 127.
"Alley Oop," 64, 75, 143.
Alleyn (Edmund), 235, 241, 250.
"Alma and Oliver," 29.
"Alphonse and Gaston," 23.
Anderson (Carl), 73.
Anderson (Lyman), 63.
Andriola (Alfred), 65, 71, 87, 92, 213.
"Andy Capp," 115.
"Anita Buen Corazon" (Spain), cf. "Little Orphan Annie."
"Apartment 3-G," 110, 111.
"Apple Mary," cf. Mary Worth.
Appleby (Barry), 115.
"Arabelle, la Dernière Sirène," 95.
"Arcibaldo e Petronilla" (Italy), cf. "Bringing Up Father."
Arnal, cf. Cabrero-Arnal.
Arnal (François), 229.
Arroyo (Eduardo), 229, 231, 237, 241, 251, 252.
"Arthur et Zoé" (France), cf. "Fritzi Ritz."
"Arys Buck," 95, 99.
"As du Ciel" (L') (France), cf. "Romano il Legionario."
"Astérix le Gaulois," 123, 127, 181.
"Atomas," 183.
Attilio (Mussino). 32, 33.
Avai (Cesare), 77, 79.
Avai (Giacomo), 77.
"Aventures de Corentin" (Les), 99, 101.
"Aventures de M. Vieuxbois" (Les), 11.
"Avventura de Capitan Coviello," 115.

"B.C.," 107, 109, 141, 143, 185, 191, 219.
Badert (A. G.), 75.
Baker (George), 85, 90.
"Banana Oil," 38.
Bara, 115.
"Barbarella," 119.
Barlog, 75.
"Barnaby," 87, 90.
"Barney Baxter," 69.
"Barney Google," 48, 49, 53, 159, 166.
Barry (Dan), 131.
Bastard, 119.
"Bat Star" (Italy), cf. "Brick Bradford."
Battaglia (Dino), 115.
"Bébé Cyanure," 125.
"Bécassine," 31, 53, 75, 170.
"Beetle Bailey," 113, 114, 165.
Bellamy (Frank), 115, 133, 135.
"Belles Images," 53.
"Belloy l'Invulnérable," 95.
"Benitin y Eneas" (Spain), cf. "Mutt and Jeff."
"Bernard Tempête" (France), cf. "Don Winslow."
Berndt (Walter), 45.
Berni (Antonio), 231, 239.
Beroth (Leon A.), 75, 171.
Bertini (Giani), 235, 241, 242, 243, 252.
"Better or Worse," 115.
"Betty," 45.

Bévère (Maurice de, called "Morris"), 99, 101, 123, 181, 185, 191.
"Bibi Fricotin," 52, 55, 79, 173.
"Bicot" (France), cf. "Winnie Winkle."
"Big Ben Bolt," 119, 180.
Bignardi, 241.
"Bilbolbul," 33.
"Bill l'Albatros, Pirate de l'Air" (France), cf. "Will Sparrow."
Bisi (Carlo), 77.
Blaisdell (Philip "Tex"), 133.
"Blondie," 45, 73, 151, 163, 167, 169.
"Blondinette" (Canada), cf. "Blondie."
Blosser (Merrill), 45.
"Bob l'Aviateur" (France), cf. "Scorchy Smith."
"Bob et Bobette," 101.
"Bob Rilet" (France), cf. "Rusty Riley."
"Bonaventura," 52, 53, 145, 179.
"Boob McNutt," 38, 39.
"Boots and Her Buddies," 45, 215.
Boshier, 229, 241.
"Bouclette Haute Couture" (France), cf. "Tillie the Toiler."
Bowen, 119.
"Braccio di Ferro" (Italy), cf. "Popeye."
Bradley, 110, 111, 173.
Branner (Martin V.), 45, 49, 180.
Brau (Jean-Louis), 233.
Breger (Dave), 85.
"Brenda Starr," 119, 184.
Brewerston, 45.
"Brick Bradford," 60, 63, 69, 75, 113, 161, 210.
Briggs (Austin), 63, 83, 92, 131.
Briggs (Clare), 27, 29.
"Bringing Up Father," 34, 45, 75, 113, 131, 135, 143, 145, 151, 157, 169, 170, 179, 191, 205, 213, 215.
Brinkerhoff, 119.
Brown (Tom), 14, 19.
Browne (Dik), 119.
"Bruin Boys" (The), 53.
Bruning, 229.
"Buck Danny," 101, 179.
"Buck Rogers," 57, 60, 63, 65, 79, 129, 163, 165.
"Buck Ryan," 101.
"Buffalo Bill," 99, 233.
"Bungle Family" (The), 45.
Burnett (W. R.), 63.
Burroughs (Edgar Rice), 57, 177.
Busch (Wilhelm), 11, 12, 21, 219.
Bushmiller (Ernie), 45.
"Buster Brown," 23, 114, 135, 145, 173, 179.
"Buz Sawyer," 85, 86, 111, 135, 173, 185, 210, 213, 223.
Byrnes (Gene), 45.

Cabrero-Arnal (José), 95.
Cabu, 185.
Cain (James), 63.
Calkins (Lt. Richard W.), 61, 69, 163.
Calvo, 95.
"Camember," cf. "Facéties du Sapeur Camember."
Camo, 95.
Caniff (Milton), 65, 68, 82, 88, 89, 91, 93, 94, 111, 131, 135 145, 167, 171, 173, 180, 187, 191, 195, 213, 216-217, 223.
"Capitaine Cormoran," 119.
"Capitaine Fantôme," 99.
"Capitaine Fouchtroff," (France), cf. "The Captain and the Kids."
Capp (Al), 33, 73, 76, 103, 131, 151, 152, 166, 173, 175, 205.
"Captain and the Kids" (The), 39, 113, 137, 179, 183.

"Captain Cocorico" (Italy), cf. "The Captain and the Kids."
"Captain Easy," cf. "Wash Tubbs."
Caran d'Ache, 9, 11, 19.
"Carol Day," 115, 116.
Carter (Ad), 45, 163.
Castillo (Arturo del), 115, 119, 219, 226.
Caswell (Leslie), 115.
Caumery, cf. Languereau (Maurice),
Cazenave (Raymond), 95, 99.
Celardo (John), 131.
"César-Napoléon Rascasse," 77.
Chandler (Raymond), 61.
"Charlie Chan," 65, 71, 83, 87.
Charlier (J. M.), 179.
Charteris (Leslie), 63.
"Chasseur de Monstres" (Le), 77, 78.
"Chaumière Indienne" (La), 7.
Cheval-Bertrand, 231, 241, 244, 245, 251.
"Chlorophylle," 126, 127.
Christman (Bert), 65, 87.
Christophe, cf. Colomb (G.)
"Cino e Franco," cf. "Tim Tyler's Luck."
"Cinque della Selena," 1, 115.
"Cisco Kid" (The), 115, 123.
"Cocco Bill," 101, 115.
Cohl (Emile), 145.
Collins (D.), 115.
Colomb (Georges), "Christophe," 15, 31, 169, 179, 187.
"Connie," 45, 65, 69, 71, 91, 113, 119, 160, 205, 215.
"Cora" (France), cf. "Connie."
Cordier (Daniel), 237.
"Cosinus," cf. "L'Idée Fixe du Savant Cosinus."
Cossio (Carlo), 77.
"Count Screwloose of Toulouse," 35, 39.
Couperie (Pierre), 45.
Crane (Roy), 47, 53, 85, 86, 91, 111, 133, 134, 159, 173, 185, 209, 210, 213, 223.
Crepax (Guido), 115, 201.
"Cri-Cri" (Le), 53.
Crosby (Percy), 45, 170.
Cruikshank (George), 7, 9.
Cuello, 241.
Culliford (Pierre), "Peyo," 123, 126, 225.
Cuvelier (Paul), 99.

Daix (A.), 77.
Dali (Salvador), 27.
"Dan Dare," 115, 133.
"Dan Dunn," 131.
Davis (Phil), 71.
De Beck (Billy), 49, 166.
Dean (Allen), 71, 73.
"Dennis the Menace," 113, 114, 151.
"Desperate Desmond," 29.
"Detective Comics," 65.
"Diane," cf. "Connie."
"Dick Fulmine," 77.
"Dick Tracy," 61, 63, 83, 87, 119, 129, 145, 165, 187, 205.
Dille (John), 163.
"Dimanche Illustré," 55.
"Dinglehoofer and His Dog Adolph," 143.
Dirks (John), 113.
Dirks (Rudolph), 19, 21, 39, 69, 113, 137, 179.
Disney (Walt), 21, 73, 75, 103, 219, 233.
"Don Panfrito" (Spain), cf. "Barney Google."
"Don Winslow of the Navy," 75, 143, 171.
Donald Duck," 73.
"Dondi," 119.
Doré (Gustave), 9.
Dowling (Steve), 101.
"Down Hogan's Alley," 19.
"Drago," 92, 185, 187.

253

Drake (Stan), 111, 167, 184.
"Dream of the Rarebit Fiend," 170.
Dumas (Jacques) "Marijac," 75, 95, 119.
"Dumb Dora," 45.
Dunkley (Jack), 115.
"Durondib et Leur Chien Adolphe" (Les), cf. "Dinglehoofer."

"Eagle Scout Roy Powers," 205, 215.
Ed (Carl), 45.
Eddison (E. R.), 177.
Edgington, 111, 173.
Edson (Gus), 49, 119.
"Electropolis," 77.
"Elmer," 45.
Enghelm, 115.
"Epervier Bleu" (L'), 101.
Erik, 95, 101.
Ernst (Ken), 109.
Etcheverry-Quello, 115, 122, 210.

"Facéties du Sapeur Camember" (Les), 15, 169, 179.
Fahlström (Oyvind), 231, 233, 235, 237.
Falk (Lee), 71, 73.
"Famille Fenouillard" (La), 15, 145, 179, 187.
"Famille Illico" (La) (France), cf. "Bringing Up Father."
"Famille Mirliton" (La) (France), cf. "Gumps" (The).
"Famille Têtebêche" (La) (Canada), cf. "Blondie."
"Famous Funnies," 69.
"Far Till Fyra," 115.
"Fearless Fosdick," 151, 175.
Feiffer (Jules), 109, 111.
Feininger (Lyonel), 27.
"Felix the Cat," 35, 37, 39, 75, 145, 183, 219.
Ferro (Gudmundson), 235.
Ferro (Ted), 91.
"Fils de Chine," 119.
Fisher (Ham), 65, 71, 83.
Fisher (Harry C. "Bud"), 29, 30, 129.
Flanders (Charles), 71.
"Flapper Fanny," 45.
"Flash Gordon," 61, 63, 64, 75, 85, 91, 92, 95, 129, 131, 137, 138, 143, 154, 158, 160, 176, 177, 191, 195, 207, 209.
Fletcher (Hank), 113.
Fogeli (Fogelberg Ola), 55.
Foldès (Peter), 229, 231, 232, 233, 235, 237, 241, 243, 245.
Forest (Jean-Claude), 119, 125.
Forrest (Hal), 69.
"Fort Navajo," 123, 191.
Forton (Louis), 33, 52, 53, 55.
"Fortunello" (Italy), cf. "Happy Hooligan."
Foster (Harold), 57, 58, 63, 66-67, 75, 84, 85, 115, 132, 141, 163, 173, 179, 182, 187, 191, 192-193, 207, 209, 210, 213, 219.
Foxwell (H. S.), 53, 54.
François (Edouard), 85.
Franquin, 99, 123, 127, 181, 225.
"Frazer," 115, 135.
Frazetta (Frank), 165.
"Freckles and His Friends," 45.
"Fritzi Ritz" (later "Fritzi Ritz and Nancy"), 45.
Fronsky (A.), 75.
"Funnies on Parade," 65.
"Futuropolis," 77, 183, 198, 199.

"G.I. Joe," 85.
Gaïtis (Yannis), 235, 243.
"Gambols" (The), 115.
"Garth," 101.
"Gasoline Alley," 46, 49, 165, 168, 169, 175.
Gately (George), 113.
Gaty (Christian), 130.
Genoves, 252.
"Gertie the Dinosaur," 29.
Giffey (René), 99.
Gigi (Robert), 130, 191, 226.
"Gil Jourdan," 123, 157, 203.
Gillain (Joseph), "Jijé," 101, 123, 124, 184, 224.
Gillam (Bernard), 19.
Gillon (Paul), 119, 125.
Giraud "Gir," 123, 125, 191.
Godwin (Frank), 45, 61, 65, 71, 113, 115, 160, 205, 207, 209, 215, 219.
Goldberg (Reuben L.) "Rube," 23, 39, 93, 145.
Goscinny (René), 123, 126, 181, 185.
Gould (Chester), 61, 63, 131, 187, 205, 219.

"Grand Duduche" (Le), 185.
Gray (Clarence), 60, 63, 113, 161, 210, 213.
Gray (Harold), 47, 49, 131, 163, 175, 205, 219.
"Great Gusto" (The), 113.
Greene (Vernon), 113.
Gross (Milt), 23, 38, 39.
Group Cronica, 236, 252.
"Guerre à la Terre," 97.
"Gumps" (The), 44, 45, 49.
"Gun Law," 115.
"Guy l'Eclair" (France), cf. "Flash Gordon."

Haenigsen (Harry), 119.
"Hagen, Fagin and O'Toole," 119.
"Hairbreath Harry," 23.
Hamlin (Vince T.), 69, 75.
Hammett (Dashiell), 61.
"Hapless Harry," 113.
"Happy Hooligan," 21, 23.
Harman (Fred), 71, 73, 213, 221.
"Harold Teen," 45.
Hart (Johnny), 107, 109, 141, 185, 199.
Hasen (Irwin), 119.
Hast, 115.
"Haut et Puissant Seigneur Baron de Cramoisy," 15.
Hearst (William Randolph), 19, 21, 23, 39, 45, 113, 129, 137.
"Heart of Juliet Jones" (The), 110, 111, 167, 184.
Heilman (Dan), 111.
Hélion, 233.
"Henry," 73.
Hergé, cf. Rémi (Georges).
"Herr Piepmeyer," 11, 103, 183.
Herriman (George), 35, 37, 103, 183, 205.
Hershfield (Harry), 29.
Hess (Sol), 45.
"Hi and Lois," 119.
"Hippolyte et Clémentine," cf. "Hi and Lois."
Hiraga (Key), 231, 235, 243, 252.
"Histoires en Estampes," 11.
"Histoires en Images," 53.
Hogarth (Burne), 5, 57, 58, 63, 77, 91, 93, 103, 113, 131, 132, 138, 141, 144, 158, 163, 167, 176, 179, 182, 185, 187, 191, 192-193, 205, 207, 209, 212, 213, 219.
Holdaway (Jim), 115.
Holman (Bill), 75.
"Hombre Enmascarado" (El) (Spain), cf. "Phantom" (The).
"Homme Masqué" (L') (France), cf. "Lone Ranger" (The).
Hubinon (Victor), 101, 179.
Huston (John), 63.

"Idée Fixe du Savant Cosinus" (L'), 15.
"Inspector Wade," 61.
Irving (Jay), 119.
Isou (Isidore), 231.

Jacobs (Edgar Pierre), 95, 97, 127, 173, 185.
Jacovitti, 101, 115.
"Jane," 45, 101.
"Jane, Daughter of Jane," 115, 116.
Jansson (Lars), 115.
"Jean Bolide," cf. "Tailspin Tommy."
"Jean Valhardi," 101, 123, 184.
"Jeff Hawke," 115, 116, 133, 161.
Jensen (C.), 45.
"Jerry Spring," 123, 124, 224.
"Jidehem," 181.
Jije, cf. Gillain (Joseph).
"Jim Boum," 77, 119.
"Jim el Temerario" (Spain), cf. "Jungle Jim."
"Jim la Jungle" (France), cf. "Jungle Jim."
"Jimmy das Gummipferd," 115.
"Jodelle," 123.
"Joe Palooka," 65, 71, 83.
"Johnny Hazard," 85, 86, 111, 167, 223, 224.
Johnson (Crockett), 87, 90.
Johnson (Ferd), 113.
Jones (Ralston), 113.
Jordan (Sydney), 115, 116, 133, 161.
"Jorge el Piloto" (Spain), cf. "Smilin' Jack."
"Jorge y Fernando" (Spain), cf. "Tim Tyler's Luck."
"Judge," 19.
"Judge Parker," 111.
"Julieta y Eva Jones" (Spain), cf. "Heart of Juliet Jones" (The).
"Juliette de Mon Coeur" (France), cf. "Heart of Juliet Jones" (The).

"Jungle Jim," 61, 63, 73, 87, 145, 207.
"Just Kids," 45, 163.

Kahles (Charles W.), 23.
"Katzenjammer Kids" (The), 19, 21, 41, 45, 49, 69, 87, 103, 113, 129, 135, 137, 143, 145, 151, 166, 169, 173, 181.
Kelly (Walt), 93, 105, 175, 179, 180, 181, 185, 219.
"Kerry Drake," 87, 92.
Ketcham (Hank), 113, 114, 131.
"Kin-der-Kids" (The), 27.
King (Frank), 46, 49, 168, 169, 175.
"King of the Royal Mounted," 71, 73, 131.
"Kit Carson," 77.
Klasen (Peter), 241, 250.
Knerr (Harold H.), 39, 41, 45, 69, 113, 137, 143, 166, 181, 183, 191.
Knight (Clayton) 69.
Kohlsaat (Roland), 115.
"Korgan, le Magicien de la Forêt Morte" (France), cf. "Viro, il Mago," etc.
Kotzky (Alex), 111.
"Krazy Kat," 35, 37, 39, 75, 145, 183, 231, 233.
Kudo, 245, 251.
Kujawski, 241, 244, 245, 252.

Lambert (Jean Clarence), 231.
Languereau (Maurice) "Caumery," 31, 33.
Lanteri (Arturo), 55.
Lapoujade, 233.
"Larks" (The), 115.
Lazarus (Mell), 107, 108, 109, 180.
"Le Franc," 184.
Le Guen, 119.
Le Rallic, 75, 95, 99.
Lemaître (Maurice), 231, 233.
Lichtenstein (Roy), 228, 229, 231, 233, 235, 251.
"Life," 19.
"Li'l Abner," 73, 131, 143, 161, 152, 165, 166, 173, 175, 205, 219.
"Liliane" (France), cf. "Connie."
"Lindy," 116.
Liquois, 95, 97.
"Little Annie Rooney," 75, 129.
"Little Jimmy," 21, 75, 205.
"Little King" (The), 73, 75.
"Little Nemo in Slumberland," 11, 24, 25, 27, 87, 139, 186, 219.
"Little Orphan Annie," 47, 49, 75, 129, 163, 175.
"Little Tiger" (The), 21.
"Llanero Solitario" (El) (Spain), cf. "Lone Ranger" (The).
"Lone Ranger" (The), 71, 73, 115.
"Looie Blooie," 143.
López (R. G.), 55.
"Lorenzo Parachoques" (Spain), cf. "Blondie."
Lovecraft (H. P.), 65.
Lubbers (Bob), 131.
"Luc Bradefer" (France), cf. "Brick Bradford."
"Lucky Luke," 99, 101, 123, 181, 191.
"Luis Ciclon" (Spain), cf. "Steve Canyon."
Lynde (Stan), 113, 114, 209.

"Macaco," 55.
McCay (Winsor), 11, 24, 27, 29, 35, 139, 155, 170, 183, 186, 205, 209.
McClure (Darrell), 75.
McManus (George), 4, 29, 30, 34, 42, 45, 91, 113, 131, 139, 155, 157, 170, 179, 191, 205, 213, 215.
McNamara, 45.
Mac Raboy, 87, 131.
Macherot (Raymond), 123, 126, 127.
Macréau, 243.
Magritte, 243.
Malaval, 241, 245.
"Male Call," 82, 87, 88, 167, 180.
"Malheurs d'Annie" (Les) (France), cf. "Little Annie Rooney."
Manca (Giovanni), 77.
"Mandrake the Magician," 71, 73, 91.
"Marc Dacier," 184.
"Marc Orian" (France), cf. "Barney Baxter."
"Marc Reynes," 95.
Marijac, cf. Dumas (Jacques).
Martin (Edgar), 45, 215.
Martin (Jacques), 95, 101, 127, 184.
Martinek (Frank), 75, 171.
"Mary Perkins on Stage," 111, 112, 221.

"Mary Worth," 109.
Mat, 77.
Mathelot (Christian), 97.
"Max," 115.
"Max und Moritz," 11, 12, 21.
Maxon (Rex), 131.
Maz, 115, 116.
"Mediaeval Castle" (The), 182.
"Merlin, el Rey de la Magia" (Spain), cf. "Mandrake."
Merritt (Abraham), 65, 177.
"Merry Marcelene" (The), 29.
Messick (Dale), 119, 184.
"Michel Tanguy," 123.
Michenet, 231, 243.
"Mickey Mouse," 69, 73, 75, 87, 135, 145, 233.
Miller (Frank), 69.
"Minute Movies," 48, 53.
"Mio Mao" (Italy), cf. "Felix the Cat."
"Miquette" (Canada), cf. "Mickey Mouse."
"Miracle Jones," 167.
"Miss Peach," 107, 180.
"Mister Cryptogame," 11.
"Modesty Blaise," 115, 116.
Molino (Walter), 79.
Moliterni (Claude), 200, 226.
Monk (Jack), 101.
Monory (Jacques), 235, 241, 245, 246–247, 251.
"Monsieur et Madame Nouveaumariés" (France), cf. "Newlyweds" (The).
"Monsieur Poche," 75.
"Monsieur Réac," 11.
"Moon Mullins," 46, 49, 75, 113.
Moore (Ray), 71, 73.
Morley (Jack), 87.
Morris, cf. Bevère (Maurice de).
"Moschettieri dell' Aeroporto Z," 77.
Mosley (Zack), 69.
"Mr. and Mrs.," 45.
"Mumintrollet," 115.
Murphy (Jimmy), 45.
Murphy (John Cullen), 119, 180.
Musial (Joseph), 113, 137.
"Mutt and Jeff," 30, 129, 139, 146.

Naccache, 229, 235.
Nadar, cf. Tournachon (Félix).
"Nancy," cf. "Fritzi Ritz."
"Nasdine Hodja," 119.
Nast (Thomas), 19.
National Cartoonist Society, 93.
"Naufragés du Temps" (Les), 119, 125.
"Nebbs" (The), 45.
"Ne'er-do-well Ally Sloper," 15.
"Neutron," 115, 118, 119, 201.
"New Fun," 65.
"Newlyweds" (The), 29, 30.
Norris (Paul), 131.
Nortier (Lucien), 95, 99, 130.
Novelli, 243.
Nowlan (Phil), 60.

O'Donnel (Peter), 115, 116.
Ohser (Erich), 75, 76.
"Ombra," (L'), 115.
"On Our Block," 45.
O'Neal (Frank), 109.
"Oompah-Pah," 123.
Opper (Frederick Burr), 19, 21, 23, 35, 205.
Orr (Martha), 109.
Outcault (Richard Felton), 17, 19, 22, 23.
Overgard (William), 113.
"Ozark Ike," 131.

Paape (Eddy), 184.
"Pam," 45.
"Pampurio," 77.
"Panhandle Pete," 29.
Parker (Brant), 107, 109.
Parker (G.), 45.
"Patrouille des Aigles" (La) (France), cf. "Eagle Scout Roy Powers."
"Paulette" (Canada), cf. "Connie."
Payne (A. B.), 54.
"Peanuts," 105, 107, 109, 143, 146, 152, 182, 199, 219.
Pedrocchi (Frederick), 79.
Pellaert (Guy), 123.
"Pekka Puupää," 55, 58.
Pellos (René), 77, 78, 198.
Percy (Bill), 168.

Périlli (Achille), 229, 231, 232.
"Perishers" (The), 115.
Perré (A.), 75.
"Petit Illustré" (Le), 53.
Peyo, cf. Culliford (Pierre).
"Phantom" (The), 71, 73.
Phillips (Irving), 109.
"Pic et Balou" (France), cf. "Perishers" (The).
"Pieds-Nickelés" (Les), 32, 33, 53, 75, 145.
"Pier Cloruro de' Lambicchi," 77.
"Pif le Chien," 95.
"Pim, Pam, Poum" (France), cf. "The Katzenjammer Kids."
Pinchon (Jean-Pierre), 31, 170.
"Pionniers de l'Espérance" (Les), 95, 97, 163.
"Pip Squeak and Wilfred," 53, 54.
"Pitchounet, Fils de Marius," 77.
"Placid et Muzo," 95.
Planen (E. O.), cf. Ohser (Erich).
"Plick et Plock," 15.
"Pogo," 105, 107, 109, 153, 173, 175, 179, 180, 181, 185, 219.
Poïvet (Raymond), 95, 97, 130, 163.
"Polly and Her Pals," 43, 49, 205.
"Poncho Libertas," 95, 99.
"Ponytail," 119.
"Pop," 55.
"Popeye," cf. "Thimble Theatre."
"Pottsy," 119.
Pratt (Hugo), 115, 198.
Prentice (John), 112, 113, 187, 196–197, 221.
"Prince Valiant," 56, 63, 66–67, 75, 84, 85, 87, 141, 143, 153, 167, 193, 207, 209, 210, 213.
"Principe Val," (II) (Spain), cf. "Prince Valiant."
"Principe Valentino" (Italy), cf. "Prince Valiant"
"Principe Valiente" (Spain), cf. "Prince Valiant"
"Prinz Eisenherz" (Germany), cf. "Prince Valiant"
"Private Breger," 85.
"Professeur Nimbus" (Les Aventures du), 15, 77, 153.
"Prosper l'Ours," 75.
Puck, 19.
Pulitzer (Albert), 19.
Pulitzer (Joseph), 19, 39, 113, 137.

Rabier (Benjamin), 12, 53, 75.
"Radio Patrol," 61.
"Ragnar le Viking," 115, 122, 210.
"Rainbow" (The), 53.
Rancillac (Bernard), 231, 233, 235, 237, 239, 245, 252.
Randall, 115, 120–121, 226.
"Raoul et Gaston" (France), cf. "Tim Tyler's Luck."
Ratcliff (Ernest), 116.
"Raúl," 55.
Rauschenberg (Robert), 233, 237, 243, 245, 250.
Raymond (Alex), 63, 64, 75, 85, 87, 91, 93, 94, 111, 138, 143, 154, 158, 163, 176, 179, 182, 191, 195, 207, 209, 213, 219, 221.
Raymond (James), 87.
Raynaud, 245.
Raysse (Martial), 239, 243.
Realidad Group, 239, 252.
Recalcati (Antonio), 231, 241, 250, 252.
"Red Ryder," 71, 73, 131, 213, 221.
"Reg'lar Fellers," 45.
Rémi (Georges) "Hergé," 79, 95, 101, 133, 163, 169, 171, 180, 191, 203, 233.
Reutersward, 229.
"Rex Morgan, M.D.," 110, 173.
Reynaud (Emile), 9.
"Ribambelle" (La), 180.
"Richard l'Aviateur" (France), cf. "Smilin' Jack."
"Richard le Téméraire" (France), cf. "Tim Tyler's Luck."
"Rick O'Shay," 113, 114, 159, 209.
Rickenbacker (Eddie), 69.
Ridgeway (Frank), 113.
"Rip Kirby," 91, 94, 101, .113, 167, 187, 196–197, 221.
Ritt (William), 60, 161, 210.
Rivers (Larry), 241, 251.
Rob Vel, cf. Velter.
Roba, 180.

Robbins (Frank), 65, 71, 85, 86, 111, 167, 187, 213, 223, 224.
Robinson (Jerry), 109.
Rose (Rudolf), 75.
Romagnoni (Bepi), 244, 251.
"Romano il Legionario," 79.
"Romeo Brown," 115.
Rosenquist (James), 241, 243, 248–249.
"Rosie's Beau," 143.
Rubimor, 131.
"Rupert," cf. "Adventures of the Little Lost Bear."
"Rusty Riley," 113, 207.

"Sad Sack" (The), 85, 87.
Sagendorf (Bud), 69.
Saint-Ogan (Alain), 55, 75, 79, 161.
Saint-Phalle (Niki de), 245, 251.
Salinas (José-Luis), 115, 122, 219.
Salomon (Alan), 235.
"Salvator," 95.
"Sam Billie Bill," 95, 99.
"Sandy Highflyer," 23.
Sarkis, 235.
"Saturno Contro la Terra," 79, 163.
Saunders (Allen), 109, 113.
"Savage World," 135.
"Scarlet Dream," 119, 191, 226, 227.
Schlosser, 241.
Schmidt (Charlie), 61.
Schrödter (A.), 11.
"Schtroumpfs" (Les), 123, 126, 225.
Schulz (Charles), 105, 107, 109, 146, 152, 182, 199.
Schwitters (Kurt), 233.
Scolari (Giovanni), 79, 163.
"Scorchy Smith," 65, 69, 71, 87, 137.
"Secret Agent X-9," 61, 63, 83, 113, 195.
Segar (Elzie), 23, 38, 39, 69, 75, 135, 183.
Seldes (Gilbert), 39, 55.
Sellier, 243.
Senarens (L. P.), 65.
"Short Ribs," 109.
Shuster (Joe), 69.
Sickles (Noel), 65, 173.
Siegel (Jerry), 69.
"Simplicio Bobadilla" (Spain), cf. "Happy Hooligan."
Sirius, 101.
"Skippy," 45, 170.
"Skyroads," 69.
Slesinger (Stephen), 131.
"Smilin' Jack," 69.
Smith (Sydney), 44, 49.
"Smitty," 45.
"Smokey Stover," 75, 143.
Smythe (Reginald), 115.
"Snoozer," 29.
Soglow (Otto), 73.
"Spirou," 78, 79, 99, 101, 119, 151, 181, 225.
"Spooky the Cat," 75.
Starr (Leonard), 111, 112, 191, 221.
Steinlen, 9.
Stenvert, 245.
Sterrett (Cliff), 43, 49, 205.
"Steve Canyon," 93, 173, 188, 195, 222.
"Steve Roper," 113.
"Still Life," 109.
Sto, cf. Tofano (Sergio).
Stokes (G.), 115.
Sullivan (Pat), 35, 37, 183.
"Superman," 69, 73, 83, 233.
Swinnerton (James), 19, 21, 205.
"Syncopating Sue," 45.

"Tailspin Tommy," 69.
"Tartol de la Clanche," 101.
"Tarzan," 57, 58, 59, 69, 83, 93, 113, 129, 131, 132, 137, 138, 141, 143, 145, 158, 176, 179, 191, 207, 209, 212, 233.
Télémaque (Hervé), 233, 235, 241, 245, 246, 251, 252.
"Téméraire" (Le), 91.
"Terrors of the Tiny Tads" (The), 27, 28.
"Terry and the Pirates," 63, 85, 88, 93, 94, 167, 171, 184, 188, 216–217, 222.
"Thimble Theatre," 39, 69, 75, 91, 123, 135.
Thomas (W. F.), 15.
"Tif et Tondu," 101.
"Tiger Tim," 54.
"Tillie the Toiler," 45.

Tillieux (Maurice), 123, 157, 203.
"Tim Tyler's Luck," 71, 73.
"Tin y Ton" (Spain), cf. "The Katzenjammer Kids."
"Tintin," 79, 101, 127, 143, 151, 159, 163, 169, 171, 180, 203.
Tofano (Sergio), "Sto," 52.
Tolkien (J. R. R.), 177.
"Toots and Casper," 45.
Töpffer (Rodolphe), 11, 12, 15.
"Topolino," cf. "Mickey Mouse."
Tournachon (Félix), "Nadar," 11.
Tourtel (Mary), 54.
13, rue de l'Espoir," 119.
"Tres Randas" (Los), (Spain), cf. "Les Pieds Nickelés."
"Tristan Triston" (Spain), cf. "Sad Sack."
"Trois Mousquetaires du Maquis," 95, 119.
Turner (Leslie), 85.
Tuthill (H. J.), 45.

Uderzo (Albert), 95, 99, 123, 126, 127, 181.

Uggeri (Mario), 115.
"Upside Downs" (The), 28, 29.

"Vampire des Caraïbes," 95.
Van der Steen (Willy), 101.
"Vater und Sohn," 75, 76, 77, 169.
Verbeck (Gustave), 23, 27, 28, 29.
"Virus, il Mago della Foresta Morta," 79.
Voight (C. A.), 45.
Voss (Ian), 235, 243.

Walker (Mort), 93, 113, 114, 149, 165.
"Wash Tubbs," later, "Captain Easy," 47, 53, 69, 83, 133, 159, 185, 213.
Watson (Keith), 115, 133.
Watt (John Millar), 55.
Waugh (Coulton), 219.
"Weary Willie and Tired Tim," 14.
Welles (Orson), 45.
Wells (G.), 65.
Wertham (Frederic), 103.
"Wes Slade," 115.
Westover (Russ), 45.

Wheelan (Ed), 49, 53.
Whitington (L.), 45.
Will, 101.
"Will Sparrow, il Pirata dell' aria," 79.
Willard (Frank), 46, 49.
Williamson (Al), 113, 133, 135.
Winner (Doc), 45, 113, 137.
"Winnie Winkle" (The Breadwinner), 45, 49, 129, 143, 180.
"Witwe Knolle," 75.
"Wizard of Id," 107, 109, 219.
Wright (David), 115, 116.
Wunder (George), 93, 94, 184, 191.

"Yellow Kid" (The), 17, 19, 21, 23, 103, 179, 209.
"Yordi" (France), cf. "Superman."
Young (Lyman), 71, 73.
Young (Murat) "Chic," 4, 45, 73, 76, 113, 163, 167, 169.

Zaboly (Bela), 69.
"Zig et Puce," 50, 51, 55, 75, 79, 161, 173.

M.L.B. INC.
FEB 26 1971
SYRACUSE, N.Y.